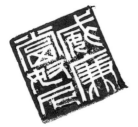

the complete
CALLIGRAPHER

the complete CALLIGRAPHER

A comprehensive guide from basic techniques
to inspirational alphabets

EMMA CALLERY

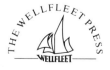

THE WELLFLEET PRESS

WELLFLEET

A QUINTET BOOK

Published by Wellfleet Press
A Division of Book Sales, Inc.
110 Enterprise Avenue
Secaucus, New Jersey 07094

This edition produced for sale
in the U.S.A., its territories
and dependencies only.

ISBN 0-7858-0032-8

This book was designed and produced by
Quintet Publishing Limited
6 Blundell Street
London N7 9BH

Creative Director: Richard Dewing
Designers: Nicky Chapman
Editor: Emma Callery
Project Editor: Katie Preston

Typeset in Great Britain by
Central Southern Typesetters, Eastbourne
Manufactured in Singapore by
Eray Scan Pte. Ltd.
Printed in Singapore by
Star Standard Industries (Pte) Limited

The material in this publication previously appeared in *The Calligraphy
Source Book, An Introduction to Calligraphy, The Encyclopedia of
Calligraphy Techniques* and *The Art and Craft of Calligraphy*.

ACKNOWLEDGMENTS
Step by step sequences demonstrated by Diana Hardy Wilson, Annie Moring and George Evans.

Every effort has been made to obtain copyright clearance, and we do
apologize if any omissions have been made.

144–146, 164–167 George Evans; 31 John Smith; 33 Jean Larcher, Ieuan
Rees; 49, 116 Dave Wood; 55 Paul Shaw; 74–6, 83, 88–90, 98–99, 102–105,
111–112, 117–120 Miriam Stribley; 77 Peter Thompson; 78–79 Arthur Baker;
84–85 Dorothy Mahoney, Pelham Books; 91 Evert van Dijk, Gaade Uitgerens;
96 Renate Fuhrmann; 97, 106–110, 122, 124–125, 128–135, 137–142 Dover
Publications; 100–101, 126–127, 136 based on Hans Meyer, Graphis; 116
Joan Pilsbury; 121, 123 V & A Museum; 162–163 Diana Hoare; 168–171
William Taunton and Diana Hoare.

Contents

Introduction 6

MATERIALS AND TOOLS 7

TECHNIQUES 15
Getting started 16
Pen practice 20
Using a quill pen 23
Using a reed pen 24
Using a brush 26

DECORATIVE DEVICES 28
Using colour 29
Flourishes 32
Raised gold 34
Gilding 36
Illumination 38
Ornament 40
Borders 44

LAYOUT GUIDELINES 47
Filling the space 48
Composition 51
Headings and sub-headings 54
Rules 56

LETTER CONSTRUCTION 57
Terminology 58
Understanding letter construction . . . 59
Roman capitals 60
The development of lower case 65
Numerals 69

THE ALPHABETS 71
Roman alphabets 72
Uncial and half-uncial alphabets . . . 80
Versal alphabets 86
Gothic alphabets 92
Italic alphabets 113
Copperplate alphabets 129

MORE ADVANCED TECHNIQUES
AND PROJECTS 143
Deciding on text area 144
Using rough sketches and thumbnails . . 146
Using a centred layout 154
Using words as images 162
Illustrations 164
Bookbinding 168

GLOSSARY 172

INDEX 174

Introduction

THE CRAFT OF CALLIGRAPHY – a Greek word meaning beautiful writing – has roots which stretch back into the mists of time. The techniques, tools, materials and some of the letter forms are much the same now as they were in the Middle Ages, and further back, but this does not mean that calligraphy has no part to play in the modern world.

The Chambers Twentieth Century Dictionary defines 'technique' as a 'method of performance'. This book is concerned both with working methods of practising calligraphers and with what they want their calligraphy to 'perform' as a result of these 'methods'. In the West, we expect to see lettering running from left to right and from top to bottom in straight lines of varying lengths. However, the calligrapher has wonderful opportunities to break free from the traditional mould and make letters perform visually as well as intellectually.

The modern student of calligraphy turns to historical models for an understanding of letter forms as they were used by earlier professionals. Before the invention of printing, calligraphy was vitally important as one of the few means of storing and transmitting the written word. For centuries scribes produced books by hand and we have much to learn from their methods.

Print is primarily for reading, not for seeing. The vast amounts of written material to which we are exposed every day make us switch off our sensitivity to lettering. Newspapers filled with sensationalism, information on every packaged product, road signs, shop signs and street names all bombard us. The act of reading has become an everyday skill that most of us take for granted.

Calligraphy helps us to 'see' what we are reading by making the words beautiful. Much of its impact relies upon producing a rhythmic texture in the writing. This beauty, however, is not necessarily peaceful. Tensions can also be used to disturb us. Seen in this light, calligraphy is a powerful tool for communicating the written word in the modern world.

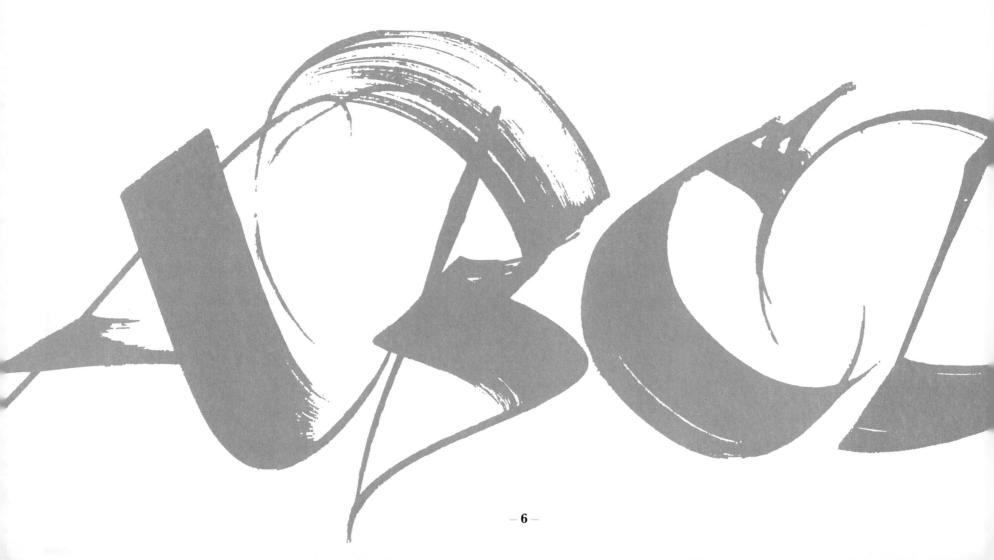

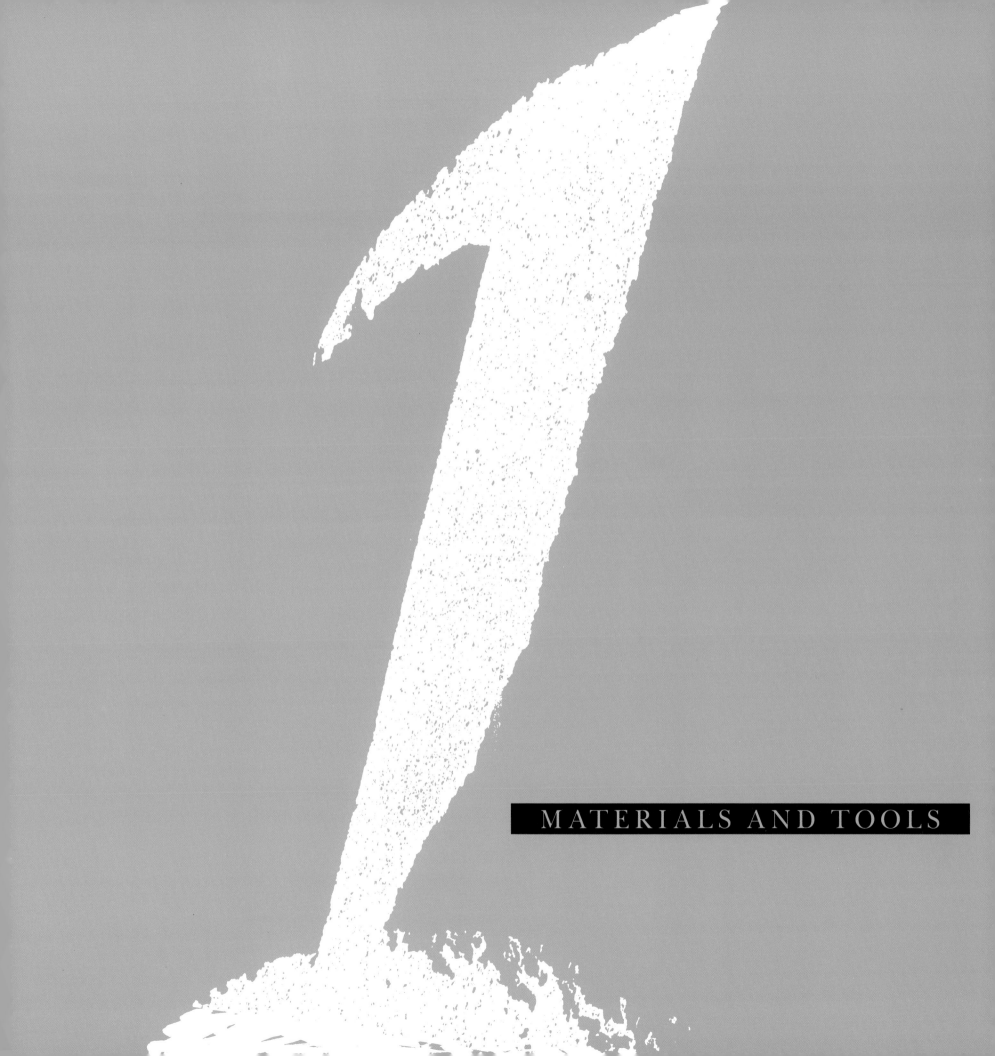

MATERIALS AND TOOLS

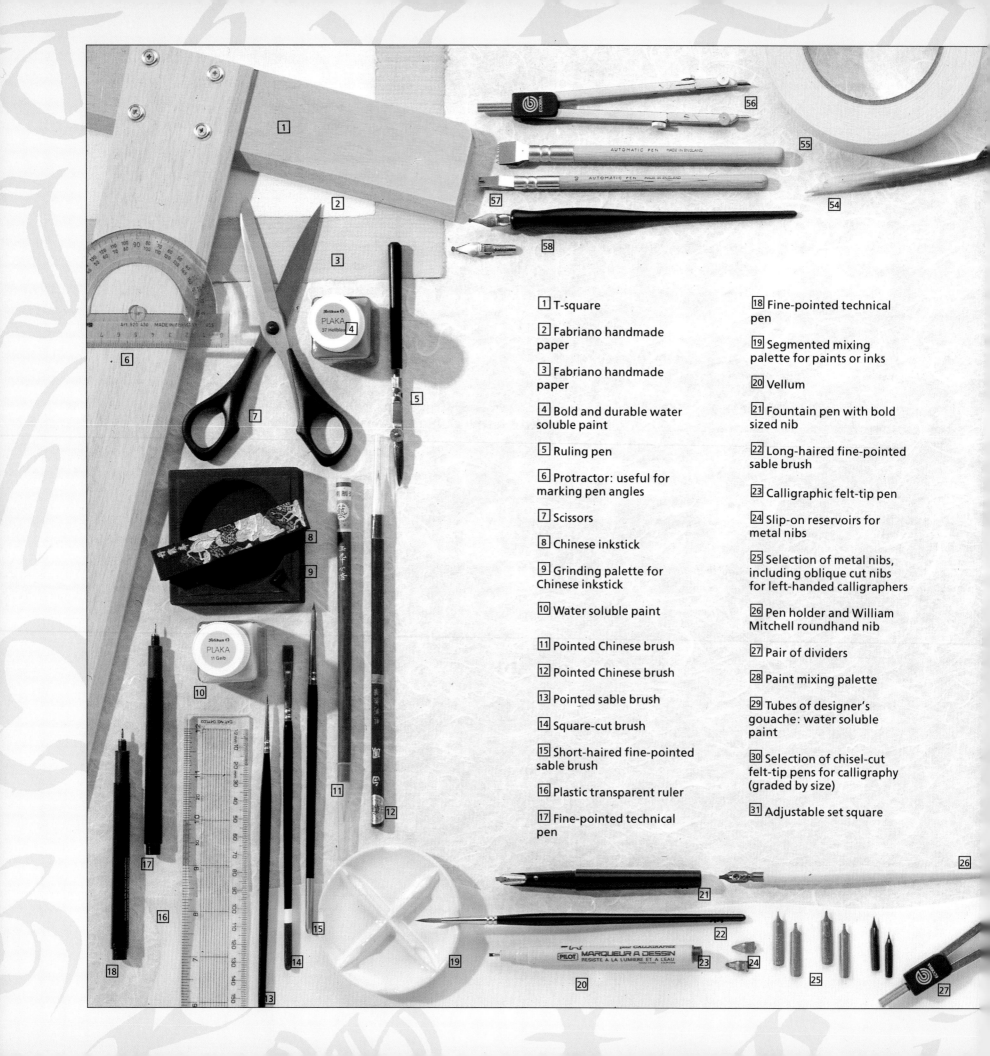

1 T-square

2 Fabriano handmade paper

3 Fabriano handmade paper

4 Bold and durable water soluble paint

5 Ruling pen

6 Protractor: useful for marking pen angles

7 Scissors

8 Chinese inkstick

9 Grinding palette for Chinese inkstick

10 Water soluble paint

11 Pointed Chinese brush

12 Pointed Chinese brush

13 Pointed sable brush

14 Square-cut brush

15 Short-haired fine-pointed sable brush

16 Plastic transparent ruler

17 Fine-pointed technical pen

18 Fine-pointed technical pen

19 Segmented mixing palette for paints or inks

20 Vellum

21 Fountain pen with bold sized nib

22 Long-haired fine-pointed sable brush

23 Calligraphic felt-tip pen

24 Slip-on reservoirs for metal nibs

25 Selection of metal nibs, including oblique cut nibs for left-handed calligraphers

26 Pen holder and William Mitchell roundhand nib

27 Pair of dividers

28 Paint mixing palette

29 Tubes of designer's gouache: water soluble paint

30 Selection of chisel-cut felt-tip pens for calligraphy (graded by size)

31 Adjustable set square

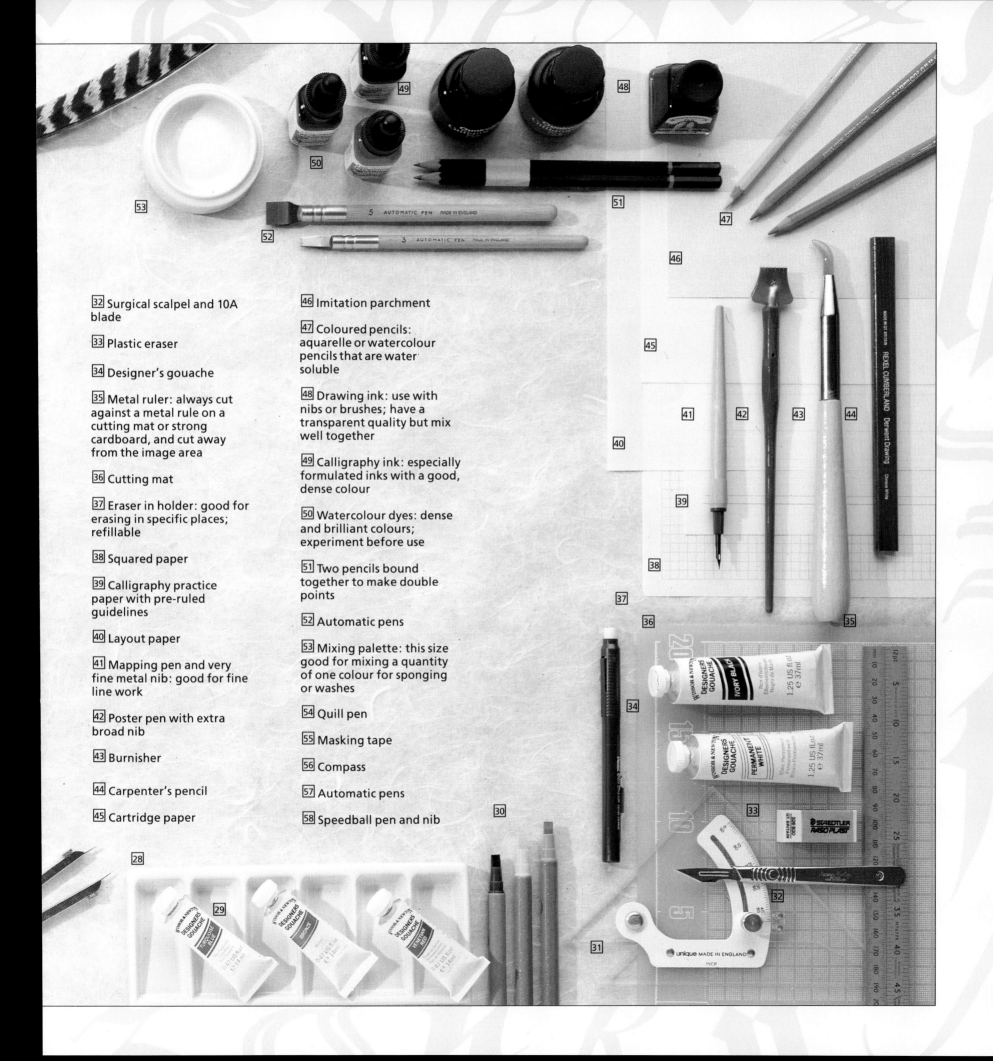

32 Surgical scalpel and 10A blade

33 Plastic eraser

34 Designer's gouache

35 Metal ruler: always cut against a metal rule on a cutting mat or strong cardboard, and cut away from the image area

36 Cutting mat

37 Eraser in holder: good for erasing in specific places; refillable

38 Squared paper

39 Calligraphy practice paper with pre-ruled guidelines

40 Layout paper

41 Mapping pen and very fine metal nib: good for fine line work

42 Poster pen with extra broad nib

43 Burnisher

44 Carpenter's pencil

45 Cartridge paper

46 Imitation parchment

47 Coloured pencils: aquarelle or watercolour pencils that are water soluble

48 Drawing ink: use with nibs or brushes; have a transparent quality but mix well together

49 Calligraphy ink: especially formulated inks with a good, dense colour

50 Watercolour dyes: dense and brilliant colours; experiment before use

51 Two pencils bound together to make double points

52 Automatic pens

53 Mixing palette: this size good for mixing a quantity of one colour for sponging or washes

54 Quill pen

55 Masking tape

56 Compass

57 Automatic pens

58 Speedball pen and nib

The craft of calligraphy does not require a large outlay: the main requirements are pen, ink and paper, and the main ingredient is a willingness to learn. Don't rush out and buy any old pen. Read these pages carefully and then decide upon your own requirements.

There is a tremendous range of materials and implements available to the calligrapher. The craft is currently experiencing a revival and many companies are entering this market for the first time, especially in the production of writing implements.

WRITING TOOLS

There are two main types of steel-nibbed pens: the pen nib with reservoir and pen holder, which requires constant filling, and the fountain-type pen, which has a built-in reservoir. The latter is a better choice for the beginner. It relieves you of the tedious task of constantly refilling the reservoir, using a paint brush or pipette which then requires washing out, before continuing to letter; full concentration is needed and so any distraction or encumbrance should be avoided.

Whichever type of pen you choose, always inform the supplier whether it is for a right- or left-handed person. There are special nibs for left-handed users where the end of the nib slopes top right to bottom left when viewed from the top. Whichever pen collection is chosen, there will be a variety of nib sizes available, although the size of, say, an Italic fine may vary between different manufacturers, whether it is for a fountain pen or nib holder.

Fountain-type pens

There are various calligraphic pens on the market. Some are purchased as an integral unit (that is, a complete pen); others are bought as a set and include a barrel, reservoir and a set of interchangeable nib units. Avoid the cartridge refill as it limits the colour of ink that can be used. It is better to buy a pen which has a squeeze-fill reservoir so that colour can be changed quite easily.

Don't be afraid to ask the local art shop or stationers to show their entire range. The larger suppliers often have demonstration pens that can be tested before finally making a decision to purchase. The choice of pens available is ever-increasing and you must ensure that you choose one which is the most comfortable for you.

BELOW Three kinds of fountain-type pens. The top two have a variety of interchangeable nib units. The third art pen is a complete unit, available in a number of metric sizes.

The ink holders, or reservoirs, are of either the squeeze or piston type and all three pens have an optional cartridge ink supply.

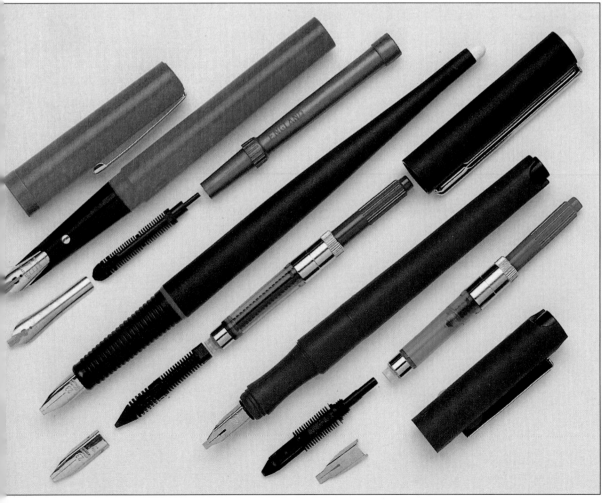

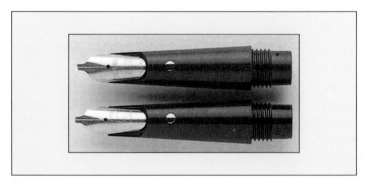

ABOVE A left-hand nib unit and a right-hand nib unit.

Nibs

Once you have gained confidence and experience with a pen, a pen holder and range of nibs is the next addition to your equipment. The range available is vast, including round-hand, script, poster, scroll and special-effect nibs. These items are sold separately or can often be bought on a display card which contains pen holder, reservoir and set of nibs. If you do decide to purchase this type of pen you will need to remove the film of lacquer with which the nibs are coated to avoid deterioration. This can be done either by passing the nib through a flame briefly or by gently scraping the surface.

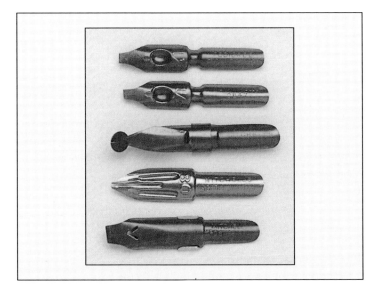

INKS

There are many inks available, and choice is made difficult by this fact. The main property an ink should have is that it should flow easily and not clog the pen. Non-waterproof ink flows marginally better than waterproof inks and watercolours. The medium should not spread on the writing surface. Unwanted feathering can be attributed either to the paper or to the ink, and you should experiment with both to confirm compatibility.

Density of colour is important in finished work, and there are inks available which are specifically stated as being calligraphic inks. These are suitable for use in fountain-type pens. There are also inks that are referred to as 'artist colour', some of which are waterproof; many

need a cleaning fluid to clean or flush the pen through after use. (Check with the stockist that such a cleaning agent will have no harmful effects.) The range of colours is wide, and most of these types of ink are miscible, giving an even wider range.

Calligraphers often use watercolour paint for embellishment. This is satisfactory for a pen and holder but not for a fountain pen. Instead of watercolour, pens can be filled with artists' retouching dye, which is translucent and the colour is very pure and water soluble. Ink and watercolours vary in light fastness; so check the label for the product's degree of permanence.

Some bottles have a pipette incorporated in the cap. This is useful for charging the reservoirs in pen holders and saves loading with a brush.

LEFT A selection of nibs.

BELOW Pen nibs and holders with an ink reservoir, and nibs with integral reservoirs and holder.

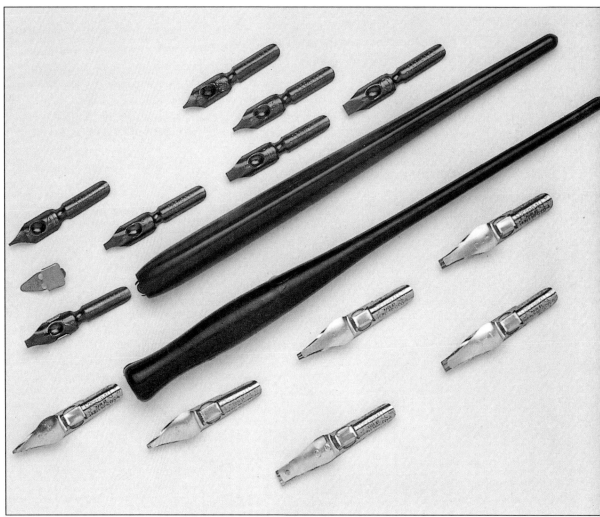

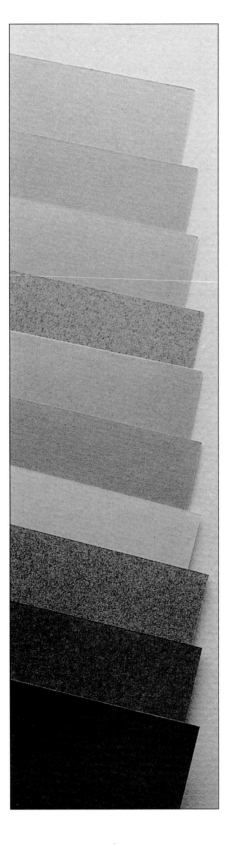

PAPER

For the beginner, a draughtsman's or designer's layout pad is ideal for roughing out ideas and preliminary penwork. Pads come in various sizes, finishes and weights. Initially, choose a paper that is not too opaque and make sure, when the paper is placed over the sample alphabets in this book, that you can still see the letterforms through it.

There are typo pads specifically made for designers' layouts. This type of pad is ideal, because it is used for tracing letters in studios when laying out work. It has a slightly milky white appearance and is not as transparent as tracing paper.

For finished work a good quality cartridge paper is ideal. Writing papers are produced in many shades and finishes, although they can be a little restrictive due to the sizes available. There are also many drawing papers which can be put to good use. It is as well to experiment with different types of paper, avoiding those with a heavy coating, as they will obstruct the passage of the nib and the flow of the ink. For outdoor work such as posters, special papers that weather well can be used, but do not forget to use a waterproof ink.

LEFT Different papers for finished work, available in pads or single sheets.

DRAWING BOARD

A drawing board on which to work will of course be required. This need not be an expensive purchase. In calligraphy, work is carried out with the drawing board at an angle. Position yourself in front of the work so that you can see it clearly without stretching. The angle of the board should ideally be about 45°. However, providing you are in a good viewing position, it may be as low as 30° – whatever suits you. Never work on a flat surface as this necessitates bending over the board and using the pen in an upright position, whereas on a sloping board the pen is at a shallower angle, helping to regulate the ink flow.

A drawing board can be purchased, with or without adjustable angles, from most art shops. Alternatively, laminate shelving board is available at most timber merchants and is quite adequate. A suitable board size is 18 × 24in (450 × 600mm). Apply iron-on laminate edges to give a clean finish. The board can be supported on your lap and leant against a table or desk, making an angle of about 45° with the desk top. A professional-looking board that adjusts to three angles can be made quite readily. The board illustrated is approximately one-tenth scale so multiply all measurements by ten.

BELOW A home-made drawing board with three adjustable angles.

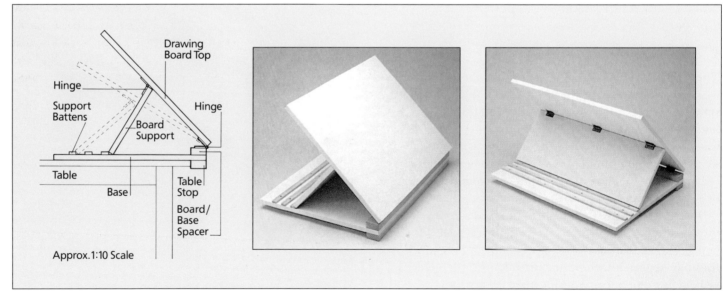

Drawing Board Top

Hinge

Support Battens

Hinge

Board Support

Table

Base

Table Stop

Board/ Base Spacer

Approx. 1:10 Scale

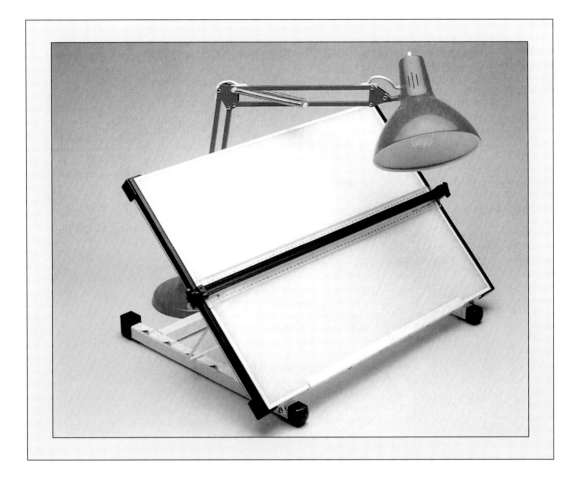

ABOVE A professional drawing board with parallel motion.

RULER

Choose an 18in (450mm) ruler, preferably with both metric and imperial calibrations. Transparent rulers with grid lines running parallel to their edges can be useful for horizontal alignment in rough layouts, where multiple lines need ruling.

A ruler with a good bevelled edge is more accurate in transferring measurements and is useful when reversed for ruling ink lines as the bevelled edge prevents ink seeping under the ruler.

SET SQUARE

A 45° set square will be required. Some have millimetre calibrations on the right-angled edges, and these are useful when laying out rectangular shapes. The square should be at least 10in (250mm) on the two shorter edges. A similar 30°/60° set square will also be needed.

PENCILS

An H or 2H pencil is needed for preliminary guidelines, which need to be fine. The leads are not too soft; so the student won't be spending a lot of time keeping a keen point on the pencil.

An HB will be required for rough layout work as it is sufficiently soft to give a good image without unnecessary pressure. A soft carpenter's pencil is ideal for initial test layouts and can be sharpened to a chisel edge to emulate the size of calligraphic nib to be used.

Propelling, or clutch, pencils have become very popular in recent years, and HB, H and 2H leads are available. A $\frac{1}{50}$in (0.5mm) lead size is preferable, as the smaller leads tend to snap easily.

ERASER

There are many erasers on the market. Choose a plastic one for paper and film.

Cut two laminate boards to the dimensions above, one for the base and the other for the top. In the same material cut a further piece for the board support and some softwood for support battens, table stop and board-base spacer. All these items measure the same width as the drawing board. In addition, six butt hinges and some chipboard screws will be required.

Screw a board spacer to one edge of the base together with a table stop on the opposite side to prevent the board from sliding when in use. Screw the support battens to the base in the positions shown to give three angles from 30° to 45° approximately.

Attach the board support to the drawing board top with three of the hinges, one in the centre and one a little distance in from each end. It is essential that the support is positioned correctly to achieve the desired angles. Fix the remaining three hinges to the drawing board, underside at the base, with the other side to the board-base spacer. Give all edges a clean finish with iron-on laminate.

CUTTING TOOL

A surgical scalpel is very useful and has an exceptionally keen edge. Replacement blades are sold in units of five per packet. Do be careful when changing the blade, it will be extremely sharp and should be treated with great respect. Always remove the blade by lifting it first from its retaining lug and then with the thumb, push the blade away from the body. Keep the fingers well away from contact with the cutting edge. When fitting a new blade, slide it on to the retaining lug, grip the blade on the blunt top edge and push it home. When the scalpel is not in use, a cork from your favourite bottle of wine will protect both you and the blade.

RIGHT When the scalpel is not in use, use a cork to prevent accidents and avoid blunting the blade.

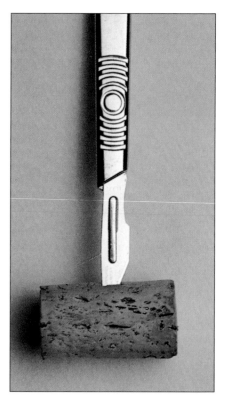

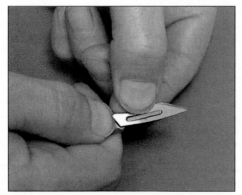

1 Ease the scalpel blade from its mounting using a thumbnail.

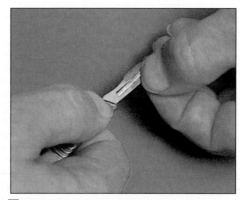

3 Place the new blade on the handle mounting.

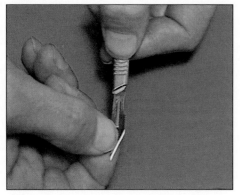

2 Pull the blade from the handle mounting by gripping the blunt edge.

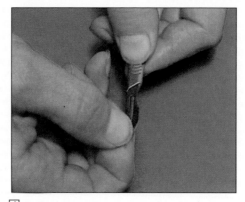

4 Push the blunt edge of the blade firmly on to the mounting gripping.

ADDITIONAL REQUIREMENTS

These include masking tape and a few large sheets of cartridge paper to cover the new board and to guard any work. Absorbent cloth, or kitchen roll, will also be necessary to wipe clean the fountain pen after filling, and the nib when the ink shows signs of building up or clogging.

Some double-sided tape and a substantial weight of card will be required, as may additional lighting if the working area lacks sufficient daylight or good artificial light. Lighting is discussed in more detail in the next chapter.

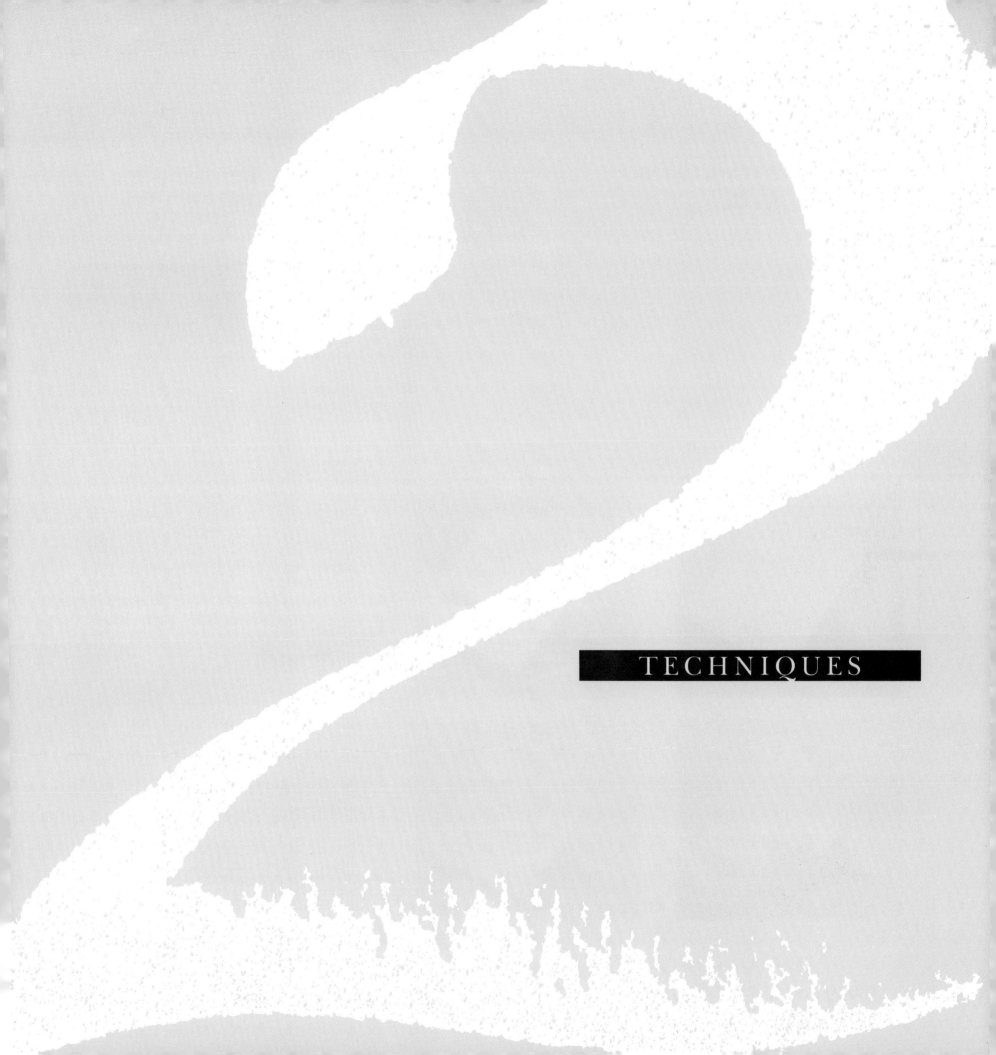

TECHNIQUES

Getting Started

The styles compiled in the following sections are basic calligraphic forms, but this certainly does not mean that they are easy. You will require determination, patience and, in order to maintain concentration, peace and quiet. To facilitate the learning progress, follow the principles laid down in this book as closely as possible. If a certain standard is asked to be maintained – for example, accurate laying out of guidelines for lettering – the instructions should be followed carefully: the use of blunt pencils to mark these out would be unacceptable because it would produce inaccuracies. Wherever possible, time-saving devices have been incorporated to assist progress. So do not try to take short cuts. This invariably ends up with you having to back-track. If you are having problems, check that you have followed the instructions correctly. Most people can letter well, when properly guided.

BELOW A card support with book in position for right-handed students.

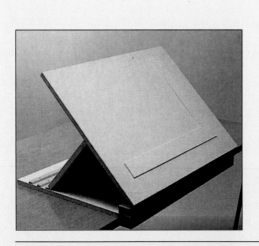

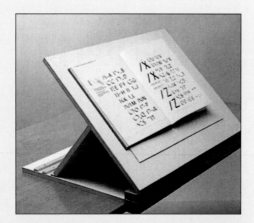

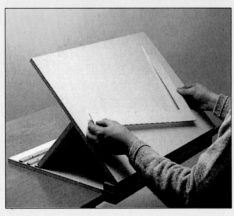

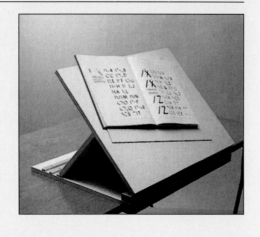

SETTING UP THE DRAWING BOARD TO TRACE

The drawing board now has to be set up so that this book can be used as a tracing reference. If you are right-handed, take a strip of heavy mounting card and position it with tape on to the writing surface. This is to rest this book on when the letterforms are traced.

For left-handed students, the card is positioned differently, because it is difficult for left-handed calligraphers to letter horizontally. The writing hand obscures the lettering produced and, even with a left-handed nib, to achieve the correct angle of writing can involve an uncomfortable pen hold. By tilting the paper the problem is lessened.

Therefore, if you are left-handed, try positioning the work with its right-hand side dropped down 15° from the horizontal, with the extra piece at right angles to prevent the book from sliding to the right. You can then try lettering a few characters. If the position is uncomfortable the angle may need to be adjusted several times.

If you find that by merely turning the paper through various degrees, you are still unable to achieve the desired angle of lettering, try grinding down the nib to form an even steeper angle. This can be done on a fine-grade India stone or fine-grade production paper (the type used by car sprayers in the preparation of paintwork).

To save undue expense, experiment first with a nib used with a pen holder before attempting to convert a fountain-pen nib. This way, at least, if the result is not satisfactory, a relatively costly nib will not have been ruined. Make sure that when grinding down the edge, a burr is not left on one side, nor the edge left so sharp as to cut into the surface of the paper to be lettered. Finally, ensure that the edge of the nib is square, not rounded.

LEFT A card support for left-handed students.

SETTING UP THE DRAWING BOARD FOR GENERAL WORK

Remove the pieces of card used to retain the book. Take two sheets of cartridge paper and cut them to a size which is 3in (75mm) less than the height and width of the surface area of the drawing board. If the board has been constructed from the illustration in this book, 15 × 21in (375 × 525mm) will be required. Place these sheets on the board surface with an equal border all around of about 1½in (40mm). Using masking tape, stick both sheets together to the board. It will be easier if this is done with the board flat. Attach one of the long edges of the sheets first, then pull the sheets taut and stick down the opposite side. Then tape the two exposed ends.

For the pad cut a further, slightly larger, sheet of cartridge which will give a border of 1in (25mm) on the drawing board and stick this with tape on all four edges so that no edge is left exposed and the sheet it taut. This will now provide an ideal writing surface. The pen does not perform well against a hard, solid surface and the backing sheets give a little spring, which is suited to the action of the nib. Once the first alphabet has been lettered, you

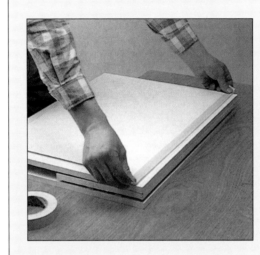
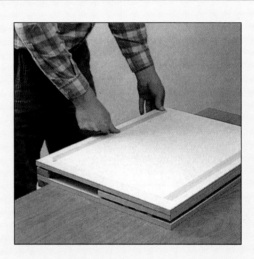

ABOVE Applying cover to drawing board.

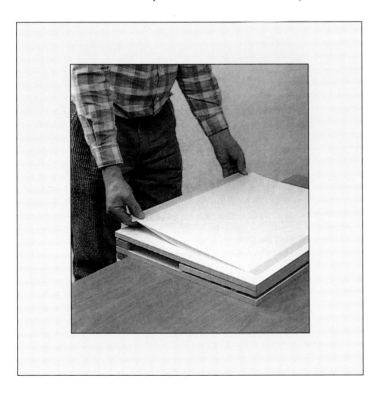

LEFT Applying padding to drawing board.

should have a good idea of the point on the board where you feel most comfortable when lettering. This position will differ with the individual and is known as the writing level.

To prevent grease from the hand being deposited on the writing sheet, make a guard sheet from a sheet of cartridge paper. It must be positioned with tape on to the pad at a level that allows you to work on the writing line.

To retain the writing sheet as it is moved towards the top of the board at the end of each line of lettering, a strip of fabric tape or card may be used at the top of the board. This is an optional extra; you may prefer the sheet to be mobile.

Always put aside a spare piece of the writing material being used to start the pen off and to practise strokes.

LIGHTING

Correct lighting is as important for the eyes as posture is for the limbs. Tired eyes and limbs are not conducive to clean, crisp calligraphy. Ideally, you should work in daylight. If you are right-handed, the light source should be from the left, and if left-handed, from the right. Light, correctly directed, should ensure that the calligrapher is not working in the shadow cast by the writing hand. Lighting therefore plays a key role in the laying out of the working area. Strong direct light, such as sunlight, should be avoided, as excessive glare from the usual white surface being worked will make lettering difficult.

You will also need artificial light from an anglepoise lamp or similar unit, either wall-mounted or standing. The direction of the source is the same as for daylight. The advantage of an anglepoise lamp is that of ease of direction or position; for intricate work, light can be directed to the point required by simple adjustment.

THE POSITION TO ADOPT WHEN LETTERING

It is important to be comfortable when seated, with the feet flat on the floor, the back straight and the drawing board positioned so that the arms can move freely.

The height of the seat or chair used is important, and consideration should be given to the height of the table or desk on which the drawing board sits. If the board is too low, the calligrapher will inevitably acquire backache through bending over it; if too high, the neck and arms will suffer through constant stretching. The ideal height will differ for each and every one of you and adjustments to seating and height of drawing board may be necessary.

HINTS ON PEN MAINTENANCE

For some, pens are not the easiest of implements to work with: they blot, dry up in the midst of a stroke or even refuse to write at all. However, many of the complaints levelled at pens are due to poor maintenance. Just like any other tool, they need a certain amount of care and attention if they are to perform properly.

Always empty a fountain-type pen of ink after use, unless it is to be re-used in a short space of time. Ink soon dries both on the nib and in the ink-feed section, rendering the implement useless. Time and effort can be saved by emptying the reservoir into the ink bottle and flushing the pen with lukewarm water which contains a drop of washing-up liquid. This simple measure is ideal for water-based inks and will keep the pen in good condition.

Occasionally it is necessary to strip down the whole nib unit and clean it with soapy water and an old tooth-brush or nail-brush. Most manufacturers would be horrified to think that such an act was necessary to clean their pens, but when changes of colour are required from, say, black to red, merely flushing the pen is insufficient to remove all

the black ink, and the red or lighter colour will be tainted if the pen is not completely clean. If a pen has been left with ink inside for a period of time, without use, it will require stripping down in the same manner. A pipe cleaner is ideal for removing ink from inside the squeeze-type reservoirs, but make sure that its wire centre does not puncture the plastic.

There are now many different waterproof inks available for use in fountain-type pens. The colour range available is so vast that most students cannot wait to try them out. The snag about waterproof inks is that, once the pen is left for a short time, a waterproof ink will dry up and be difficult to remove with a water-based solution.

There is a cleaner available which is primarily used by airbrush artists for removing the colour from the airbrush. This solution is ideal for a thorough strip-down operation. The fluid has no harmful effect on the pen and removes even the hardened ink, but it is always best to ask the supplier if it is safe to use on plastics. If the ink stops in the middle of a stroke, remove the barrel and squeeze or turn the reservoir, depending on the type of pen, until the ink reaches the nib. Make sure you have a paper towel at hand to prevent a disaster.

A pen that is drying or missing during writing may have insufficient ink, or the split in the nib may have become widened by pressure. To solve this problem either fill the pen or reduce the split in the nib by squeezing both sides together. Also check that the nib and ink duct are free from particles picked up from the paper surface. Ink will not take to a greasy surface. To remove such marks, a good proprietary light fuel may be used. Test a sample of the same paper to ensure that the petrol does not leave a stain.

Rulers and set squares (triangles) should be cleaned only with warm soapy water. Abrasive cleaners will damage the plastic and remove the calibrations.

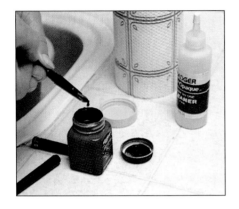 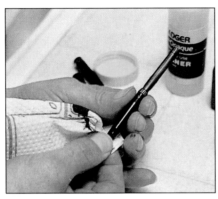

1 Emptying the ink from the pen.

2 Removing the nib and ink feeder from its housing.

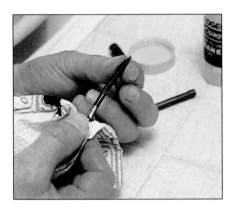 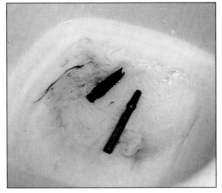 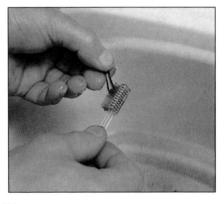 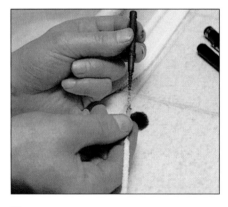

3 Separating the nib from the ink feeder.

4 Washing out the housing and ink holder, or reservoir, in water.

5 Using a toothbrush soaked in cleaning fluid to clean the parts.

6 Using a pipe cleaner soaked in fluid to remove all the ink from inside the ink holder or reservoir.

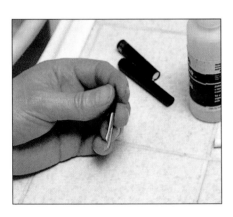 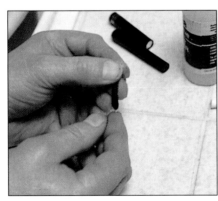 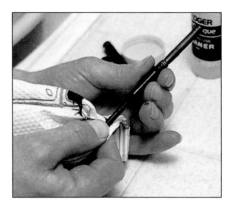 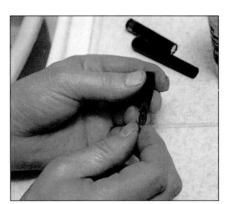

7 Aligning the nib and ink feeder before re-assembling the pen.

Pen practice

It is the angle of the nib in relation to the direction of writing and stroke which gives the letterforms their characteristics. A style that is formed with the nib angle at 30° to the writing line will have a different visual appearance to that lettered at 45°. This is because it is the angle that determines the weight of each stroke and the stress of the round letters. Because the angle is maintained from letter to letter, with the exception of one or two strokes, a certain quality and rhythm is created throughout the letterforms.

Because the pen angle is 30°, a vertical stroke will only be as wide as the image the nib will make at that angle and not equivalent to the full nib width. In a round letterform, there is a point at which the whole of the nib width is used due to the pen travelling in a semicircle.

The maximum width of stroke – 'the stress' – will be exactly 90° to the thinnest stroke, which is fortunate for round letterforms because, if the nature of the tool used did not produce this automatically, round letterforms would appear thinner than vertical ones of the same weight. Indeed, when letterforms are freely constructed with a pencil and filled in with a brush, compensation has to be made to the curved thick strokes, increasing them in weight to give an optical balance with straight strokes.

Weight of stroke is determined by the angle of the pen and the direction of travel. Diagonal strokes will vary in weight depending on the direction of the stroke. Strokes made from top left to bottom right are more consistent than those formed top right to bottom left. Horizontal strokes are of a uniform width. These variations are acceptable in pen lettering and give the forms a natural, unforced appearance. The alphabet is constructed from common vertical, horizontal, diagonal and curved strokes.

Letterforms within the alphabet have common likenesses and, although there are 26 characters, the strokes that are repeated within the capitals and lower case are frequent. This repetition makes the task easier: once the basic strokes used in letter construction are mastered, the forming of individual letters is relatively simple. The ability to produce the strokes with confidence comes from practising them on layout paper.

FORMING STROKES

Unlike handwriting, where the pen is lifted from the paper only occasionally between words or necessary breaks in form, calligraphic lettering dictates that the pen is lifted after each stroke. It is the combination of strokes which creates the letterforms.

The pen is nearly always used with a pulling action towards the letterer. Horizontal strokes are made from left to right. The nib should glide across the sheet with just enough pressure to keep it in contact with the writing surface.

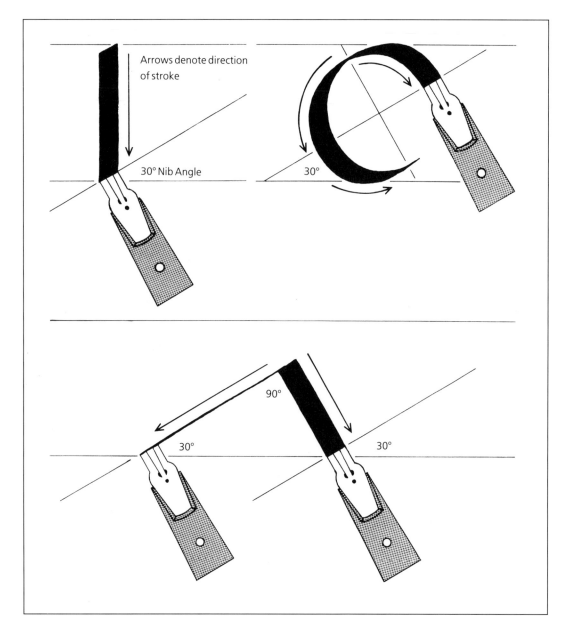

Arrows denote direction of stroke

30° Nib Angle

30°

90°

30°

30°

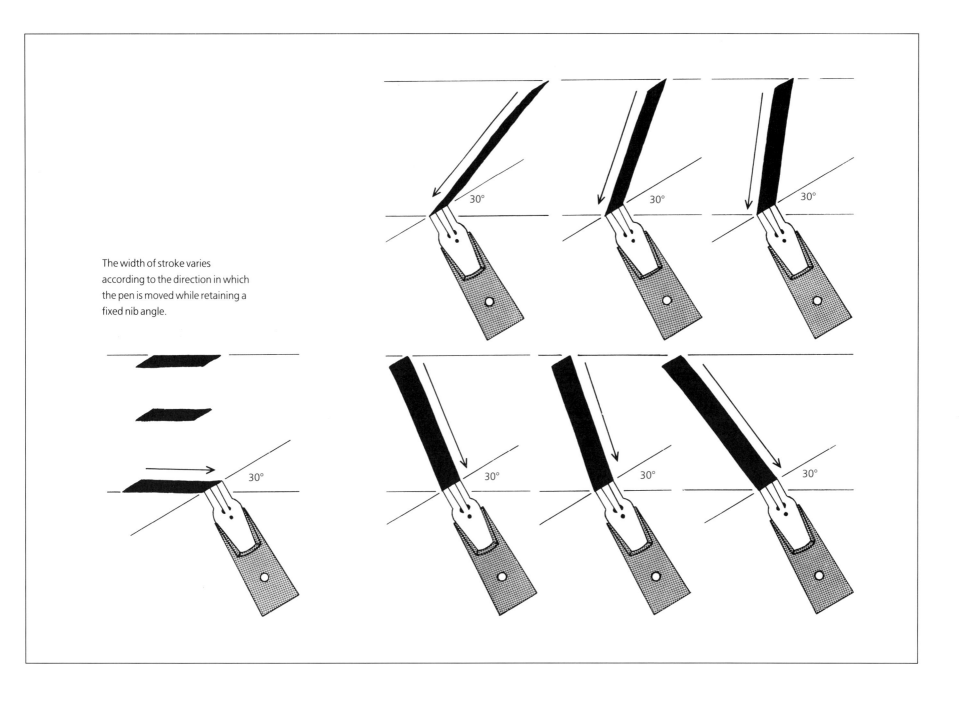

The width of stroke varies according to the direction in which the pen is moved while retaining a fixed nib angle.

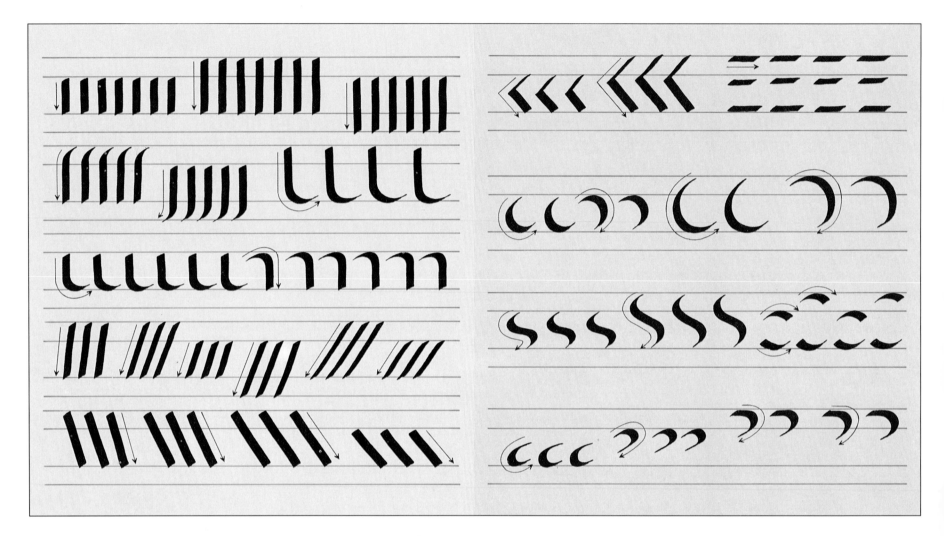

It is at this point that problems often face the newcomer to calligraphy. It is essential that the pen angle is maintained while producing the stroke, whatever direction is taken. This usually takes all of the your concentration and can result in the nib not being in contact with the paper throughout the movement. This skipping will cause an uneven weight in the stroke, and the result will be patchy.

Control over the pen for small letters is with the fingers for the up-and-down movements, with the wrist being employed only slightly for rounded letters. When forming larger letters, say over ¾in (20mm), the movement is from the shoulder with the whole arm moving down the writing surface. The height of letter at which the transition from finger to arm movement is made is dependent upon the dexterity of the individual.

The exercise requires mainly finger and wrist action with, perhaps, some of the longer, diagonal strokes needing arm movement. The third and little finger rest on the paper and help to support the pen holder.

BASIC LETTER STROKES

Begin by tracing over the forms given in the exercise. To do this, a nib that is of the same size as that used here will be required. Take a nib and compare it with the nib and width of stroke marked at the side of the sample exercise. It will be beneficial if the size can be matched exactly, although a small variation will not matter at this stage. The main aim of the exercise is for the student to become familiar with the action of the pen and to develop a rhythm when forming the images.

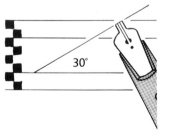

ABOVE These simple strokes form the basis of letter construction.

Using a quill pen

The development of the formal Roman capital alphabet, with its elegant proportions parading a fine balance of thick and thin strokes, demanded a writing implement with flexibility and the ability to produce fine lines.

The quill pen had all the characteristics required to write early scripts. It enabled scribes to write legibly, establish a rhythm, and produce good, rounded shapes with a consistent weight of stroke, as required.

The variations possible in preparing the nib of a quill strongly influenced the hands for which it was used. The nib could be cut at a variety of angles, or could be sharpened to a very fine point. The angle of the pen could also alter the strokes and the forms described on the page. This resulted in instruction books being made, containing illustrations of how the quill pen should be held and its angle of manipulation. There are many fine engravings that show a scribe manipulating a chunky instrument. This is the quill pen. Some pictorial references show the barbs of the feather intact, which is not convenient for writing.

There are many excellent sources of quills. The primary flight feathers of geese, swans, and turkeys are ideal. For delicate work, crow and duck quills provide a very fine shaft. The natural curve of the quill is important, so that the instrument sits comfortably in the hand. Left-handed calligraphers should select quills from the right side of the bird, and right-handed calligraphers from the left.

The quill needs to be thoroughly dried out before it can be prepared and cut for use. During the drying process, the natural oils are eliminated. Ideally, this should be done naturally, but that could take many months. A source of gentle artificial heat can be substituted. Exposure to the heat source is very brief, otherwise the quill is rendered too brittle. The heating alters the quill from the original opaque soft-textured form to a harder, clarified shaft.

There are several methods of applying heat and each calligrapher needs to find the one that produces the right flexibility and hardness according to personal preference. The simplest method of heating is to position the quill about 2in (5cm) above an electric hotplate and rotate it slowly for about 10 seconds.

After heating, scrape off the greasy membrane from the outside of the quill and remove the pith from inside. When you have polished the quill it is ready for cutting. A suitable length is 7–8in (18–20cm). You can shape the quill nib with a surgical scalpel or sharp steel knife. To maintain the writing quality, it can be retrimmed frequently.

CUTTING A QUILL

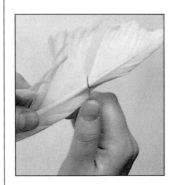

1 Strip the barbs from the shaft. Using the back of a pocketknife, scrape the length of the barrel to remove the outer membrane. Rub the shaft with a rough cloth.

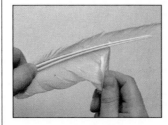

2 Before cutting, the quill must be hardened and clarified. First, cut off the sealed end of the barrel, then soak the quill in water overnight. The next morning, heat some sand in a shallow tray or pan. Take the quill from the water and shake it vigorously. Using a long point, such as a knitting needle, push the 'coil' inside the quill to the end. Spoon hot sand into the barrel and, when it is full, plunge it into the heated sand for a few seconds. Then cut the top off the quill.

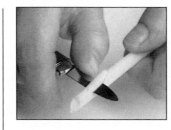

3 Make an oblique cut, long and slanting, downward to the tip of the quill.

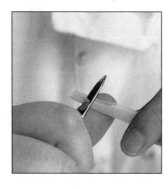

4 Make another oblique cut below the first to shape the shoulders of the quill. This gives the familiar stepped arrangement of shoulders and nib tip. Remove any pith remaining in the shaft. Make a small slit in the shaft to aid the flow of ink down to the writing tip. Do this very carefully: a length of ¼in (6mm) is adequate.

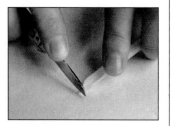

5 Work on a smooth, hard surface, such as glass, for the final shaping of the nib. There are two ways of holding the nib for this stage. The first is to rest it on the edge of the glass, underside down. The other method requires more care: place the nib underside uppermost and hold it firmly. Make a clean cut down the nib tip in a single vertical movement. Pare the nib finely and obliquely on the topside to complete the quill.

USING A QUILL PEN

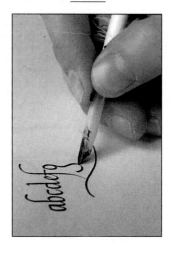

Use a brush to load the quill pen with ink, and begin to write. If used often, the nib will need to be recut.

Using a reed pen

Reed pens, among the earliest forms of nibbed writing instruments, were commonly used by Middle Eastern scribes because of the plentiful supply of sturdy and suitable reeds in their regions. The Egyptians, too, made reed pens and soft reed brushes for writing on papyrus. The Romans, having adopted the use of papyrus, found the reed pen a most suitable instrument with which to write. It was sometimes referred to as a 'calamus', after the particular species of palm that provided the raw material. Cut to shape, the reed pen was used to apply ink to parchment and linen as well as papyrus.

A reed pen can be made quite easily and certainly cheaply. Garden cane is the material most commonly available now that provides an equivalent to the original type of reed. The hollow cane is easily cut to length and shaped, using a sharp knife, to form a writing nib. Inspect the cane carefully to make sure it has no splits or imperfections that could result in any number of disasters when you start using it to write. Cut it to a manageable length – 8in (20cm) is recommended.

The cane, being nothing but a hollow tube, provides an excellent reservoir for ink. You must take care not to let it flood the writing, so work on a flat or only slightly inclined surface. In common with most calligraphic implements, the reed pen resists a pushing motion and you obtain best results from pulling the stroke.

In comparison with the quill, the reed pen has less flexibility. It cannot sustain such fine and accurate shaping, and the overall effect of work written with this pen may not be as eloquent. It does have excellent qualities, however, which make it a valid implement for many styles of writing. The calligrapher can select canes of different sizes and prepare a varied range of nib widths accordingly. The resulting bold letterforms are highly effective in poster work, headings, and titles, and can be matched to specific jobs where a particular nuance is sought.

The Romans used the reed pen in the execution of their square capitals and rustic hands. The method of holding the pen between the index and middle fingers must have influenced the way Rustica letters evolved, with thin uprights and thick cross strokes. Other variations occurred with these letterforms, including a slight pull to the right in curved strokes and a condensing of the overall shape, especially as compared to the roundness of the Roman capitals.

MAKING A REED PEN

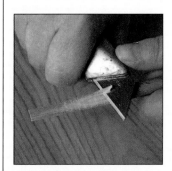

1 Assemble the materials – a suitable reed or cane, a sharp knife, and a hard surface to cut on. Soak the reed or cane for at least 15 minutes, then cut it with a sharp knife while it is still wet. Cut the cane to a comfortable working length – about 8in (20cm). The first cut, shown here, is an oblique slash down toward one end.

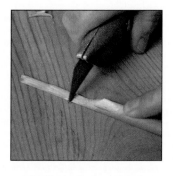

3 Firmly hold the pen on the cutting surface and trim the end to nearer the eventual nib length. Turn the pen through 90° and make a small slit down the centre of the nib, at right angles to the writing edge.

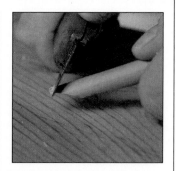

5 Make a small diagonal cut on the upper side of the nib, down towards the end. This will produce a fine writing edge.

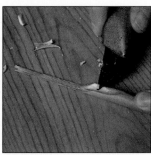

2 Shape the shoulders of the nib. Then, using the point of the knife, clean out any pith inside the cane which has been exposed by the first cut.

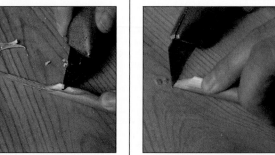

4 If the nib seems too thick, very carefully pare it down to make it thinner. Holding the nib underside up, make a vertical cut across the nib end.

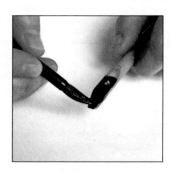

6 The reed pen is now ready to use. A brush is used to transfer ink onto the underside of the nib.

USING A REED PEN

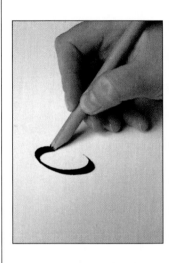

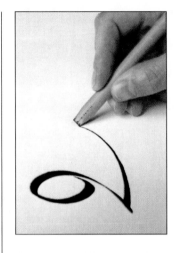

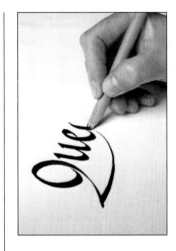

1 A reed pen has a different 'feel' to a metal-nibbed pen; because it is made all in one piece, it feels almost like an extension of your hand and is very pleasurable to use. The width of the strokes made with a reed pen is dictated by how wide the nib has been cut. This illustration demonstrates the firm and solid strokes which this simple instrument is capable of producing.

2 The reed pen has the ability to produce both the extremely fine lines and the thick strokes required for calligraphy. Holding the reed pen at the prescribed pen angle, a fine line is extended from the tail of the letter. To complete the line the right-hand side of the nib is lifted off the paper, and the left-hand side of the nib drags wet ink into a hairline.

3 The lower-case letters are written confidently, and show how a nib made from an inflexible material can produce very well the familiar characteristics of calligraphy.

4 When working with a reed pen, always keep the top side of the nib clean. Take care not to overload with ink, as this could result in blotting or smudging. This example shows an excellent balance between the thin and thick strokes, and a fine hairline extension to the last letter. This was performed by dragging wet ink with the left-hand corner of the nib.

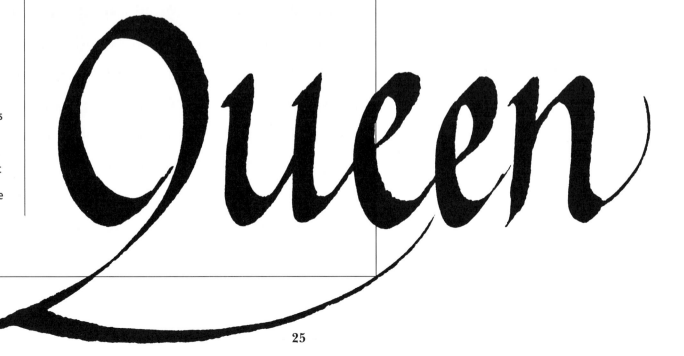

Using a brush

The best way to learn the possibilities of brush lettering is to work on quite a large scale and freely, in an informal style. Something of a hidden agenda exists when you work with brushes. This is particularly in evidence when the amount of ink or paint on the brush diminishes, providing the potential for interesting textural contrasts. For example, if the ink runs dry in mid-letter, you can make a positive feature of the change of emphasis, rather than dispensing with the work as 'no good'.

You can experiment further by laying patches of wet colour side by side and letting the different colours merge. A pre-planned colour selection can produce some exciting and extremely interesting results.

Broad, flat, or square-tipped brushes produce bold lettering. Manipulation of the brush angle, particularly when doing a horizontal stroke, creates further interest.

When working with brushes, you will soon realize that, having worked a successful solution in rough form, recreating the exact same image in the finished work is not so easy. This must be regarded as an exciting advantage of brush lettering, not as a deterrent. Because of the free movement of the brush, a good understanding of letter shapes is essential if you are to achieve convincing brush lettering.

Discovering which brush to use, in order to achieve the required impact, is truly a matter of trial and error. Favourite solutions will reveal themselves over a period of time. Get to know the marks of as many brushes as possible. The traditions of Eastern calligraphy are founded in the use of brushes, so include Chinese bamboo brushes in your selection. The hairs of these brushes come to a fine point and make marks quite different from those of square-cut watercolour brushes. Your attempts at lettering with pointed brushes may result in images related to Oriental brush-writing styles. Study of Eastern brush techniques can only make an enriching addition to the repertoire of the Western calligrapher.

Brush lettering can be incorporated in a wide range of designs, creating strong visual effects with an enticing air of informality. The image of brush lettering, for example, as a headline above the more formal writing of the broad nib can be highly effective. In this role, brush lettering played a major part in advertising design of the 1930s and 1940s. If you look at examples of advertising design from that period, you will see the potential of using freely written brush script with formal typeset copy.

ARRANGING LETTERS

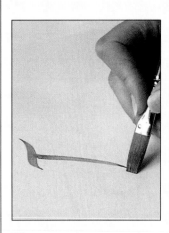

1 Working with a large square-cut brush permits much freedom of individual expression. The first letter provides an anchor from which the remaining letters can hang or around which they can be grouped.

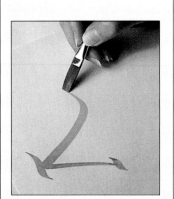

2 The letters are constructed in the traditional manner of following a stroke sequence. The brush is held at an angle either suitable to the chosen style of lettering or to produce the intended weight of stroke for a particular piece.

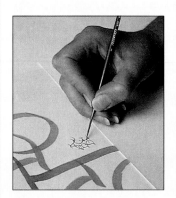

3 Pleasing arrangements can be arrived at, often unintentionally, when practising lettering with a brush. An extended stroke to create a swashed letter is easily accomplished with a brush.

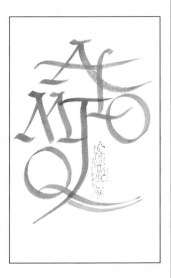

4 Place a sheet of clean paper under your writing hand to keep the writing surface clean and free of grease.
Allowing the design to grow, without adhering to any preconceived ideas, often produces pleasing results.

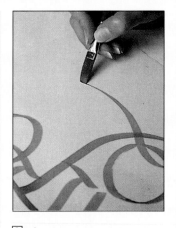

5 The introduction of a second colour and a different weight of letter provides two immediate contrasts. Delicate strokes made with a fine-pointed brush further contrast with the weight of broad strokes made with a flat brush.

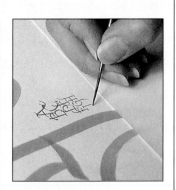

6 The completed piece illustrates contrasts of colour, letter size, and style. Consideration has been made of the space occupied by the freely written individual letters, and of their collective arrangement.

EXPLORING SINGLE LETTER SHAPES

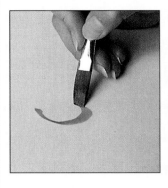

1 Practising single letter shapes with a large square-cut brush provides an excellent method for learning about letter construction.

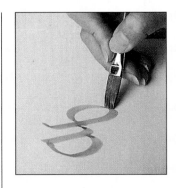

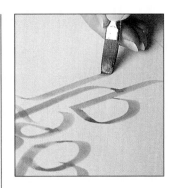

3 Using a brush provides a flexibility of physical approach not available with other instruments. The springiness and lightness of touch of the brush hairs on the page, compared with the rigidity of a steel nib, allow much freedom of movement across the page.

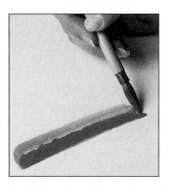

5 The head of the brush is kept at a consistent angle to enable thin and thick strokes to be formed.

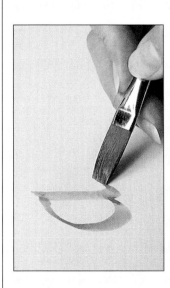

2 The sequence of strokes which make up the letters is the same as that used with a pen.

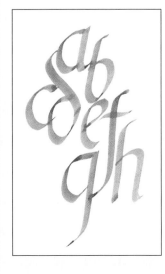

4 The opportunity to dispense with the confines of guidelines is a chance to experiment with offsetting letters on the page.

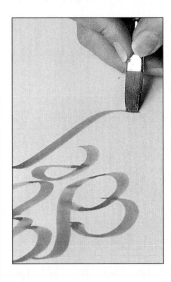

6 Even if some of the letters do not 'feel' right, do not abandon the piece: the purpose here is simply to practise manipulating the brush. Exercises like this one should be approached in a relaxed manner.

USING A POINTED BRUSH

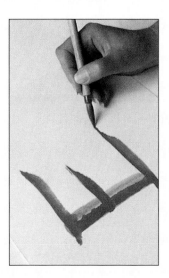

1 A pointed brush, of the kind used for Chinese calligraphy, is excellent for practising freely constructed letters. Chinese brushes are designed to hold much more paint or ink than a traditional Western watercolour brush.

2 Chinese brushes are also versatile: fine strokes can be produced with the tip, and broad strokes with the body.

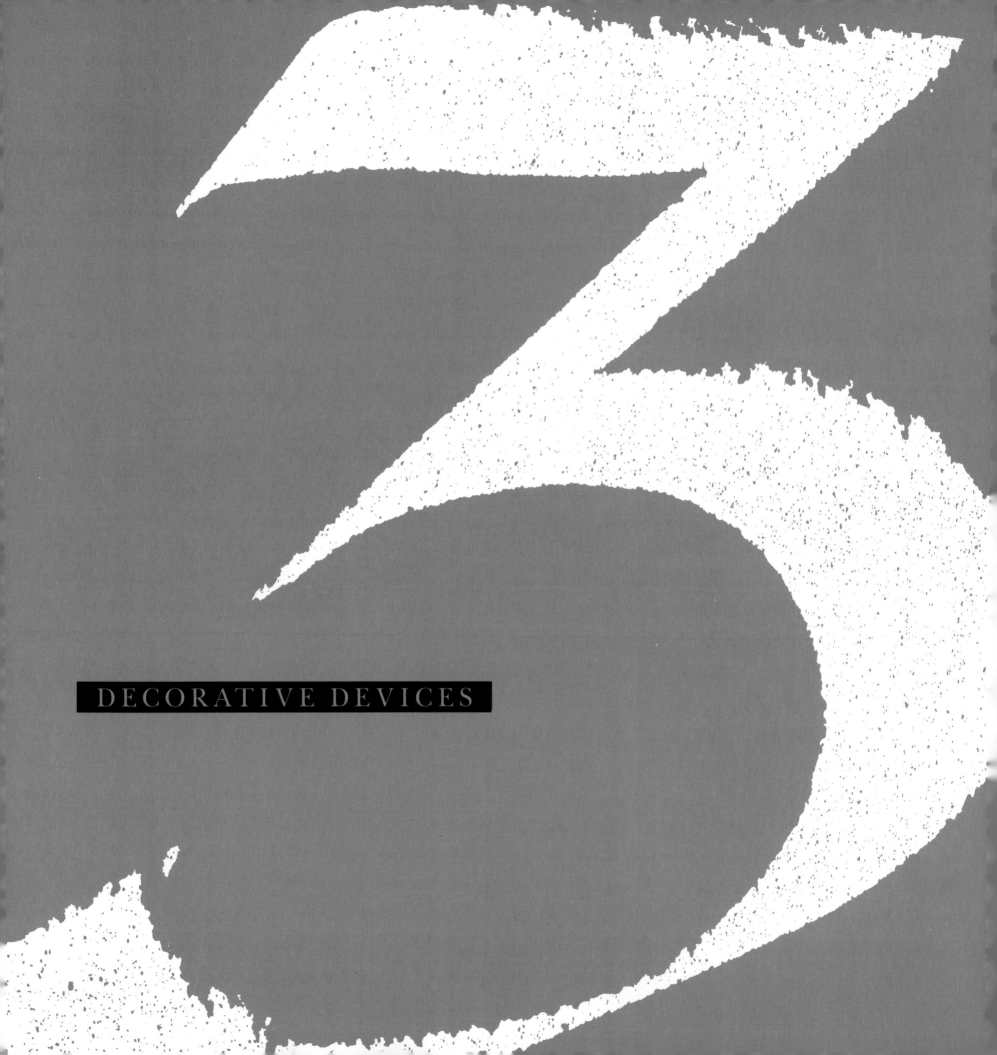

DECORATIVE DEVICES

Using colour

The introduction of colour into a calligraphic work instantly adds substance and gives another dimension to the piece. In past centuries, as now, the use of colour was dictated first by the availability of materials and second by the requirements of the work. Pellucid, uncomplicated colour decoration was applied initially to draw attention to specific information and to contrast with the dense blackness of the text.

Colour made from rubrica, a red earth, was commonly applied to manuscripts not by the scribes themselves, but by rubricators, experts at employing the pigment. The 'rubric' which they applied might be the title, a heading or an initial letter in the manuscript, notes of instruction in the margin of a text, or an entire paragraph.

The opportunities for including colour to some degree paralleled the development of the scripts that they both accompanied and utilized. The Versal letter, for example, heavily ornamented, blossomed on the pages of broad-pen scripts, creating immediate interest and contrast.

The range of colour applications remains largely unchanged since the time of considered and glorious ornamentation of illuminated manuscripts. Colour can be included as an entire pictorial piece, as a single capital letter at the beginning of the text, or as individual letters throughout the work.

There is an extensive range of materials supplying colour for the calligrapher. The two most useful sources of colour to be laid down for finished work are coloured inks and paints. Some consideration needs to be given to selecting the right medium for the work. The medium must be suitable for application with the intended writing instrument, giving sharp edges and hairline serifs or decoration as required. You must also consider the permanence of the works. Inks with an inherent transparency will have a tendency to fade, unlike opaque designer's colours or gouache.

The paper must also be chosen carefully. If you're using watercolours, a paper that can absorb the added moisture will be necessary.

INKS

For single-colour work, a good quality calligraphy ink can be used. These inks are specially formulated, are waterproof, and have good permanence. They provide a substantial finish to the calligraphic stroke.

USING A LARGE BRUSH

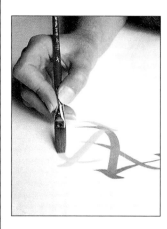 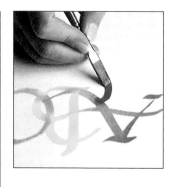 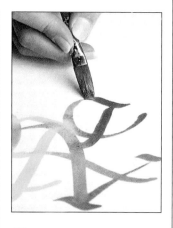

1 Working with colour and a large brush is an adventure, and one from which much can be learned. The freedom of movement afforded by the brush, combined with the search for an interesting layout and arrangement of colour, is also good for developing personal concepts for use in later works.

2 Placing a second colour over a first, while the latter is still wet, can produce exciting results.

3 Occasionally this wet-in-wet technique results in a muddy mess; but the enjoyment experienced and the discoveries made through your experiments are, initially, more important than achieving a perfect result every time.

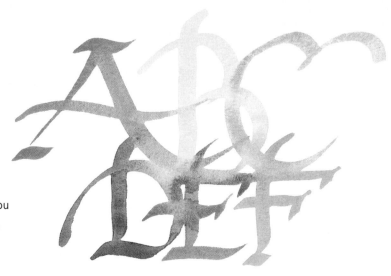

4 Experience will tell you how much time to allow between applications of colour to achieve a more controlled result.

Drawing inks, available in many brilliant, transparent colours, require no mixing, although they can be mixed with each other. Ready to use, they are a good choice for practice strokes and roughing out colour areas, either in text or decoration, even though the final work may be executed in another medium. The fluidity of the inks makes them ideal for this purpose, and they can be used directly with nib, brush, or ruling pen.

Concentrated watercolours or dyes are mediums that give a very bold finish and can be used directly from the container or diluted with water.

PAINTS

Watercolour is the medium most frequently employed by calligraphers. Individual preference dictates whether to use paint from a pan, cake, or tube. These colours, which need to be mixed with water to create a workable consistency, mix easily with each other to furnish an extensive palette.

Watercolours provide a luminous effect. The principle of watercolour work is that the light comes from the substrate – usually white paper. Layers of colour can be applied separately, overlapped, or built up one on another. This must be done carefully with fresh colour to benefit fully from the effect of these pigments.

Designer's gouache provides a superior source of solid colour, not obtainable with translucent watercolours. The opaque colour sits on the substrate and light is reflected from the painted surface, so white or coloured paper can be used without fear of losing the vibrancy of the paint hues. Water is used to thin and mix gouache and does little to diminish the brilliance of the colours. Colour can be laid thinly as a single layer or be strengthened by painting wet into wet, or colour mixes can be made in the palette.

APPLYING COLOUR

When working with any colour system, always mix more than the job will require and keep a note of the colours you use and their proportions in the mixtures. You will need to practise mixing colours to a good working consistency so that the paint flows in a manner that will achieve the intended results.

Do plenty of rough workings and test the substrate for absorbency. Always have a sample of your selected paper

PREPARING TO USE PAINT WITH A NIB

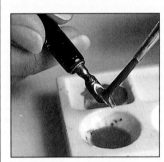

The paint is prepared in a palette. Water is carefully added with a brush or eyedropper so that the paint does not become too thin. It is always advisable to test for consistency and colour match on a scrap of paper. Use a brush to transfer a small amount of the paint onto the nib.

USING A NIB

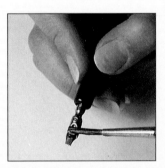

1 Hairline extensions to letters are often easier to form with paint than with ink. Paint takes longer to dry and so enough residue of liquid is available to pull down with the corner of the nib. Load the nib carefully with a brush before starting to work.

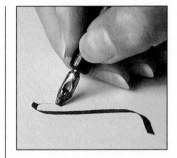

2 When executing fine lettering with paint, the nib will require frequent cleaning. This is best done between letters to prevent clogging and to maintain the crisp edge required of the lettering style.

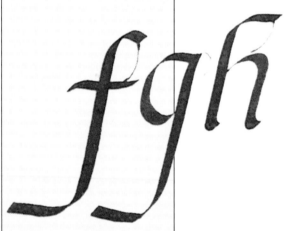

3 When working with colour, care must be taken to maintain an even distribution of colour tone, unless an irregularity is being exploited. The hairline extensions are made by lifting the nib, and dragging wet paint with one corner of it. This can be easier to achieve with paint than with other media because paint takes longer to dry. A pool of liquid, ready to be pulled into an extension, remains at the beginning or end of the stroke for longer.

PREPARING A COLOURED GROUND

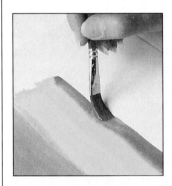

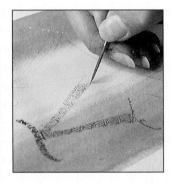

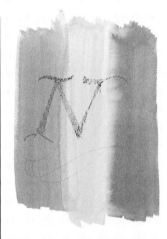

[1] Although most calligraphy is done on white or cream paper, a coloured ground can often add an extra dimension to a work. To create a delicate wash of colour, use thinly-diluted watercolour paint applied to pre-dampened paper with a broad flat brush. Colour-washing works best on heavy or absorbent papers. Be sure to mix plenty of paint so you don't run out half way through, and apply the wash quickly to avoid streaks and runs.

[2] Allowing different drying times between the application of adjacent colours will permit some of the colours to merge into each other. In well planned and more complicated works, this can add background interest and suggest visual ideas that can be exploited.

[3] Make sure the paint is absolutely dry before attempting to write on the sheet.

RIGHT JOHN SMITH – The choice of a dark coloured paper adds an extra dimension and depth to this work. The gouache, with its excellent opacity, sits well on the coloured ground. The contrasting colours used for the words by P B Shelley work well together, especially in their arrangement of broken lines. The grouped lines, with colour overlapping, add movement to the work, designed to a circular format and transformed visually into a spiral.

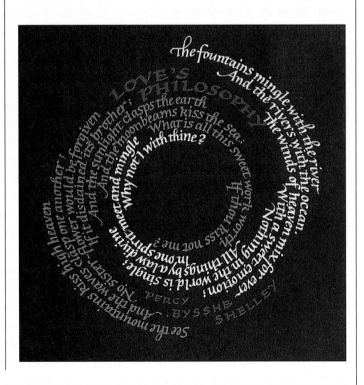

or board on hand on which you can test the colour, for both consistency and colour match. Mix the colours well, check that you have the required colour, and keep on checking and stirring so that the colours do not begin to separate.

There are two agents that you can use to improve paint consistency. The first is gum arabic. Most designer's colours use this as an ingredient. It aids the handling or flow of the paint and slightly increases the gloss of its finish. The other agent is oxgall. Both agents improve the adhesive quality of the paint. When using gum arabic or oxgall, add them to the paint mix very carefully and only one drop at a time. Use a toothpick or matchstick to apply the drops, not a brush.

If you are using a pen, load the nib with a brush, then check that it is not overloaded either by flicking the pen (well away from the final piece) or by writing a small stroke on a scrap sheet.

Working with paint, in particular, necessitates cleaning the nib or brush frequently. This should become a habit and be done even if the tool does not seem to require cleaning. It is better to do so before a disaster mars the work.

When the medium is mixed with water, the liquid tends to collect at the bottom of the letter strokes. This may be the intention, and can be exploited to the advantage of the work. However, you need to lower the angle of your work surface towards the horizontal.

Understatement, deliberately limiting the amount of colour, can result in a superior finished work as compared to a piece where colour is overstated and the impact is lost. Colour intended to provide contrast and draw attention to the work must also supplement it; but if the lettering is not well executed, the colour cannot save the work.

Flourishes

Flourishing, the ornamental embellishment of a letter or letters, requires some study before it can be used effectively. There are innumerable examples that you can refer to, in books, manuscripts held in museum collections, and the work of engravers on glass or metal. In all these examples, a wealth of challenging ideas can be confronted. Look for common elements and develop a personal working language for flourishing. Make sketches, and, where possible, put tracing paper over the flourishing and trace the flowing lines. Discover the shape formed by the flourishing, what space it occupies, how thick lines cross thin lines and diagonals run parallel.

The most obvious context for flourishing would seem to be as an extension of formal scripts, but this is not its only place. There are plenty of opportunities, but proceed with caution. In learning when and where to apply flourishing, bear in mind that the basic letters must be well formed.

In work that technically could form the basis for splendid flourishing, the nature of the words, or of the job itself, may dictate otherwise. Studying the text together with the guidelines of the brief will quickly reveal whether the work should be treated to a subtle or elaborate amount of flourishing – if any at all. There are occasions when a measure of controlled flourishing is quite sufficient and the result is more effective for the restraint applied. Other situations provide a challenge that should be met with flourishing that is innovative and inventive.

Begin with simple solutions, always remembering that the strokes must be perceived as a natural extension of the letters, not as additions. They should flow freely and be naturally incorporated into the whole design. They should not bump into or obscure the letters of the text. Always plan flourishing well in plenty of rough drafts.

Practise with a relaxed arm movement, using whatever instrument feels most comfortable. A fine pointed nib works well. Experiment with taking thin strokes upward and working the down strokes with more pressure applied. Applying pressure on upward strokes is disastrous – the nib digs into the paper and ink splatters.

Accomplished and elaborate flourishing can look wonderful, but needs much study and practice. As you gain confidence, flourishing will become quite a logical extension to much of your calligraphic work. Signwriting, memorial inscriptions, civic documents, certificates, letterheads and single-letter logos, and delicate personal messages all provide potential for flourishing.

USING A POINTED BRUSH

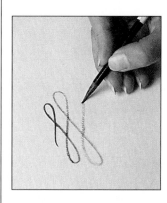

1 Successful flourishing requires practice so that the strokes can be accomplished in a relaxed manner and flow naturally. Flourishes should blend with the work and not appear too contrived. A pointed brush is an excellent tool to assist in developing a rhythmic and fluid style.

3 Flourishing exercises can be interesting pieces in their own right. Here the addition of red dots, made with the tip of the brush, provide a finishing touch.

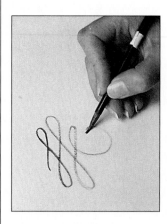

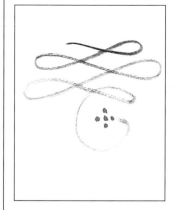

2 The brush moves with great agility to create expressive arcs and lines. Varying the pressure on the brush produces lines that vary from thick to thin in one continuous stroke.

4 Practise making traditional flourishing shapes and simple marks before attempting to apply the lines as letter extensions.

USING A SQUARE-CUT BRUSH

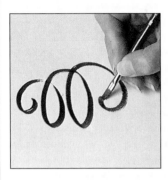

1 A small square-cut brush will mimic the thin and thick lines of a broad nib, but not create too much resistance in its movement.

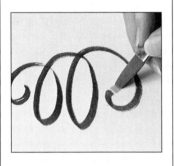

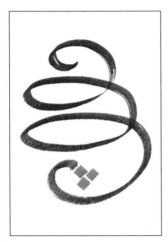

2 A large square-cut brush is used here to add red dots as a finishing touch.

3 Exercises like these will demonstrate how thick and thin strokes evolve, especially when using a square-cut brush. They will also help develop your ideas on layout.

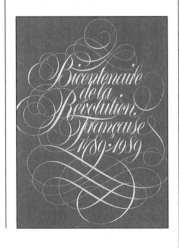

RIGHT JEAN LARCHER — An exuberant display of flourishing using Copperplate-style lettering. The final piece was produced by silkscreening one colour in reverse. The artwork was prepared in black on scratchboard.

USING DOUBLE POINTS

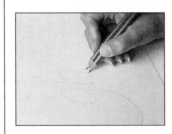

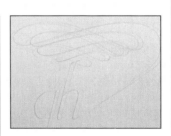

1 Employing double points to make flourishes provides an opportunity to introduce letters to the exercises. The double points are treated in the same manner as a square nib, but can be manipulated with greater freedom of movement across the page.

2 Double pencils allow an energetic flourish to emerge and be applied as an extension to a letter. The flourish on the italic H is drawn to resemble a ribbon unfurling.

BELOW IEUAN REES — An energetic but controlled flourish which adds great interest and balances the work. Note how the bold lines which form the basis of the flourishing are parallel.

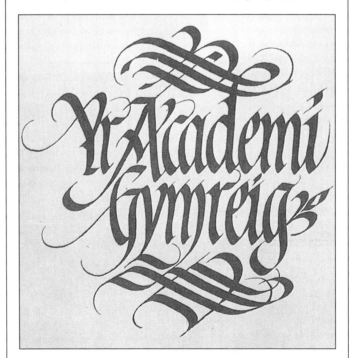

Raised gold

Among the finest medieval manuscripts are those that include the application of gold. Elegant capital letters and complex patterns adorn the pages in a grand demonstration of the manuscript as an item to be admired and revered. To produce such fine work, lengthy processes of preparation were assiduously followed. First, the preparation of the substrate, then the selection and treatment of pigments for colour decoration, and, finally, the ground for the gold leaf. The processes for applying raised gold remain largely unchanged since medieval times. The work is planned and the text written out, leaving the gilding until last. The gold is laid on a prepared ground and, when dry, is brought to a high lustre by burnishing.

Raised gold is a particularly fine effect of gilding, as the leaf is laid on a raised ground forming a low 'cushion', a three-dimensional element that causes the gold leaf to reflect even more brilliance than when it is laid flatly. It catches all the available light that falls on the page as it is viewed and turned.

Gesso provides the ideal ground for raised gold decoration. This is, basically, a mixture of plaster and glue that can be applied with a quill or brush. It has a slightly tacky surface that receives the gold leaf evenly. When dry, it is solid but relatively flexible, so that it will not crack when a page is handled. Preparation of the gesso ground is the most lengthy procedure involved in applying raised gold decoration.

Gold leaf is sold in booklets in which the fine gold is interleaved with tissue. Other metallic leafs are available: palladium, derived from platinum and silver. The burnisher used to bring up the shine on the gold after it is dry is traditionally made of agate or hematite.

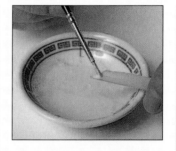

1 Prepare the gesso by breaking up the coloured plaster into a cup or a small dish. (The plaster is coloured so that when applied to the page, it will show up against the background.) Add a few drops of glair – a solution of egg-white – or distilled water to make the gesso into a workable medium. Leave the mixture to dissolve for at least 20 minutes.

2 Cover the gesso with distilled water and mix to a smooth, creamy consistency. The end of a quill pen, or a bone folder, can be used to stir the solution and get rid of any air bubbles. If bubbles persist, a drop of oil of cloves dripped from the end of a toothpick should solve the problem. The gesso is now ready to be used with a quill or metal nib.

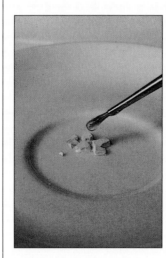

3 The best substrate for working on is vellum. Care must be taken to ensure that the vellum is free of all impurities such as grease or tackiness. To do this, treat the surface with pumice, and then carefully brush off all the powder.

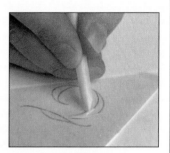

4 Lay the vellum flat on a sheet of glass. Flood the letter with gesso to give a raised 'cushion' effect. When the letter is completely filled in with gesso, allow a minimum of 12 hours for it to dry. The drying letter can be left overnight, and the gold applied next day. Sometimes the final result is better for the waiting. Laying the gold must be done quickly, so it is important to have all the necessary materials and equipment on hand before you begin.

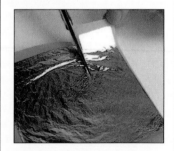

5 Gold leaf is a very fine material, so take extra care in its handling. The scissors used to cut the leaf should be cleaned with silk, to stop the material from sticking. The gold leaf is interleaved with tissue paper. Cut through both layers to a size slightly larger than the letterform.

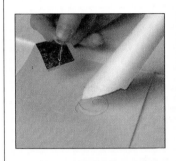

6 Holding the gold leaf with its backing sheet ready, blow gently through a paper cylinder onto the gessoed letter. The still-tacky gesso is now ready to receive the gold. This must be done quickly.

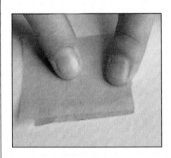

7 Apply firm pressure through the backing sheet, to encourage the gold leaf to adhere to the gesso. Remove the tissue backing sheet, and replace with a piece of parchment.

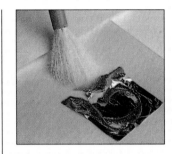

8 Using a hematite or agate burnisher, rub firmly on the crystal parchment. After working with the burnisher, remove the parchment.

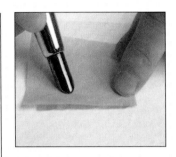

9 Clean the burnisher on a piece of silk, and burnish the gold leaf directly. Work the gold leaf around the raised letter, paying particular attention to pressing the gold into and around the edges.

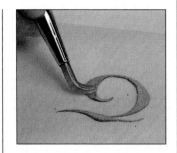

10 Using a dry soft-haired brush, remove the excess gold leaf from around the letter. Use light, short brush strokes to flick the gold away, rather than dragging the brush.

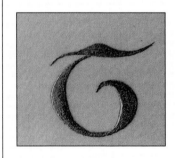

11 Continue light brushing until all the gold leaf surrounding the gilded letter is removed. A second layer of double gold leaf is now placed over the gilded letter. Crystal parchment is again placed over the gold and firm pressure is applied. Clean off the excess gold with a soft brush as before.

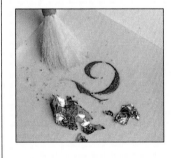

12 Here, a toothed agate burnisher is used to work the gold leaf to a final brilliance and smoothness. This burnisher is specially shaped to ensure that the leaf is worked into the edges and rounded parts of the letter.

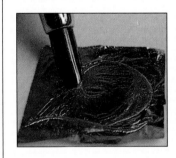

13 The gold leaf is now burnished until it is completely smooth and shines brightly when it catches the light.

Gilding

There are two distinct techniques of applying gold decoration to calligraphic design. One is the flat method of gilding, the other raised gold. The true art of illumination stemmed from the practice of applying a medium with a metallic finish that would reflect any surrounding light, although the term also referred to the introduction of any colour in order to draw attention to something in the text.

Many of the finest manuscripts of the past two thousand years are richly adorned with gold. In Greece, where the concept of working with gold may have arrived from the East or from Egypt, there were early references to some of the scribes as 'writers in gold'. There is evidence to suggest that by the second century, Rome was influenced by the Greek example. Gloriously ornate manuscripts were produced solely for the wealthy citizens. The exorbitant cost of materials, particularly gold and vellum, prohibited their use to most people. To make vellum, early scribes meticulously prepared the skins of calf, kid, or lamb, if necessary staining them to the colour required for the baseground of the manuscript. Sometimes the entire skin would be gilded. This involved many processes including, after the initial washing, beating, stretching, and drying, smearing with egg whites, and then more washing, drying, rubbing, pressing, and polishing and finally applying gold leaf. Egg whites were usually used as the fixative for the application of the gold.

The many ancient recipes for preparing to work with gold read like an alchemy instruction book, the only difference being that the scribes already had the precious metal. Other metals were also used, including silver, brass, and copper. If none of these were available, a scribe could simulate gilding using tin and saffron.

Great care is required in the application of gold, as it remains an expensive commodity. Gold leaf, or sheets of gold transfer leaf, is excellent for decorating a page with a highlighted initial letter, filling in an ornament, or providing a baseground. The leaf must be laid on an adhesive ground. The process of laying gold leaf is very delicate, as it is a fine material.

The less lustrous powdered gold is obtainable loose or in cake form. When mixed with distilled water to a working consistency, it creates a reasonable finish. Gum arabic used as a binder improves its adherence to the page. Powdered gold can be applied with a quill pen, nib, or brush and is a direct and less complicated medium for gilding than gold leaf. Both types of gold can be burnished when absolutely

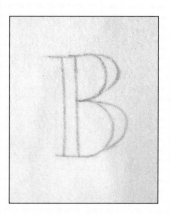

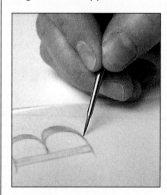

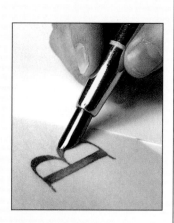

1 One of the most accessible methods of applying gold to a work is the modern flat method. Begin by preparing all the equipment and materials. Then make a very light pencil outline of the letter to which the gold is to be applied.

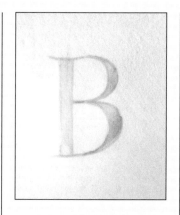

2 Ammoniac is the traditional compound used as size. PVA, a plastic adhesive, also works well, although it does not have the inherent long-lasting qualities of ammoniac. Mix the size with a little gouache and, if necessary, some water. The colour provided by the gouache will make the letter clearly visible on the page. Paint the outline and fill in the letter with the mixture using a small pointed brush.

3 Allow the letter to dry completely. Depending on the working conditions, this could take from 30 minutes to one hour.

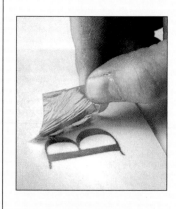

4 Carefully cut out a piece of gold leaf large enough to cover the letter completely. Breathe on the letter to create a tacky, adhesive surface ready to receive the gold leaf. Press the gold down firmly with the thumb, working gently over the area being gilded. Apply a second layer of gold in a similar manner if required.

5 Brush away the excess gold leaf with a soft, long-haired Chinese brush. Burnish the letter with great care using a burnisher made from agate or hematite.

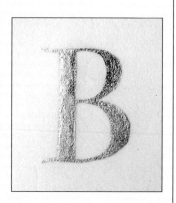

6 The use of PVA will not give the superior quality of finish obtained with raised gold. However, the method provides a more accessible way of applying gold and can produce pleasing results.

dry, but powdered gold never attains the gleaming surface quality of burnished gold leaf.

Inexpensive alternatives to real gold are naturally inferior in quality, especially in surface finish. Various metallic gouaches, inks, and felt-tip pens are available. These are all excellent for use in rough drafts and may in some circumstances be suitable for finished work.

PREPARATION FOR GILDING

There are two materials that can be used as the size to prepare the surface of a page for gilding. One is polyvinyl acetate (PVA), a plastic adhesive. It consists of resin in suspension in water, together with plasticizers and stabilizers that prevent separation of the resin. When PVA is applied to a surface, the water evaporates and the resin particles coalesce into a continuous film.

The other size, ammoniac, requires preparation. Supplied in solid form, it must first be reduced to fine granules and soaked overnight in distilled water. Next, stir the ammoniac and strain it through a fine mesh of cheesecloth or nylon. Gently heat the strained mixture and strain again. The straining process may have to be repeated several times until the resulting liquid is of a suitable consistency for use with a pen. Any ammoniac not used can be stored in an airtight container.

Before applying either type of size, colour it slightly with some gouache so that you will be able to see it clearly on the page. Check the work surface is level, so that the size will not collect at the bottom of a letter stem or decoration. You can apply size with a pen or brush.

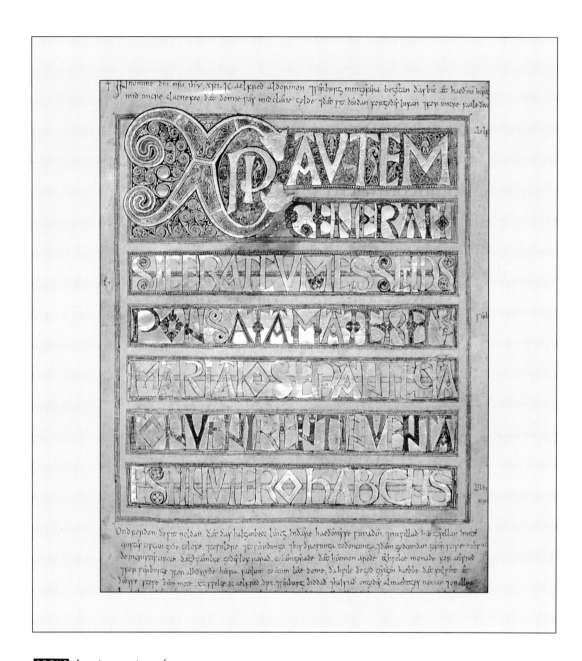

ABOVE An extravagant use of gilding is displayed on this page from the Codex Aureus. An interesting balance has been achieved in applying the gold alternately to a line of letters, and as a background to the next line. Traditional elements of ornament decorate the page.

Illumination

Originally, illumination referred to the simple act of including colour, usually red lead, in a manuscript with the body of the text written in black. This was done to draw attention to a particular passage by identifying the first letter or word of the section in colour. Some minimal colour decoration may also have been used.

In time, the interpretation of illumination expanded to include manuscripts on stained vellum adorned with gold or silver. The letters and decoration executed in the precious metals reflected the surrounding light. Also included were richly ornamented pages displaying a profusion of colour.

Initially, the scribe responsible for writing the text added the ornamentation but, in time, as different aspects of the work developed, other craftspeople joined the workshops. However, the illuminator, as the most skilled, became a designer, colourist, and illustrator.

Illumination is really about the calligrapher's own experience, especially in terms of design sensibility and

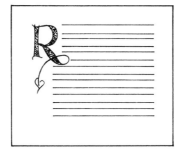

BELOW This spread from an early sixteenth-century French Book of Hours has an uncomplicated layout. A decorative border frames the Humanistic script inscribed test, which has minimally illuminated initial letters. The illustration is surrounded by an architectural device in a style common at the time of the Renaissance.

The presentation of a piece of calligraphy can be enhanced by the introduction of a decorated letter. The letter may be very simply decorated, grossly distorted, or heavily embellished with marks, lines, and symbols, forming ornate patterns. Careful thought must be given to the positioning of the letter in relation to the body text and to the layout of the page as a whole. Some of the traditionally used arrangements are illustrated here.

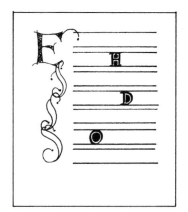

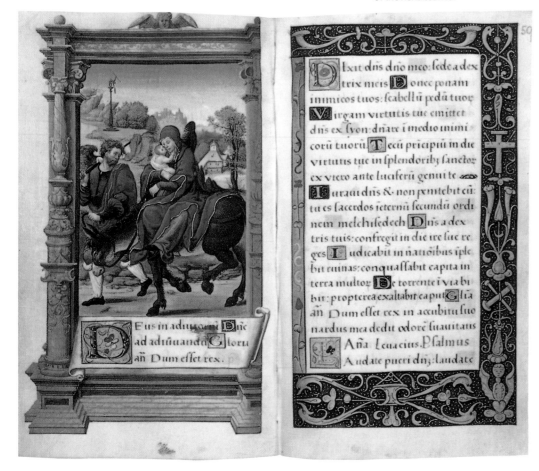

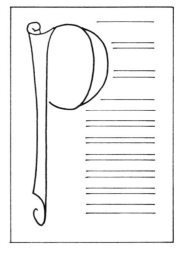

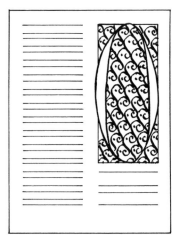

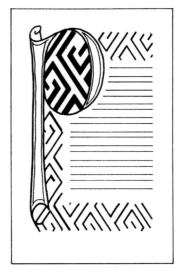

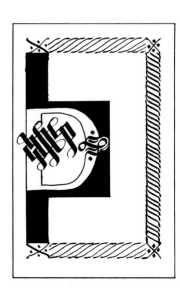

colour sensitivity. It presents a wonderful opportunity to exploit pattern, from the most simple to the outrageous, as well as colour, texture, and pictorial imagery. There are no rules to follow, but you can understand the range of possibilities if you spend time looking at some fine examples of the illuminated page.

Excellent examples of illumination can be found in museums, libraries, art collections, and books. To begin to appreciate the intricate nature of these works, make sketches and notes of solutions that appeal to you. Looking at the works can be quite an overwhelming experience, so start by studying one section at a time. For example, select an enlarged letter shape and observe its origins – perhaps Roman, Rustica, Uncial, or Versal. Is the letter distorted or elongated? Which areas of the letter are decorated? Does the decoration extend to counter spaces inside or outside the letter?

Work through the ways in which each of these areas have been manipulated. Observe where patterning is repeated, or identical motifs are employed, sometimes with simple variations. Follow foliage or knotwork patterns and notice the shapes of the spaces they occupy – circular or triangular, for example.

Breaking down a complex design into understandable sections helps to demystify the art of illumination. The same procedure can be extended to borders, margin decoration, and the whole relationship of the illumination to the text. At the same time, you can study the quality of the colour work and gilding to see which techniques might be appropriate for your own illuminations.

Lots of rough drafts and colour experimentation are the cornerstones of good illumination. This is an opportunity for great freedom of expression in calligraphic design. Build a checklist of design considerations so you can refer to the options. Basic ingredients are dot, line, shape, and colour. Many patterns can be built, for example, based solely on dots or circles. Treatment for an initial letter may include enlargement, elongation, creating a picture that incorporates the letter, applying texture to the body of the letter, or letters made out of patterns, leaves, or animals. The same ideas are suitable for counter spaces and borders.

When working out the area to accommodate the illumination, do not ignore the text area. Indicate text with lines in your rough drafts and aim towards a balanced look for the final work.

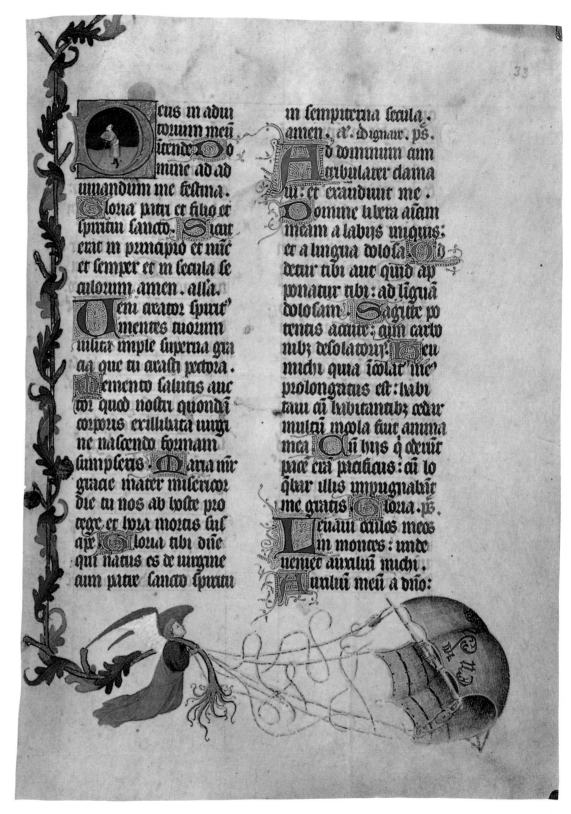

ABOVE A page from the Egerton manuscript has a refined border on one side which continues off the top of the page. At its base, the foliage border is linked with the illustration, dragged along over the shoulder of an angel. A miniature painting is contained in the counter shape of the first initial letter. Linear and spiral patterns and trailing fine lines decorate the Lombardic Versal letters, and the strong influence of Uncial letter shapes is clear.

Ornament

Changes in artistic style can often be seen as running parallel to social and political changes occurring in particular places and times. The evolution of ornament falls within this pattern of events, reflecting the rise and decline of early civilizations and the interchange of ideas between different cultures brought about by trade, military conquest, and religious influences.

An example of this was the development of decorative patterning derived from Islamic silk fabrics. Following ancient tradition, the silk weavers incorporated goodwill expressions in their designs. With the increase of trade around the Mediterranean, the art of silk weaving spread and the Muslim fabrics were copied, including the inscriptions. As the words were incomprehensible to European weavers, the scripts were copied as mere scribbles. Gradually, some of the Arabic letters were put into more symmetrical forms for mechanical weaving, resulting in 'mock Arabic' devices.

The Romans, more concerned with expanding their boundaries and creating wealth than with developing an artistic identity, initially took their influences from Etruria and Greece. As their wealth and power increased, they employed Greek teachers and, in time, established their own recognizable monumental works. Roman ornamental style subsequently overpowered that of the Greek masters. The Romans used ornament in a naturalistic manner as shown in their architecture; decorated capitals with curling leaves, entablatures with ox heads and lions, rosettes, and festoons were all incorporated.

The collapse of the Roman Empire heralded a linking of Christian ideals and the remains of classical art. With strong Byzantine influence, ornamental art underwent a transformation. By the fifth century, the symbol of the cross was included in many inscriptions and provided a base for all-over patterns and the development of the 'gammadion' device. The greatest exponents of ornament were the scribes of Ireland responsible for the fine Celtic tradition.

Succeeding centuries saw a flourishing of key patterns, intricate knotwork, spirals, mosaic, and geometric patterning. Elements from the natural world were drawn on, including vegetation – both imagined and real – leaves, flowers, palm fronds, lotus, acanthus, and vine. Animals were an important feature, making a major contribution to ornament design – dogs, lions, lambs, snakes, eagles, doves, peacocks, fish, and fantastic imaginary beasts. In

BASIC METHODS OF ARRANGEMENT

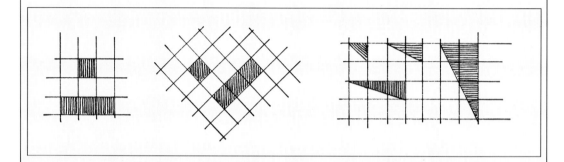

1 The best starting point for learning to apply ornament is to study the basic construction methods. Simple patterns can be generated on a network of lines crossing each other at different angles. Begin by building patterns along the lines placed at right angles to one another and at equal distances (squared paper is useful here). Fill in individual shapes to produce squares and diamonds, and adjacent squares to produce oblongs. Introducing oblique lines that cut across the squares and oblongs produces triangles.

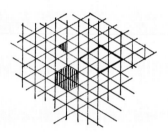

2 To create ornament based on hexagonal shapes, the lines are placed at an angle of 30°, and crossed by vertical lines.

3 Placing lines at an angle of 45°, and crossing them with vertical and horizontal lines creates octagonal shapes.

medieval and Renaissance manuscripts, miniature paintings and detailed figurative illustrations incorporated within the letters reflected the life of the time.

DESIGNING CALLIGRAPHIC ORNAMENT

Ornament may fill an entire margin, create a border for the text, or a background for a capital letter. Delicate patterns and repeated symbols can complete a line where the text falls short and does not align. The intention in using ornament in calligraphic design is to achieve absolute harmony throughout the entire work and it must

DEVELOPING METHODS OF ARRANGEMENT

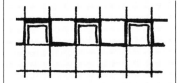

1 Altering the lines and shapes applied to the basic network of lines begins to extend the language of ornament. Here the horizontal and vertical lines provide the framework of a pattern used extensively in heraldry, known as embattled.

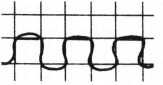

2 Here the lines of the embattled pattern have been curved to create a meander.

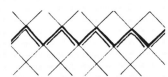

3 A squared grid, set at 45° to the horizontal, creates the diamond, which is used here as a framework for the chevron zigzag.

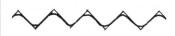

4 Using the same network, but curving the apexes of the zigzag, creates the wave.

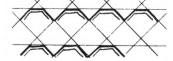

5 The same network, with the addition of horizontal lines, is the basis for the blunted zigzag and the interlaced patterns.

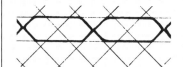

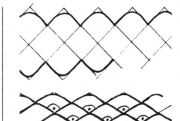

6 The geometric lines of the zigzag are here rounded to produce the scallop. The interlaced pattern is adapted to produce the scale pattern.

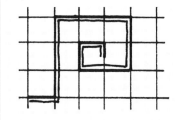

7 The squared network provides the foundation for construction of the fret. This familiar geometrical figure forms the basis of many fine ornamental borders.

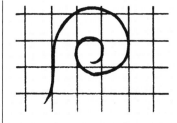

8 The spiral is created by rounding the straight lines and sharp angles of the fret.

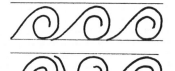

9 The wave and the running scroll are adaptations of the spiral.

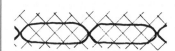

10 The interlacing constructed on the network of crossed diagonal lines can be enlarged to form a double wave or meander.

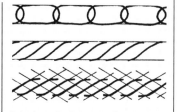

11 By converting the rectilinear network to one of circles and ellipses, further ornamental elements can be added to your repertoire. These include the chain and cable.

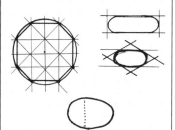

12 The curved series evolves from a softening of the basic shapes. The octagon becomes a circle. The oblong and some proportions of the diamond are altered into elliptical shapes. The ellipse and the circle produce the oval.

be planned in from the start, not added as an afterthought attached to a plain work.

Special attention needs to be paid to proportion and the symmetry of shapes and colours. Begin by including simple geometric figures that constitute the basic vocabulary of ornament: square, circle, triangle, oval, and lozenge. Introduce a connecting element with lines, chains, spiraling cables, interlacings, zigzags, waves, or a running scroll. Repetition of any of these motifs can create pattern areas within the design. More ambitious solutions can be attempted by starting with basic shapes and then including simple motifs from the natural world.

Consider carefully, through rough working sketches, the power of a simple design solution, incorporating selective ornament with an elegant letter. Compare this with a fussy and over-embellished design where the strength of the letter shape is diminished.

The size of ornament should relate closely to the scale of writing and size of the page. If the ornament is in a manuscript book, the scale should remain consistent

LAYING OUT ORNAMENT

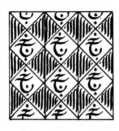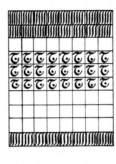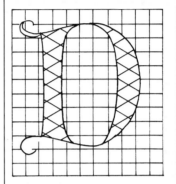

1 The diagrams on the previous page illustrate some of the elemental forms and lines found in styles of ornamental art, and upon which more elaborate details can be built. The same principle of networks is used here to show some of the methods of laying out ornament. The method shown here involves filling in each square.

3 Diapering and checkering can be effectively combined to create solid patterns.

5 Applying the ornament in rows, and leaving some rows void, creates striping. Versions of striping constructed in a narrower vein are called banding.

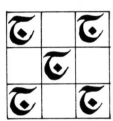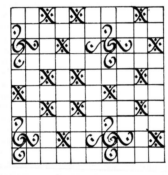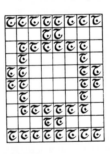

2 Working on the same squared grid, but omitting alternate squares. This method is known as checkering.

4 Employing the same principle, but allowing larger spaces between the filled-in areas. This is referred to as spotting or powdering.

6 A combination of striping and banding produces another layout, called panelling.

COMBINING ORNAMENT
AND LETTERS

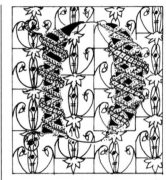

1 Working with these methods of organizing ornament provides a valuable foundation for illumination and decoration. In this example, the basic squared grid is drawn, and the letter is superimposed. The letter has a network of lines arranged at 30° to the horizontal.

2 Using the arrangements of lines, ornament is applied to both the letter and the base ground. The squared grid provides the basis for a repeat pattern. To repeat this particular pattern, the lateral repetition has been achieved by lowering the pattern to fit two sections together.

throughout the volume. Take care in selecting the ingredients of ornament drawn from the natural world – use a good model. If the ornament is imagined and repeated, be consistent in the repeats: work from a well-prepared finished rough.

Spirals, knotwork, frets, and other linear forms require careful attention. The construction methods of Celtic ornament provide the best key to this kind of interlacing. To avoid confusion, complete each stage of the construction before moving on to the next stage.

GEOMETRIC DESIGN

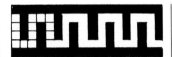

1 Fret patterns can be used as borders on their own, or they can be incorporated with ornament, and embrace an enlarged letter. The basic structure of fret patterns can be used as a framework for decoration not comosed solely of straight lines. The simplest forms use lines which are all either vertical or horizontal. The distance between the lines is the same as the width of the lines. As with other basic ornament structures, using squared paper will help you to plan your designs accurately. This geometric border is six widths wide, the top and bottom lines are continuous, and the vertical lines are three widths high. Developing this nature of analysis is the best method of understanding how to construct these designs.

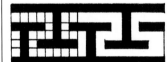

2 This pattern is seven widths wide. It is an expanded version of the first example, with the introduction of horizontal lines. In these patterns the 'negative' shapes formed by the ground (in this case, the white of the paper) are as important to the appearance of the finished design as the 'positive' shapes of the marks made.

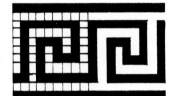

3 This pattern, known as the key pattern, provides an excellent example of a design in which the white space is almost as pleasing in shape as the black form. The balance of black and white is important in fret designs.

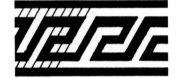

4 The introduction of slanting lines to the framework produces a sloping fret. Here the horizontal lines are retained, but the vertical lines are replaced by lines set at an inclined angle.

5 The pattern below is of interlacing strap work. To build patterns in this style, begin working with vertical and horizontal lines, and lines placed at a 45° angle. This particular example has been expanded and used at a flatter angle.

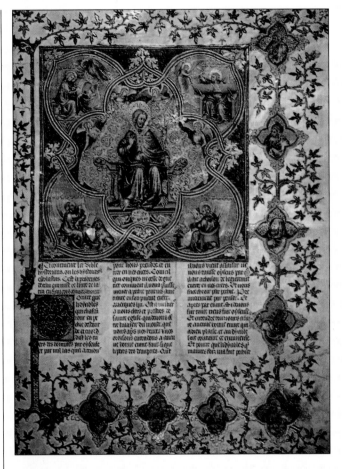

ABOVE In the wide margins of this page from the fourteenth-century *Bible Historiale*, decorated 'barbed' quatrefoils containing individual portraits set against patterned backgrounds are placed at evenly spaced intervals. The vine provides a linking device, and anchors the pictures to the page.

Borders

Borders can be incorporated very successfully in many designs. Surrounded totally or in part by a border, a block of text or lines of information on a card can be greatly enhanced. Verses of a poem can be separated by a single line of patterning. Borders should complement the calligraphy; they should not overpower the text, or look too timid.

Borders define a space and can 'tidy up' a piece of visual work, but cannot save it if the letterforms and spacing are not well-planned in the first place. To demonstrate the power of the border, take a freely drawn piece of lettering or ornament and simply surround it with straight lines. The difference in visual impact is immediate; the effect is the same as framing a picture.

There are four basic components of border design: repeat horizontal marks, or filling-in worked as a continuous running pattern; a series of vertical marks; a fusion of horizontal and vertical elements; an arrangement of panels. Put more succinctly, the simplest options are spot, horizontal, vertical, and oblique marks.

Borders should be related to the nature of the work. This is more obvious in other craft areas, but should not be ignored in calligraphy. You can render the writing without embellishment and, without loss of meaning or intent, surround it with a highly decorative and well-constructed border that provides great visual and aesthetic impact.

It takes careful consideration and artistic judgement to achieve the correct proportions of a border and its overall value in the work. There is no reason for a border to be straight or for the boundaries to be parallel. It can surround an irregular space and have straight lines on the outer perimeter.

The corners of borders need careful planning. When you have made a clear decision as to the nature of the join, whether it is to be oblique, square, or joggled mitre, the object is then to design with the join, not to accentuate or necessarily conceal it.

Sources of ideas for borders abound. You will find it useful to start building a border repertoire. For example, you might make a study of brick bonds, embroidery, or wrought- and cast-iron objects. Such items provide a wealth of line qualities, shapes, and patterns that can all be incorporated into border design. Make sketches with a pencil, then put tracing paper over your sketch and, using a nib, go over the drawing in ink, selecting simple repeated components. Use these to create an original border.

JOINS FOR BORDERS

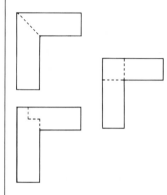

The structure of a border framing a work needs consideration. Frames are formed in several ways, including oblique, square, and joggled mitre. The corner is the best place to start when designing a border to form a full or semi-enclosure.

POINTED BRUSH BORDER

1 When designing borders, experiment with different tools and media to add further variety to the strokes and marks. For example, manipulating a pointed brush, with designer's gouache, can produce varying weights of mark.

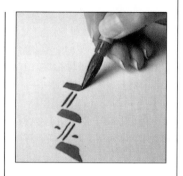

2 Applying a little pressure and pulling down quickly through the stroke produces a contrasting bold line.

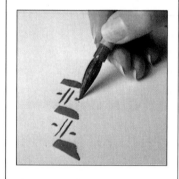

3 Delicate dots can be added using the tip of the brush. Control of the dot size is dictated by the pressure placed on the brush as it rests on the paper.

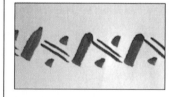

4 The dots in this completed simple border pattern were made by placing the point of the brush on the paper, then pulling it slightly downward as it was lifted off the paper.

BORDERS: BASIC STROKES

The broad pen can be used to produce simple and pleasing marks which, either alone or in combination, can be repeated to create a decorative border. Changing the pen angle will increase the variety and interest even within the same border.

FELT-TIP BORDER

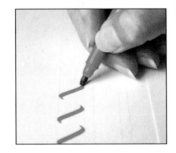

1 Felt-tip pens with chiselled nibs are useful for working out border patterns, being quick to use and available in a variety of colours. Employing basic broad pen strokes, a line is worked through to the end.

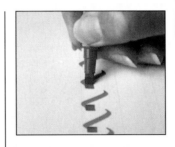

2 Turning a thick pen to an angle of 90° to the horizontal writing line, square dots are placed at the top of the slanted line.

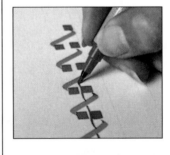

3 Dots are placed at the base of the slanted line. Then the same pen, held at about 10° to the horizontal, is used to produce a thin, graceful stroke.

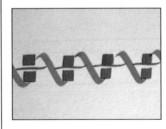

4 This red and green border could have more lines and shapes added, or, as here, be regarded as complete.

TOOLS AND TECHNIQUES

Mix and match techniques in your designs: for example, use broken rules interspersed with dots made with a broad nib. Almost any tool is suitable for building up a border – brush, pen, felt-tip pen, or pencil. Introducing colour to a border requires some planning but used well, colour is very effective.

Working on squared paper will help to build your confidence, giving a framework to the design as you twist and turn the broad nib to invent new arrangements. This exploration also makes a good practice exercise or 'warm-up'. Spend some time roughing out the design of the border, especially on the critical decision as to whether it will form a full or partial enclosure for the text. A semi-enclosure is most likely if a decorative heading is part of the piece.

If confident line drawing is one of your strengths, the border might include small concealed images relating to the text.

CARTOUCHE

Although not strictly calligraphic, the cartouche is a device worthy of consideration. Cartouches evolved from an ancient art applied to paper and parchment labels used to hold inscriptions or badges. The edges were cut in an intricate manner that resulted in ornamental curling of the labels, usually into scroll forms. The shapes evolved further in the forms of shields, and eventually panels were cast or carved to enclose an inscription, although they were sometimes left blank. In either state, they constituted an important element in design, especially to offset or draw attention to a more engaging ornament.

Calligraphers can refer to old cartouche designs as a rich source of ideas applicable to name cards, heraldic work, quotations, and many other calligraphic works.

BLACK AND WHITE BORDER

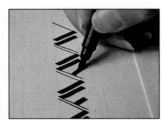

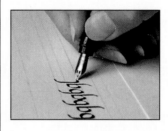

1 The width of stroke varies according to the direction in which the pen is moved while retaining a fixed nib angle. Here a black felt-tip pen, held at an angle of 45° to the writing line, produces thick downward strokes.

3 A short, thick stroke is inserted between the major lines of the pattern to break up the white space. The lines are first applied along the bottom of the design, before working through the top row.

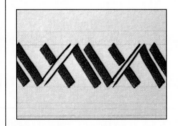

2 Holding the pen at the same angle and moving in an upward direction produces thin strokes.

4 The thin and thick strokes form a simple and basic pattern. The application of additional shorter strokes to break up the white space produces a more interesting and pleasing result.

LETTER BORDER

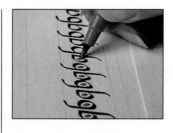

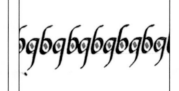

1 Borders constructed from letter shapes can be used successfully, especially if the letters are chosen to represent or allude to something referred to in the piece they surround. If no obvious links present themselves, letters that contrast with or balance each other can be selected.

3 The inclusion of a spot colour, as a simple device, can add a surprise element and further disguise the actual letter shapes.

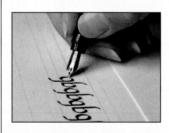

2 Repeating the letters, with their elegant proportions and thick and thin strokes, leads to a perception of an arrangement of shapes rather than actual letters.

4 The final picture perfectly illustrates how the letters have become mere vehicles in the creation of this border. The work has a balance of black and white and reads as a row of shapes and lines, rather than letters.

BROAD BRUSH BORDER

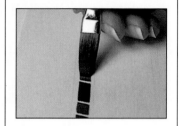

1 A brush with a square-cut end can be used to create a border composed of simple repeated shapes.

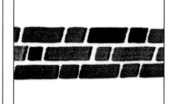

2 This example is based on a brick bonding design. The same arrangement can be made using a broad nib.

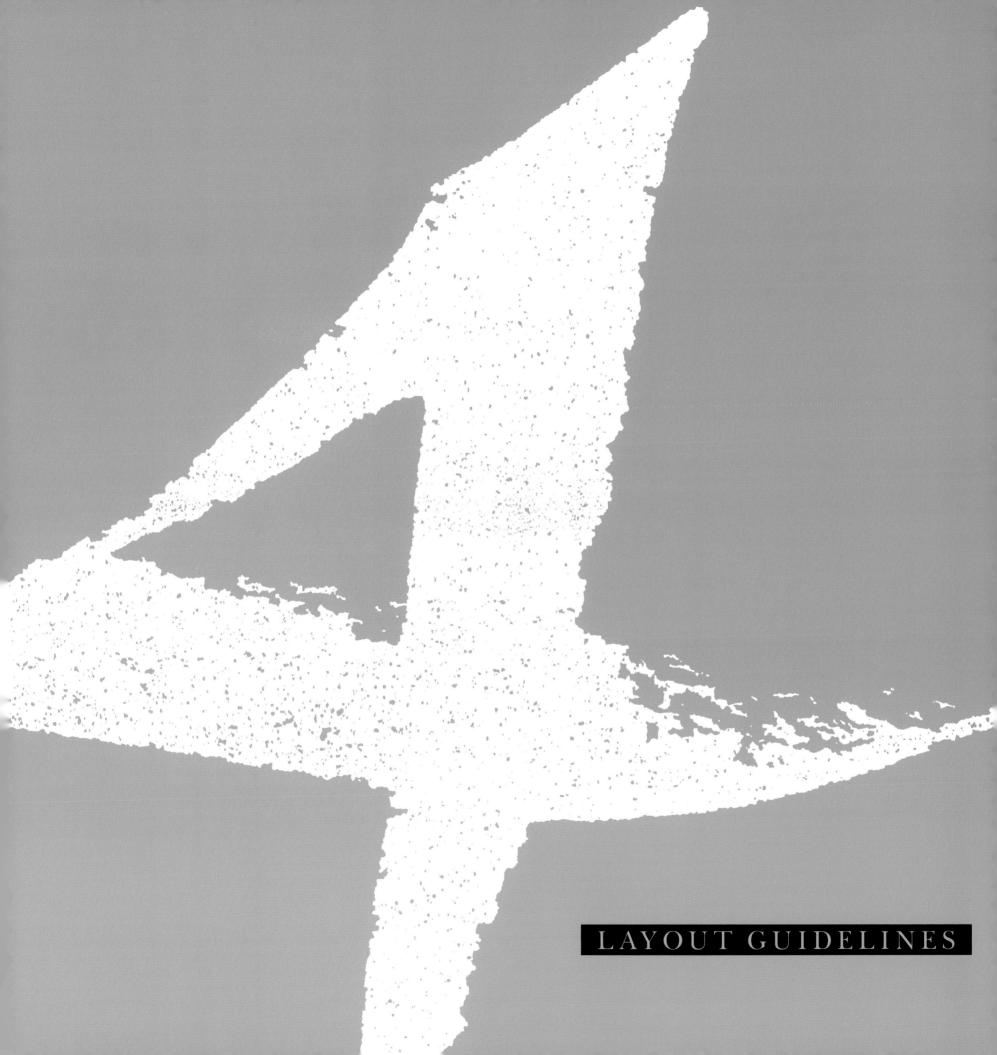

LAYOUT GUIDELINES

Filling the space

For many calligraphy assignments, there are recognized, standard formulas on layout to be followed. This is particularly so for certain official documents, certificates, ecclesiastical services, and invitations. Some other types of work may also be commissioned with guidelines provided by the client. However, planning the layout – arranging the words or groups of words to fit the page, and determining their size, weight and style – will still be necessary.

For all layouts, there are many decisions to be made. In order that nothing is overlooked, a good working practice is to draw up a checklist or list of actions. This may cover the following elements of the work: heading, subheading, text, name of author, date, name of calligrapher, decoration. If the work is an invitation, the list of information includes name, place, date, time, and so on. This list-making, breaking the job down into parts, helps you to determine the visual and literal importance of each item of information.

Scanning the words will provide more valuable information to contribute to the layout and begin to provide answers to questions, such as the following – what are the words about; what style of lettering lends itself to the mood or occasion; who is this for, and who will read it (which may affect size and shape); does it need decoration or colour; what kinds of materials would be suitable; where is the piece to be displayed, and is it to be printed or used as is?

FORMAT AND MARGINS

The size and shape of the work may not be a foregone conclusion, in which case, you can determine these elements when playing with rough layouts. If the shape is not round, square, or irregular, it will be a portrait or landscape rectangle.

Margin widths are an important factor in the design. The relationship of the margins to each other will help to balance the entire work. Generally, equal margins around the whole piece do not work well visually. The two most commonly used options are: sides and top of equal depth and the base slightly deeper; or sides of equal proportion, the top slightly less deep and the base deepest of all.

Visual faults occur if the margins are not planned carefully. Too much surrounding white space will cause the words to be lost, or to appear to float in the centre of

CREATING MARGINS

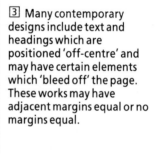

1 The areas of white space surrounding a piece of work are integral to the design of the page as a whole. One method of achieving a balanced and pleasing effect is to calculate the margins in ratios of 2:2:2:3. In this format the margins at the top and sides are equal and the base margin is slightly deeper.

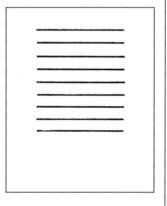

2 A second ratio for calculating margins is 1½:2:2:4. In this case the top margin is narrower than the two sides and the base margin is the deepest.

3 Many contemporary designs include text and headings which are positioned 'off-centre' and may have certain elements which 'bleed off' the page. These works may have adjacent margins equal or no margins equal.

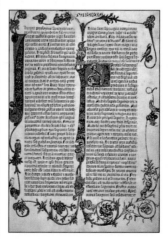

ABOVE The early typefaces mimicked the letterforms developed over many centuries by the scribes. Gutenberg's 42 line Bible illustrates this imitation, which extends to the layout and decoration of the page.

LETTER SPACING

laeio laeio
oo ll ooll

Good letter spacing is vitally important for legibility and overall appearance of any written work. The style of the lettering provides the clue to correct spacing. Some hands are round and open and dictate a need to allow space for the letters to 'breathe'. Conversely, straight, angular styles, such as some Gothic hands, demand less space.

WORD SPACING

Ljkoqruovkco

The width of an O is a good general guide for determining the space between words.

the page. Unless a small amount of white space is an integral part of the design, the words will appear cramped and the work unbalanced. Mounted and framed pictures in a gallery best illustrate traditional proportioning of margins.

Some designs do abandon a regular and properly proportional margin arrangement. These are designs in which, for example, the colour or decoration, or a rule, runs off the page. This is a called 'bleeding off'. This is a perfectly valid solution and can be used very effectively in contemporary works. Look at lots of examples in printed matter – such as books, magazines, advertising leaflets, or posters – and identify how other designers have used this method.

RIGHT DAVE WOOD – An advertising leaflet aimed at calligraphers. The list of available equipment provides a textural ground, over which an enlarged Copperplate elbow nib is superimposed. This is a successful and original concept: it includes all the relevant information and presents it well.

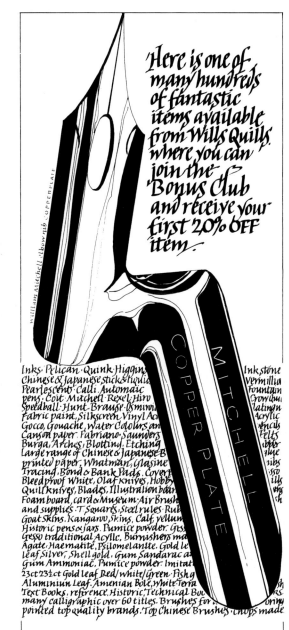

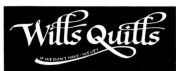

STYLE

When you have determined the importance of the order of the information to be transcribed and have become more familiar with the subject of the text, you may have a preference for the choice of lettering style. If this is not yet the case, read the copy again and try matching a feeling or mood to the words – elegant, gentle, quiet, tasteful, sombre, excited, blunt, outrageous, colourful, and so on. This exercise should also give you initial ideas for the design that will evolve as you sketch out lots of roughs.

Calligraphic design is sometimes tight and controlled, but also has great potential to be extrovert and free. Depending on the nature of the work, subscribe to the most applicable mood. Do not apply rigid layout methods to words that resound with life and energy. Equally, do not take a light-hearted approach to the design for a serious and solemn text. Think of the mood and colour of the words while roughing out various ideas as to how they can be fitted to the page.

On your rough layouts, indicate areas of text with lines, and get an idea of where the line breaks will occur. It is not necessary to transcribe all the words laboriously in early rough layouts, but include some indication of special features such as bold lettering, capital letters, patterns, illustration, bullet marks, borders, and rules.

As you work on the ideas, there should come a time when you feel that the design is beginning to 'gel'. At this point, working more toward the finished size of the piece, you can include more detail. In turn, this should lead to a finished rough complete with colour concepts and the basic structure of any patterns, borders, and illustrative material.

The finished rough provides the model for the final work. A working practice will develop as confidence grows, and some procedures will become more condensed and automatic.

The layout should create harmony on the page and be pleasing to the eye. Nothing should appear jarring. Collect ideas in a notebook and make a cuttings file of solutions that inspire you. Renew and update your file as both design styles and your personal preferences change.

CENTRING TEXT

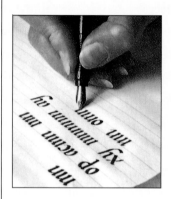 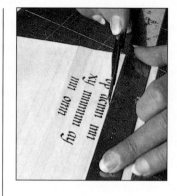 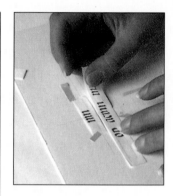

1 Many calligraphic works lend themselves to a centred layout. There are several methods of centring; making up a dummy layout is a quick and accurate way. Begin by transcribing the text in the chosen style and size. Write the text with the correct word spacing and in the individual lines that will make up the final piece.

2 Cut out each line as close to the writing as possible. Fold each strip in half so the first and last letters cover each other. The fold marks the centre point of the written line. Alternatively, simply measure the half-way point between the outer stroke of the first and last letters and mark this centre point very lightly in pencil.

3 On a clean sheet of paper lightly mark with pencil the vertical centreline. Assemble the strips and align each fold or centre mark with the pencil line. Tab each strip into position with masking tape. Pay attention to the space between the strips, especially if a final decision on this space has not yet been reached.

LETTER SPACING

Letter spaces are nearly identical, depending on which letters are adjacent. Aim for a balance between the counter spaces of the letters and the spaces between letters to achieve a balanced rhythm to the whole work.

WORD SPACING

Until you become more familiar with lettering styles, produce evenly spaced words. As a guide, allow the width of an O between words.

INTERLINEAR SPACING

Allow enough space between lines of words to ensure that ascenders and descenders do not become entangled. Take particular care if you intend to include flourishing.

Composition

PLANNING THE PIECE

When planning a piece you will need to determine the size of the lettering so that all the information can be fitted. For a poem or list of items, select the longest single line and use that as a guide when working out the size of the letters. The size of the lettering is determined by the width of the nib, so the words have to be written out in the chosen style in nibs of various sizes before discovering the size that fits. The examples below illustrate the different line lengths obtained by using a variety of nib sizes, ranging from very broad to fine. Each uses the same number of nib widths for the height of the letters.

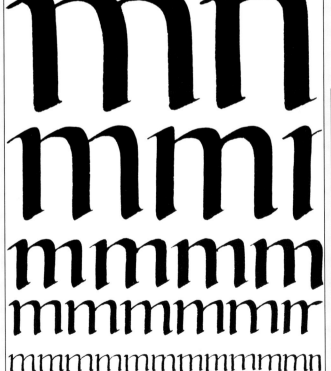

REVERSING OUT

Calligraphy, with its strong patterns of black and white, lends itself well to reproduction in print. A work designed for reproduction in black on white, or on a colour, can be given further dimension by reversing out part of the design. This can be done as artwork by hand, but it is easier to submit the piece to be reversed out as finished artwork in black on white to a printer, who will do it photographically in the darkroom. Further interest can be added by having part of the design – a box or rule – bleeding off the page.

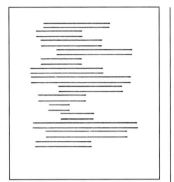

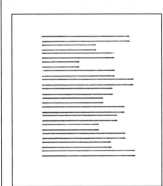

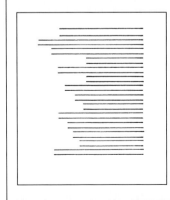

EXPLORING DIFFERENT ALIGNMENTS

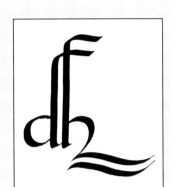

☐1 An asymmetrical arrangement of lines on the page.

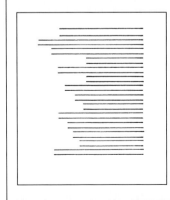

☐3 This text has lines aligned left and right; that is, it is justified left and right.

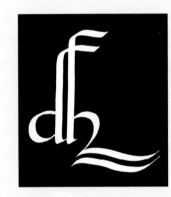

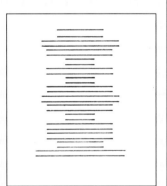

☐2 On this page the left-hand margin is aligned ('ranged left') and the right-hand margin is unjustified ('ragged right').

☐4 A centred arrangement of lines is a pleasing layout for many calligraphic works.

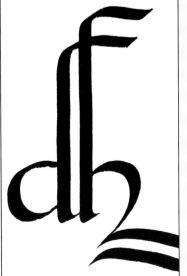

☐5 Here the 'ranged right, ragged left' alignment produces the opposite effect to number 2. This style does not make for easy reading, so is best suited to short pieces of display text.

ASSESSING DEPTH

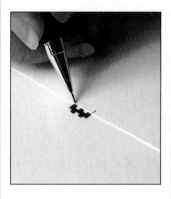 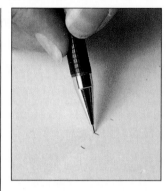

1 A depth scale is a useful item for ruling up and determining the depth of a piece of work. On the edge of a piece of paper or board, mark the height of the letters as determined by the number of nib widths.

2 Calculate the amount of space required between the lines and mark this on the depth scale. To do this, measure the amount from the base line of the letter height. Starting at the same point on each side of the paper, mark off the line depths and interlinear spaces. Use either pencil or the points of dividers, and keep the marks as close to the edge of the paper as possible.

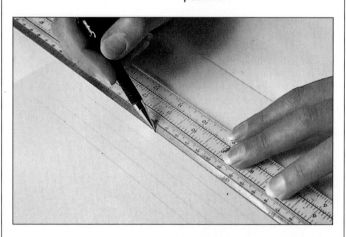

3 Rule up the writing lines using the marks as a guide. If using a T-square or parallel motion, mark off the line depths on one side of the paper only.

LINE LENGTH

There is no rule that covers all eventualities. In time, you will develop the ability to make a visual assessment based on the proportions of the letters in relation to the proposed size of the work. In some pieces, the longest line will provide the guide for the width of the work. Try out different line lengths by using different nib sizes.

LETTER STYLE

Do not use too many different styles. The advantage of pen lettering is the ability to change the weight and size of the same style to create an impact without introducing another hand.

MARKING UP

To prepare the text, transcribe all the words in the chosen style and size onto layout paper. Carefully cut around the words, phrases, titles, and so on, and compose them on a sheet of paper the same size as the final work.

ALIGNMENT OR JUSTIFICATION

The way the lines fall on the page is an important consideration. There are recognized ways that this can occur. Centred text is evenly distributed on either side of a centreline. Justified text aligns on both left-hand and right-hand margins. Alternatively, the work can be ranged (aligned) left and ragged (uneven) right, or vice versa, or the lines can form an asymmetrical arrangement.

For all methods of alignment, the rough transcribing of the hand and all the spacing requires special attention. If a space is enlarged in the final version, then the line will be, for example, off-centre.

DEPTH

A useful item for ruling up and determining the depth of a work is a depth scale. This provides a practical method of fitting the lines to text. The basic mathematical formula for determining depth in an evenly spaced work is: number of lines of text × letter height + number of interlinear spaces × space height.

Calligraphic design is design of a very specific nature, either predominantly or wholly concerned with the visual arrangement of words. Numerous decisions contribute to the production of a harmoniously arranged work. Some solutions present themselves quite easily, while others are of a more quirky nature.

It is advisable to develop a personal checklist of design elements. This will be of enormous benefit, as there are so many considerations that have a serious effect on the final work as a whole. Some resolutions become automatic as your working knowledge develops. If the work is for a client, it is possible that many of the ingredients of the design have been specified already.

Give your attention first to the text or copy. You must establish a measure of familiarity and understanding while building a feeling for the words as you read them through. Ask questions as the reading proceeds: what is this about, who will read it, what is important, will it be held or read at a distance?

Some solutions come immediately into focus from the reading, including the purpose and conditions in which the text will be read. In the early stages, you may have ideas about embellishment – it becomes more obvious whether the text is suitable for flourishing, or should have a border, or bullet points for highlighting specific and important information. At this stage, such thoughts are merely conjecture and may change, but your first impressions are worth noting.

Next, pay attention to the lettering itself: the height, weight, and style must be determined, and also whether some or all of the letters might be executed in colour. In answering your earlier questions, you will already have eliminated some letter styles. From the choices remaining, you can attempt to match the mood and inference of the words.

Deciding on the right style for the work is very important. It should be appropriate to the function of the piece: for example, a complicated Gothic hand or overtly flourished letters would be a disastrous choice for a public notice in which immediate legibility is essential.

Remember that you can introduce emphasis with a change to the weight, height, and colour of the lettering. For example, a heading written in bold upper-case letters in colour will contrast well with a text written in smaller upper- and lower-case letters of the same hand in black. This could make a better design than combining two

SUBSTRATE SHAPES

1 The overall shape of the substrate on which the work is to be executed is important. This is a portrait shape. Work can be planned to occupy any space within this area; it does not have to be centred.

2 The landscape shape is also a rectangle. The long sides are on the horizontal. Work can be placed anywhere in the space. Try experimenting with different layouts, both symmetrical and asymmetrical.

3 The square is the third shape in this group. Work can be arranged to dramatic effect within this geometrically regular figure.

distinct letter styles. Some changes of height and weight also create texture and introduce movement.

The size of the finished work may be predetermined. If it is not, you must focus on the format and dimensions of the piece. Is it to be landscape or portrait or square? Perhaps it is to be reproduced for an item that will be sent through the mail. What sizes of envelopes are available, and is the work to be folded?

The choice of a particular paper or board can often be resolved by the nature of the words to be written. If this is not the case, follow basic rules for selection. Look for colour, weight, and surface finish that will complement the calligraphy. All the materials you use are of great importance. The paper should enhance the work as a whole, but it must also be a sympathetic surface for the chosen medium.

Putting together all of the decisions made so far, you can now proceed with rough drafts. Do lots of roughs, nurture the ideas, and learn to trust your intuition. Do not throw away any scribbles: ironically, the first draft is often the best solution.

For some more practical examples of composition see pages 144–5, 146–53, and 154–161.

Headings and sub-headings

Many factors combine to make a calligraphic design successful. One is the presentation of the work as a whole, and an important contribution to this is the treatment of the heading or title.

The role of the heading is multifaceted. The word or group of words has to attract the attention of the viewer – to the whole work and to the title itself. Having captured the focus, it must allow the reader to read the text. It has, therefore, to stand out and be emphasized in some way. Bold lettering, contrasting colours, good letter spacing, and careful use of rules or decoration are all effective devices for catching the eye, but in so doing they must not render the information illegible.

The position of the heading is important. In order to make a visual impact on the reader, the words need to be placed slightly apart from the main body of the text. This does not mean that they stand in total isolation; there are several solutions to creating this space apart from just physically separating the title and text.

The first considerations are the size, weight, style and colour of the letters. Then, although the name suggests that a heading should be at the top of a page, this is certainly not the only place, nor, for some works, the best place visually.

The information given by the title is important and must be seen to relate to the whole design. A heading is not an appendage. However, you can experiment with headings in different positions on the page. A single-word title could run vertically down one side of the page. If the text is composed of individual verses or independent pieces of information, the heading could be located in the middle of the page and centred.

Alternatively, it could run across the base of the work, be placed at an oblique angle, or aligned at one side. Look for the solution that offers the most visual impact without loss of meaning.

Study early and modern examples of calligraphy to see how the problem has been solved before. Observe the variety of solutions and do lots of roughs, working thoroughly through as many options as possible. Mark in the body of the text with lines, ruled if necessary, to indicate the area it will occupy, so you can better perceive the balance of space.

If a heading has not been supplied and one is required, you must give careful thought to the wording. The heading should be thought of as a descriptive statement of

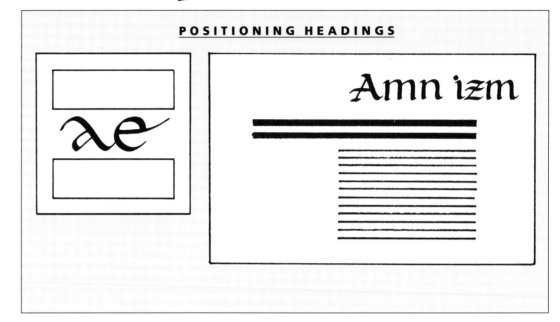

POSITIONING HEADINGS

the contents of the text, expressed both precisely and succinctly.

If you have to include the name of an author, a date, or a reference relating to the text, consider this at the same time as the heading. Often it is this important data that can create a balanced feel to the work. Do not neglect it; like the heading, it is not an afterthought.

SUB-HEADINGS

It was a relatively common practice of the early scribes to include in their manuscripts one or more lines of words with letters of a smaller size than those of the title, but larger than the text. The words would appear below a heading or after a decorated letter. Usually, they simply formed the beginning of the text, on occasions extending to quite a lengthy introduction. The concept can be most effectively employed and often works particularly well combined with a decorated or dropped capital.

Expert scribes used numerous variations of this arrangement and the best way to understand them is to spend some time looking at the manuscripts. Keeping reference notes and sketches of unusual layouts will help you to expand your repertoire.

Although some difficulty may arise in working out the letter size to fit the available space, this practice can make a good contribution to achieving a finely balanced work.

Headings serve many purposes and their design and placement deserve careful consideration. Experiment with different arrangements on the page to find the most suitable and aesthetically pleasing solution. It may be useful to use a grid system to assist in working out the layout of the page. Most printed matter – books, magazines, and newspapers – is designed using a grid, enabling the designer to align the work in a clean, legible manner, both horizontally and vertically. Look at some examples and see how the text and images are laid out on the page, often in columns of a specific width. Rough sketches are initially sufficient for working out the position of a heading. Once an idea has evolved, begin to work some of the text into the sketches.

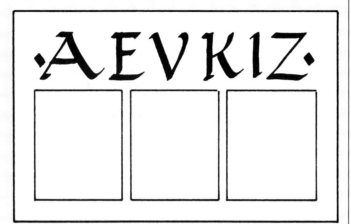

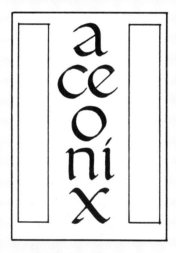

BELOW PAUL SHAW – The red words of the title of his work are ranged right, an alignment method that requires good planning. The letters of the alphabet have been placed centrally to the work. Here, they are both an illustration and a heading. The names of the authors are treated as sub-heads in size and position of lettering.

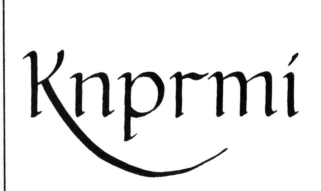

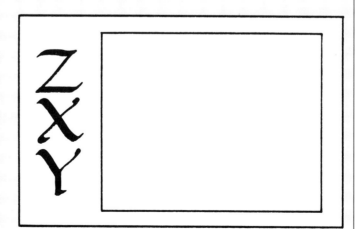

Rules

The ruling pen is an excellent instrument for drawing up rules of various widths. It can be used with ink or pen, so is versatile for introducing or enhancing colour work. The pen consists of a handle to which two stainless steel blades are attached. One blade is straight and flat, the other bows slightly outward. The tips of the blades almost meet: the space between them forms a reservoir for ink or paint. By adjusting a thumbscrew on the bowed blade, you can alter the distance between the blade tips, which dictates the thickness of the line made by the ruling pen.

The medium is loaded into the pen with a brush, or using the dropper supplied with some ink bottles. No ink or paint must be left on the outer edges of the blades, as this could flood the paper if it comes into contact with the ruler used to guide the pen. The pen must be operated with both blades resting on the paper. Its movement discharges the fluid held between the blades.

Although the thickness of the line can be considerably varied by adjusting the pen, some rules may be of a thickness that is best achieved by drawing two parallel lines and filling in between them with a small brush.

A ruling pen attachment is often found in a standard compass set. It can be used in place of the pencil lead normally inserted in the compass, so that you can draw perfect circles of ink or paint.

For fine work, the ruling pen has perhaps been superseded by the technical drafting pen, also available as a compass attachment, but for the ability to produce rules of different weights and colours, the ruling pen remains unsurpassed.

USING A RULING PEN

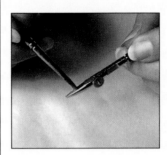

☐1 Use ink, or paint mixed to a fluid consistency. Insert the colour between the blades of the ruling pen with a dropper or brush. Wipe off any excess medium from the edges of the blades.

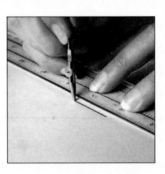

☐2 Place the ruler flat on the surface with the bevel edge sloping inward and hold firmly. The thumbscrew on the curved blade of the pen should face outward. Hold the pen at a slight angle to the ruler to avoid paint or ink flooding underneath the edge. Keep the drawn stroke light, smooth and steady, with the points of both blades on the paper to ensure an even flow of medium. It may be necessary to do a 'dummy run' to check that the width of the line is correct.

USING A COMPASS

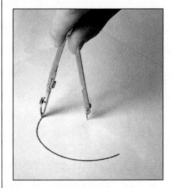

Load the blades of the compass attachment with liquid medium, place the centre of the pin of the compass onto the paper and draw the blades over the surface.

BRUSH RULING

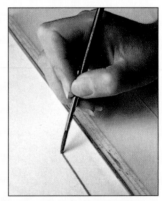

When using a brush to rule lines, avoid smudging by holding the ruler at a 45° angle to the paper so that the edge is not actually touching the paper. Gently draw the brush along the ruler, keeping the ferrule against the ruler's edge to ensure a straight line. When the line is completed, remove the ruler carefully to avoid smudging.

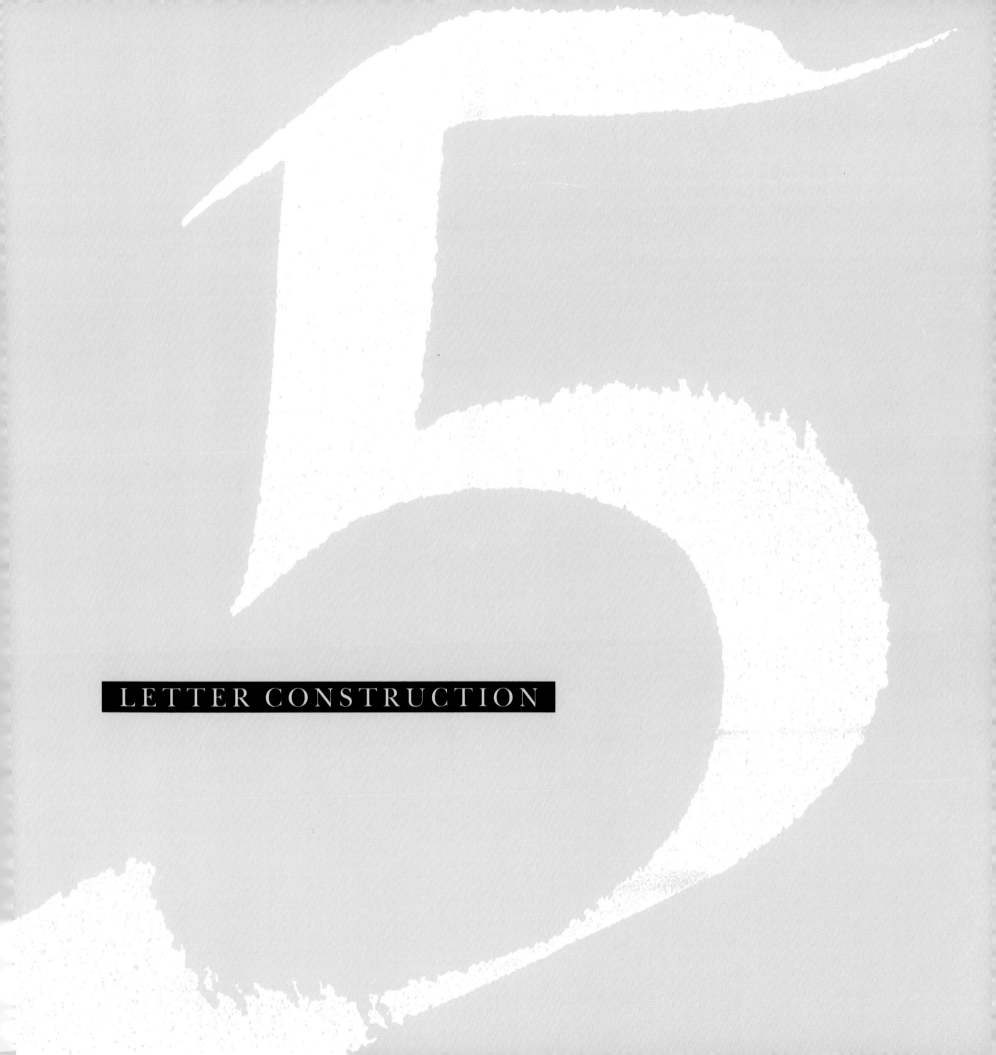

5

Terminology

In order to fully understand letter construction, you will need to understand the terminology used to describe the constituent parts of letterforms. When analyzing a particular style, this nomenclature is used to define the various elements in a concise manner. There is no standard nomenclature to define constituent parts of letters but many of the terms are self-explanatory. The terminology used here is based on that employed by letter designers and therefore may differ from that found in calligraphic references. Many descriptions are repeated from letter to letter as these terms are used generally throughout the alphabet and are not necessarily confined to a specific letter. The parts and names illustrated refer to the Quadrata capitals (majuscule) and a complementary lower-case (miniscule) alphabet although most of the terms can be employed to define other forms.

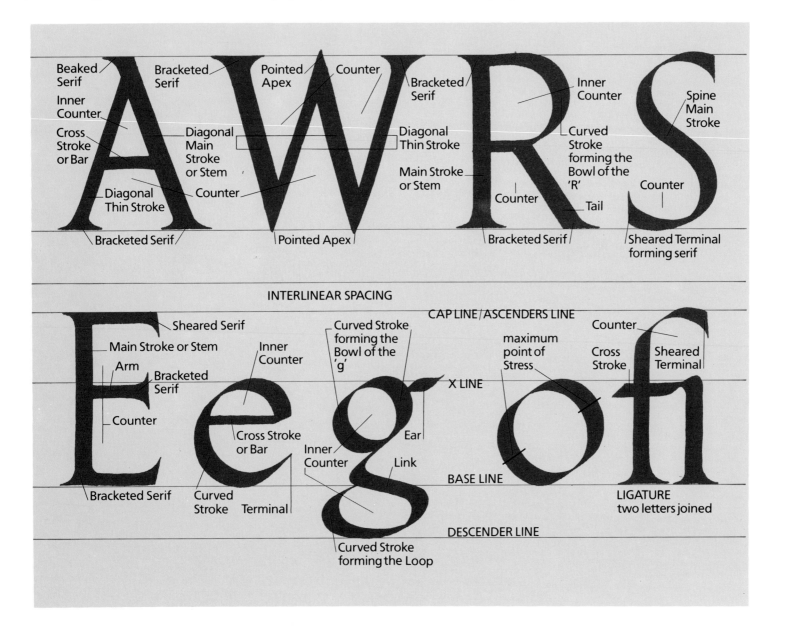

Understanding letter construction

Quadrata is the criterion on which all subsequent styles are based. It is therefore most important for you to understand this fine, proportioned alphabet.

Roman is not just the name of the country of origin but is used more generally to describe any style appearing in a vertical attitude. The capital alphabet contains more straight lines than curves, and many letters have a combination of both vertical and horizontal strokes giving a squarish appearance, hence the word quadrata. There is an architectural, geometric quality within the style which would account for the harmony created when lettering is used on buildings in stone.

Capital letters can be defined as having a uniform height throughout; that is, they are written between two parallel lines. The letters are contained without a capital or cap line (top line) and a base line, with the exception of the letters **J** and **Q** which break the base line in some styles. The lines are also marginally broken by minor optical adjustments to certain letters where pointed apexes and curved strokes slightly overlap.

There are now two fixed points, the capital and the base lines, between which to construct the letters. There is, however, a problem as you will need to decide how far apart the lines should be drawn. Consider the proportions of the letters opposite. There is a definite relationship between the capital height and the width of the main stroke. In Quadrata, the stem divides into the capital height 10 times, giving a ratio of 1:10. It is important to evaluate this ratio, as misinterpretation will result in an untrue reproduction of the style.

Once the height and weight ratios have been established, give consideration to the construction of individual letters. The Romans were a practical and efficient race, and their ability to rationalize and organize is reflected in the formal appearance of their design. The alphabet which follows has been produced with a pen and is based on formal Roman characters. If the forms are analyzed, it will be noticed that there are similar characteristics between certain letters, the **E**, **F** and **L** for example.

It is also apparent that the widths of letters are not identical and that each character occupies a given area in width while retaining a constant height. This width is known as the unit value of the letter, the **M** and **W** being the widest and the **I** and **J** the narrowest.

When letters are placed on a gridded square, an immediate visual comparison between the letterforms is

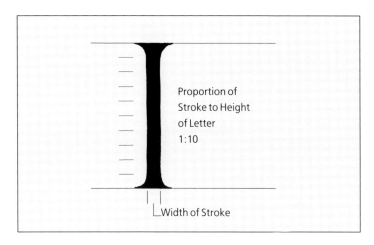

Proportion of
Stroke to Height
of Letter
1:10

Width of Stroke

possible. The grid illustrated has been divided into units of stem width for convenience, giving an initial square for the capitals subdivided into 10 units of height by 10 units of width. The lower blank portion is for the lower-case letters, which appear after the capitals. The lower portion will then be used to accommodate the descenders.

Incidentally, the words 'lower case' are a printers' term, now in common use to describe minuscule letters. It derives from the typesetters' cases which contained the metal or wooden letters. The capital letters of an alphabet were stored in the upper case and so are sometimes referred to as such, with the small letters stored in the lower case. Although concerned with calligraphy here, the common terms for majuscule and minuscule letters – capitals and lower case – are better employed and this is the terminology used from now onwards.

When analyzing the construction of individual characters, fix their images firmly in your mind. The proportions of this style will be found to be indispensable as you become more involved with letterforms, and the ability to draw on your experience of the classical Roman style will help you when analyzing other letterforms. The letters fall into six groupings, from the widest to the narrowest characters.

This alphabet has been lettered with a pen to illustrate proportion; it also shows that a classical Roman style can be achieved calligraphically. It is not necessarily helpful for you to begin lettering with this style for the construction of the letterforms is difficult in as much as they are not easily reproduced with a square-ended nib. However, within the sample alphabets on pages 71–79 there is a Roman style for use with the pen.

Roman capitals

GROUP 1

The **M** is one of the widest letters of the alphabet, occupying slightly more than the square with the diagonal strokes breaking the grid at both sides. The true Roman **M** has pointed apexes, along with the **A** and **N**, which are easily cut with a chisel; but when a pen or brush is employed, other forms of ending the strokes are more natural.

In order to achieve a pointed apex, the pen strokes end short of the cap and base lines and are then brought to a point. The apexes project beyond capital and base lines in order to obtain optical alignment with letters ending in square terminals or with beaked or bracketed serifs. Because the apexes of the **M** in the example alphabet end in a beaked serif, this will naturally be carried through to the **A** and **N** to give continuity. The straight, thin strokes in the **M** and similar letters are approximately half the thickness of the main stroke, but these strokes do alter because of the fixed lettering angle of the pen in relation to the direction of the strokes.

The **W** is perhaps the widest letter of the alphabet. It does not appear in Roman inscriptions but is a medieval addition to the alphabet. In Latin inscriptions **V** stood for both the **U** and **V** sounds – hence the name 'double U', drawn as two **V**'s virtually joined together, with minor adjustments. The **U** symbol was a later development, perhaps to avoid confusion.

Forming a Pointed Apex

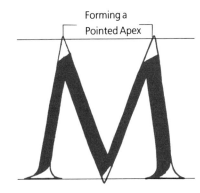

GROUP 2

The **O** sets the standard for all curved letters and the **Q** can be said to be an **O** with an added tail. It is advisable to make note of the point at which the tail joins the curved stroke. Some letters, unfortunately, have a tail which appears to emanate from the lower left-hand curve of the letter, as an extension. This is undesirable as the tail is most definitely a separate stroke.

The widest point of the thick stroke of the **O** is marginally wider than that of the stem of the **I**. In a free-drawn letter, that is, a letter drawn and then filled in, this is an optical adjustment made to compensate for the tapering or thinning of the stroke towards the thinnest part of the letter. Without this alteration, the curved stroke would appear optically thinner than the stem of the **I** (see page 64).

In calligraphy, the adjustment to thicken the curved strokes is automatic because of the oblique angle of the pen to the direction of writing. The thin strokes are substantially thinner than half the width of the main stroke, due to this same action of the pen. If desired, these thin strokes can be thickened to compare more favourably with the straight, thin strokes.

The widest point of the curved stroke is known as the 'maximum point of stress' and in this example it can be said that the letter has diagonal stress with oblique shading. There are many styles which have horizontal stress with vertical shading.

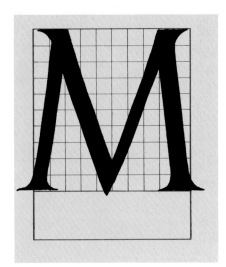
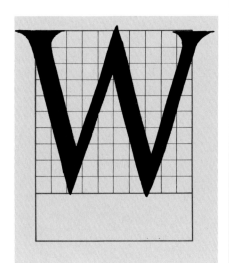
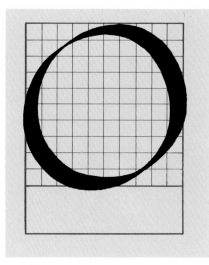
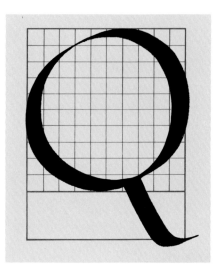

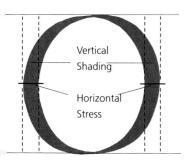

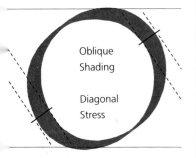

GROUP 3

The **C**, **D** and **G** take up about nine-tenths of the width of the gridded square. Because they are all rounded forms, the top and bottom curves project slightly over the cap and base lines. This is to ensure that the round letters appear the same height as those ending in flat serifs. Without this refinement they would appear smaller.

The **C** follows the left-hand curve of the **O**, but the upper and lower arms are somewhat flattened. The upper arm ends in a sheared terminal which is slightly extended to form a beak-like serif. In Quadrata, the lower arm also ends similarly. This serif is extremely difficult to produce with a pen.

G follows the lines of the **C**, with the stem of the **G** rising from the lower arm to within five-tenths of the letter height and terminating in a bracketed serif.

D follows the right-hand curve of the **O** with the upper and lower curves extending from the initial cross-strokes, so slightly breaking the cap line and base line. The stem appears slightly thickened towards the base cross-stroke where it is joined with a curved bracket. The serifs are bracketed on the left hand of the stem.

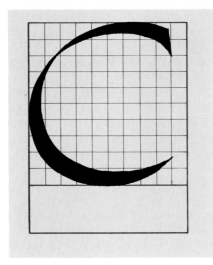

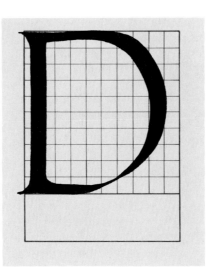

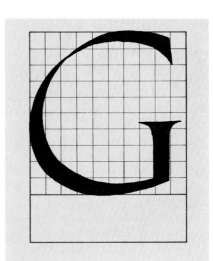

GROUP 4

This is the largest group of letters and includes **A**, **H**, **K**, **N**, **R**, **T**, **U**, **V**, **X**, **Y** and **Z**, all of which occupy approximately eight-tenths of the gridded square.

The **A**, **V**, **X** and **Y**, being letters formed from triangular elements, should appear almost symmetrical. The **V** and inverted **V** shapes should be balanced, not leaning to right or left. The cross-stroke of the **A** is positioned midway between the apex and the base line.

The cross-bar of the **H** should be slightly above the centre line; otherwise it seems to be slipping down the main stems. The two diagonal strokes of the **K** meet at a point which, too, is slightly above the centre, making the lower counter fractionally larger than the upper counter.

The pointed apex of the **N** should protrude below the base line with the upper left-hand serif being beaked. Both the upper part of the bowl of the **R** and the curved stroke of the **U** project above the cap line and below the base line respectively. The top of the lower cross-stroke which joins the bowl of the **R** is positioned on the centre line. A careful note should be made as to where the tail of the **R** meets the bowl.

The cross-bar of the **T** is sheared to the lettering angle on the left and right sides, ending in a slight serif. The spurs added to the serifs protrude above the cap line.

The **Z** is a problem letter as the main diagonal stem requires a change of pen angle to thicken the stroke. Otherwise the stem would appear as a hairline-thin stroke. This makes it difficult to execute with the pen.

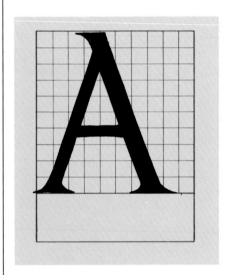
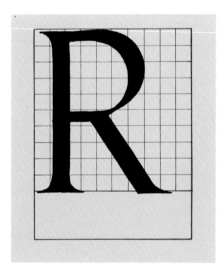
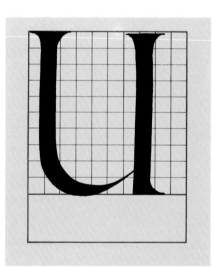
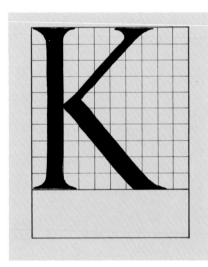
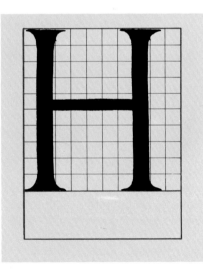
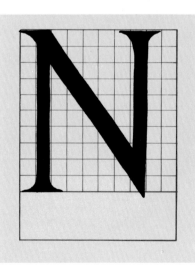
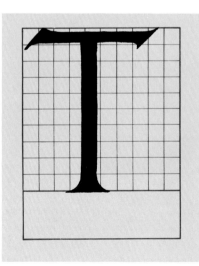
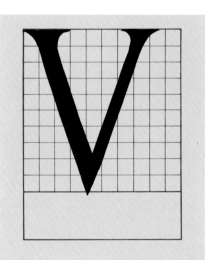

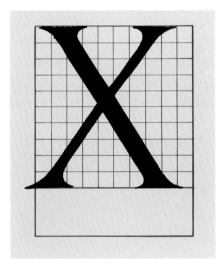

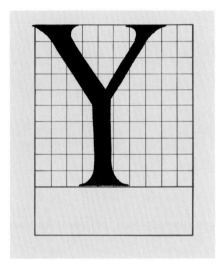

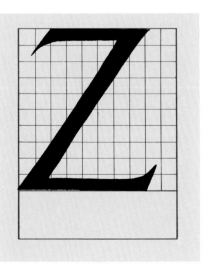

GROUP 5

Within this group are the letters **B**, **E**, **F**, **L**, **P** and **S**, each letter occupying about half the width of the gridded square. The upper bowl of the **B** is smaller than the lower and therefore the intersection is above the centre line. This is intentional: if both bowls were equal in size the letter would appear top-heavy.

The upper arm of the **E** is slightly longer than the middle arm, which is placed high on the centre line, making the upper counter smaller than the lower. Again this is optically necessary. The lower arm projects a little beyond the upper arm with both ending in sheared, bracketed serifs.

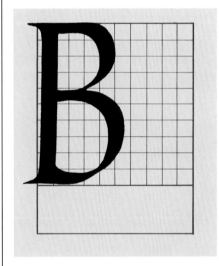

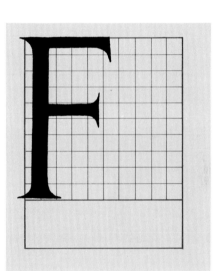

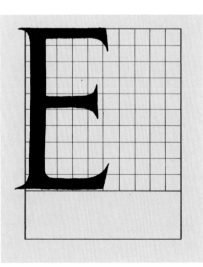

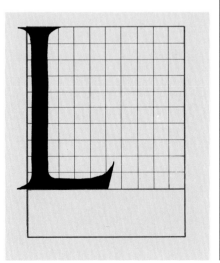

The **F** may be regarded as an **E** minus the lower arm. The **L** is an **E** without the upper arms. The stem at the cap line has the addition of a bracketed serif on the right.

The letter **P** at first glance resembles a **B** minus the lower bowl. Closer inspection will show that the bowl is larger than the upper bowl of **B**. The cross-stroke joins the bowl to the stem below the centre line.

The upper counter of the **S** is smaller than the lower counter, with the letter sloping slightly to the right. The diagonal spine is of uniform thickness until it tapers to meet the curved arms. The **S** is a diagonally stressed letter, having this characteristic in common with the **A, K, M, N, R, V, W** and, in this alphabet, the **Z**, which is the only letter with a thick diagonal stroke running from top right to bottom left. The upper and lower arms end in sheared terminals and fractionally extend to form beak-like serifs. Being the only letter with diagonal stress it is important for balance that the lower counter is slightly larger than the upper counter. This gives the **S** a slight forward tilt, making it one of the hardest letters in which to achieve a good poise.

GROUP 6

The **I** and **J** take up approximately three-tenths of the gridded square. The **I** is a simply constructed letter. Nevertheless, it is important because it sets the standard for the alphabet in height and stem width.

The **J** does not appear in the inscription on the Trajan Column where its present-day sound is represented by an **I**. **J** is written like an **I** minus the base-line bracketed serif, where the stroke continues through the base line and curves to the left, ending in a pointed terminal. The length of the stroke is contained within the descender area.

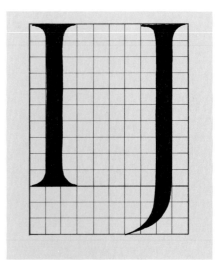

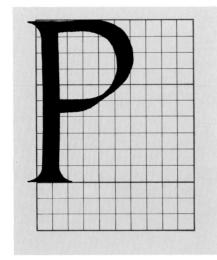

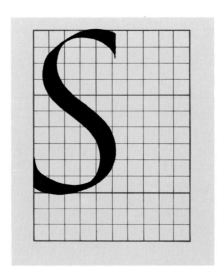

The development of lower case

The Quadrata and Rustica capitals were followed by Uncial, born of the need to write more quickly while still maintaining a formal style. Uncial is a true pen form with a simple construction and comparatively clean finishing strokes. Uncial was the literary hand for fine books from the fifth to the eight centuries. The letterforms were more rounded than traditional Roman capitals. The chief characteristic letters within the style were the **A**, **D**, **E**, **H** and **M** and, although they were still written between the capital and base lines, certain letters, namely the **D**, **F**, **G**, **H**, **K**, **L**, **P**, **Q**, **X** and **Y**, began to have longer stems which marginally broke through the cap and base lines.

Uncial was followed by Half-Uncial and here some letters are seen predominantly to break through the writing lines forming ascender and descender areas. Letterforms were modified, notably the **a**, **b**, **e**, **g** and **l**, with the remaining letters receiving only minor amendments, if any at all. Half-Uncial led the way for other minuscule scripts to be developed.

Towards the end of the eighth century, with the revival of learning, came a reform of the hand in which works of literature were to be written. The emperor Charlemagne, who governed a vast area of Europe, commissioned the abbot and teacher, Alcuin of York, to rationalize and

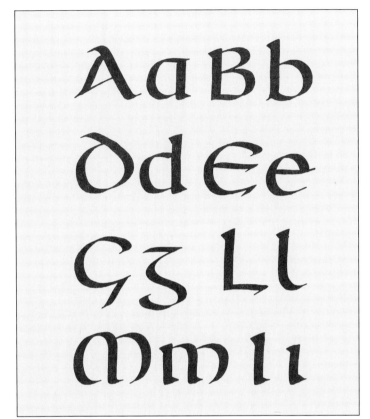

LEFT A comparison of the Uncial and Half-Uncial letterforms.

LEFT An example of Uncial and Half-Uncial lettering from the *Book of Kells*.

standardize the various minuscule scripts which had developed. Alcuin studied the former styles of Quadrata, Rustica, Uncial and Half-Uncial and developed a new minuscule as a standard book style. This has become known as the Carolingian minuscule after its instigator, the emperor Charlemagne. Calligraphy now entered a new era with this distinctive true pen form.

Although the Romans used mainly capital letterforms, a classical lower-case alphabet, together with Arabic numerals, has been included here to complement the capital forms previously described, and to give you an insight into their construction. The letters and numerals that follow are of classical proportions and, once their relative widths and construction details have been mastered, knowledge of them will stand you in good stead for lettering the sample alphabet in this book.

The letters have been placed on a grid which consists of squares of stem width: thirteen units deep, with four units allocated for the ascenders (those letters which reach the cap or ascender line, the **h** for instance), six units for the x height (that portion of the grid which contains letters such as the **s**) and three units below the x height (to accommodate the descenders of letters such as the **g** and **y**). The characters have been grouped together with common widths, starting with the widest and ending with the narrowest.

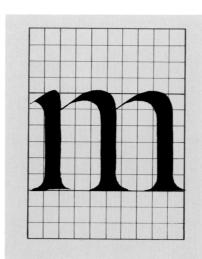

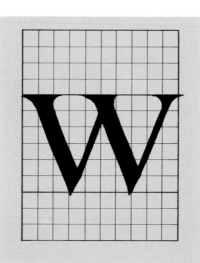

GROUP 1

The lowercase **m** and **w** occupy approximately 10 units, and both letters are contained within the x height. In the **m**, observe the point at which the curved shoulder of the second stroke meets the stem of the first – the second shoulder intersects at the same height. The serif of the first stroke and both shoulders, because they are curved, are positioned so that they break the x line to give optical alignment with the letters **v**, **w**, **x**, **y** and **z**; their tops are either bracketed serifs or, in the **z**, a cross-stroke.

The **m** is not two **n**s joined, as the inner counters of the **m** are narrower than that of the **n**. The apexes of the **w** extend slightly below the base line and the inner apex is the x line. This shows that the diagonal strokes are positioned correctly.

GROUP 2

Each letter in this group occupies about seven units. The group comprises **d**, **g**, **h**, **k**, **n**, **p**, **q**, **u**, **x** and **y**. There are three letters with ascenders (**d**, **h** and **k**), four letters with descenders (**g**, **p**, **q** and **y**), and three contained within the x height.

In the **d**, at the point where the lower curve of the bowl meets the main stem, there should be a triangular space formed by the upward movement of the curved stroke. The upper serif of the main stem projects slightly above the ascender or cap line.

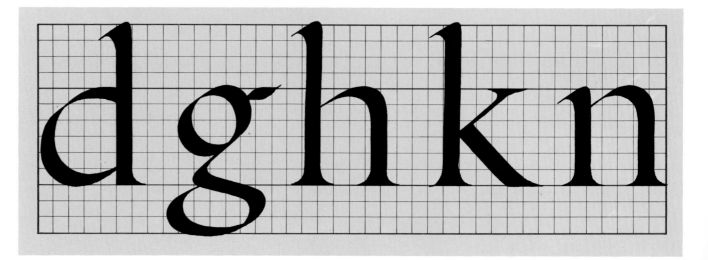

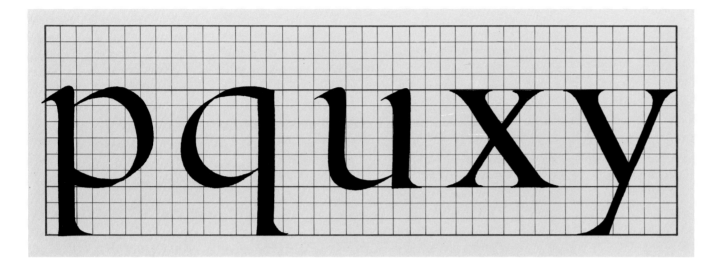

The old-style **g** is very difficult to master. In this style the bowl does not take up the whole depth of the x height: instead it occupies just over three units. It then joins the link which carries down to the base line and then turns sharply to the right and ends forming the right side of the loop. The loop is accommodated within the three-unit descender area. The ear is attached to the bowl at the right side, leaving a v-shaped space.

The **h** and **n** are formed in a similar fashion, although the **h** has the first stem lengthened to form the ascender, with the serif extending over the ascender line. The letter **n** can be taken as an **h** without the ascender. The ascender stem of the **k** is like the **h** and the diagonal thin stroke and the tail intersect just above the centre of the x height.

With the **p**, the join of the lower part of the bowl to the stem is somewhat flattened. A serif is attached to the bowl at the top left-hand corner. The **q** is not a **p** in reverse but is totally different in character, having no serif at the x line and with the upper stroke of the bowl being straightened to meet the stem.

The **u** is not an inverted **n**. The upper serifs protrude beyond the x line and a space is left where the curve makes its upward movement to meet the second stem. In the **x**, the point of intersection of the thin and thick strokes is above the x-height centre, making the lower counter larger than the upper. The diagonal thick stroke of the **y** does not reach the base line but is intersected by the thin stroke, which follows through to the descender line where it ends in a flat, bracketed serif.

GROUP 3

The two letters in this group take up approximately six-and-a-half units width. The **b** is an ascending letter, the main stem swinging to the right before it meets the base line. The **o** is contained within the x height with the exception of minor optical adjustments at the x and base lines.

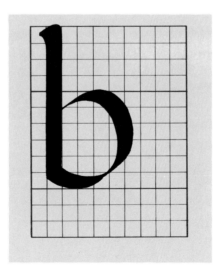

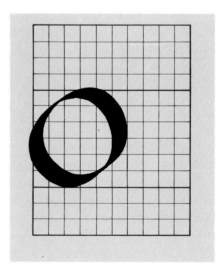

GROUP 4

This group contains the **a**, **c**, **e**, **f**, **v** and **z** and, with the exception of **f**, they are all contained within the x height.

The **a** starts from a pointed, curved arm which leads into the main stem. The bowl starts from the stem above the centre line of the x height and moves to the left before the downward curve. It rejoins the stem above the base line, leaving a triangular shape. The **c** follows the left-hand stroke of the **o**, the upper arm being slightly straightened and ending in a sheared terminal which is extended to form a beak-like serif. The lower arm ends in a pointed terminal. The **e** follows the **c**; the upper arm, however, is not straightened but flows round. End the stroke obliquely. The bowl is formed by a cross-stroke which is positioned above the x-height centre.

The **f** is an ascending letter, starting its main stroke below the ascender line with the arm projecting to the right and ending in a sheared, beak-like serif. The cross-bar is positioned just below the x line. The **v** and **z** both follow the same construction as their capital counterparts.

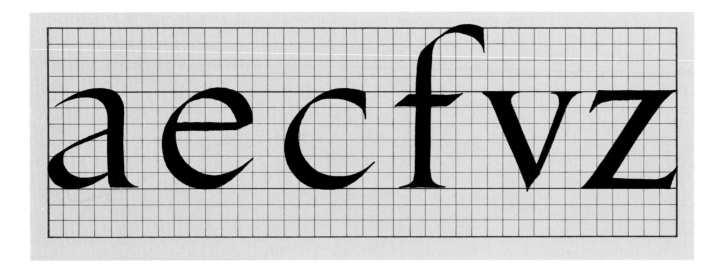

GROUP 5

This grouping contains three characters, about five units wide: the **r**, **s** and **t**. From the main stem of the **r** there is a small shoulder stroke which should not be overdone – if it is too long it can interfere with the lettering of the character which follows. The **s** is constructed in the same manner as its capital.

The main stem of the **t** starts obliquely, a little way above the x line, moving to the right before reaching the base line and ending in a pointed terminal. Like the **f**, the cross-stroke is finished with a slight upwards movement.

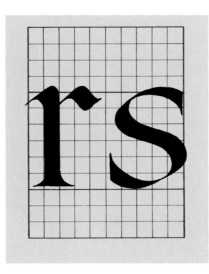

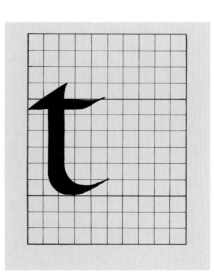

Numerals

GROUP 6

The **i**, **j** and **l** fall into this narrow-letter group. They are easily constructed, with the humble **i** and **j** setting the pattern for straight letters. The dot over the **i** and **j** can be round or flat and is usually positioned about midway between the x and ascender lines. The **j** initially follows the **i** but extends below the base line where it curves to the left, ending in a pointed terminal.

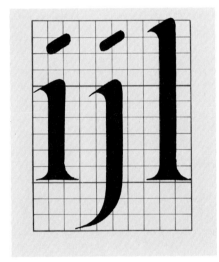

The Romans used letters of the alphabet for their numeric reference. We are all familiar with the Roman-style numerals when applied to a clock face, but perhaps not so with M = 1,000, D = 500, C = 100 and L = 50. It takes little imaginatiion to see that mathematical calculations could be made easier by changing the symbols. The Arabs did exactly that and based their system on 10 numeric signs, the 'Arabic numerals' we use today. They can be either of uniform height ('lining numerals') or of varying height ('old style' or 'hanging numerals'). In the latter style, the **1**, **2** and **0** appear within the x height, the **6** and **8** are ascending numerals and the **3**, **4**, **5**, **7** and **9** are descending characters.

The main characteristics of the numerals need little explanation, but a few points should be noted. For example, if numerals are not constructed carefully they can appear to be falling over. This is because they are mainly asymmetric in form, with the exception of the **0**, **1** and **8**, which are basically balanced.

If the curve of the **2** is allowed to project beyond the base cross-stroke, it will appear to be leaning to the right. If the tail of the **9** is not carried sufficiently far to the left, the figure will appear to lean to the left; if too far, it will look as if it is leaning to the right. The **9** is not an inverted **6**. The join of the small curved stroke to the main curved stem alters in each case, making the inner counters slightly different in shape.

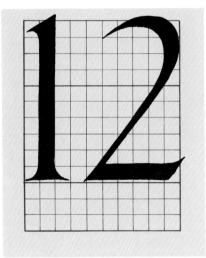

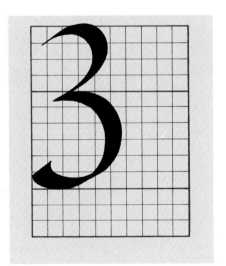

The upper counters of the **3** and **8** should be smaller than the lower; otherwise the characters will be top heavy. The cross-bar of the **4** is fairly low on the stem so that the inner counter does not appear too small. The diagonal stroke of the **7** cannot extend too far to the left: once it goes beyond the alignment of the upper stroke, it makes the letter look as if it were leaning backwards. If the cross-stroke of the **5** is too long, it too can appear to lean to the right. Finally, it should be noted that the numeral **0** is compressed and not a letter **O**.

Within our written language there are, of course, many other symbols such as parentheses, exclamation marks and question marks, to name but a few. These will become natural enough to create once you start practising calligraphy.

The character **&** is known as the ampersand. This is possibly a corruption of the mixed English and Latin phrase 'and *per se* and'. It is an ancient monogram of the letters **e** and **t**, the Latin word *et* meaning 'and'. The *et* in this instance is not reflected in the character on the grid, which occupies nine units in width. The upper bowl is much smaller than the lower with the angle of the diagonal stroke cutting through to form a semicircular counter and the tail ending in a bracketed serif. The upward tail to the bowl ends with a bracketed serif above the centre line.

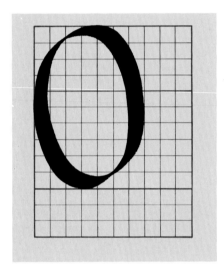

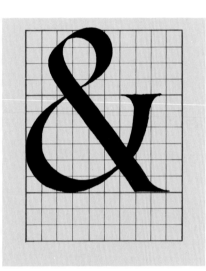

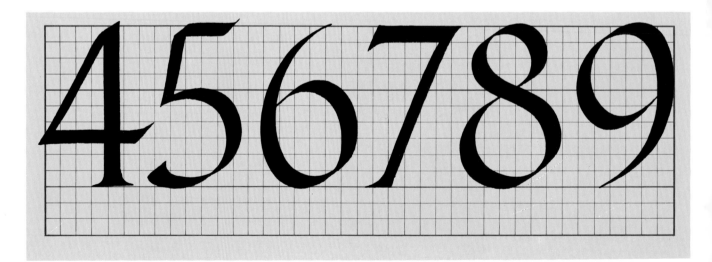

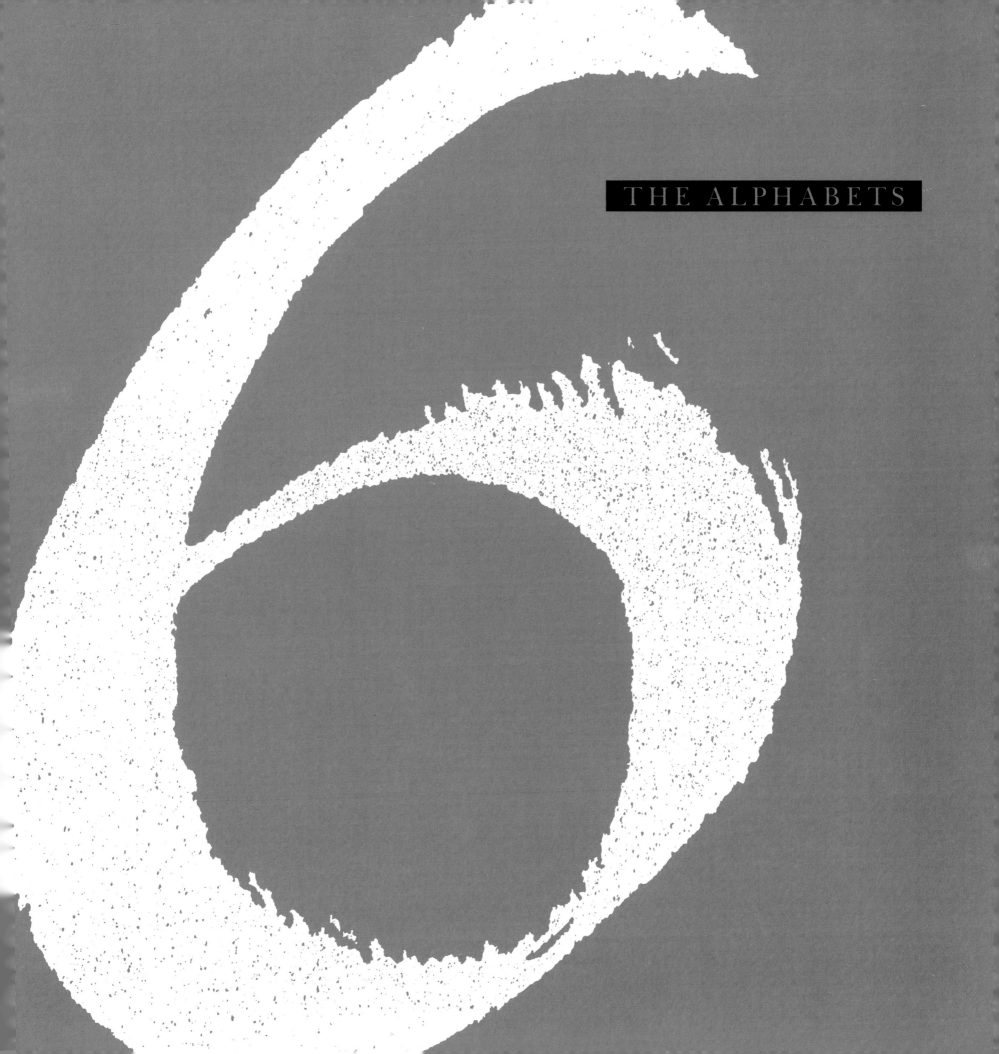

THE ALPHABETS

Roman alphabets

The great legacy of the Romans includes fine letterforms of splendid proportions and sublime elegance. In keeping with other developments in Roman culture, the letterforms matured over several centuries. The shapes of the letters have a strong connection with the introduction of the rounded arch and vault into architectural style.

To record an event, Roman capitals were extensively used incised in stone or marble, on monuments, tombs, and arches. Many fine examples of this alphabet, executed by Roman master craftsmen, can still be found. The execution of the letters was not confined to the chisel. Reed brushes and pens and quill pens also produced the perfect proportions and balance of elegant thick and thin strokes.

The Roman square capitals incised in stone were called *capitalis*. When practised with a square-cut reed pen or quill, they were known as *Quadrata*. The Quadrata required exceedingly painstaking execution to achieve the forms correctly. Quite quickly, the Rustic forms succeeded the round forms for use in manuscripts. These were letters of a style that could be written at greater speed and with some economy of materials. The square capitals continued to be well represented in headings, initial letters and special applications, as they are to this day.

In the classical Roman alphabet of 23 letters lie the origins of modern letter forms in the western world. The letters **J**, **U** and **W** were added during the Middle Ages.

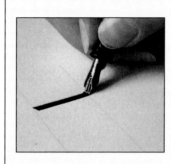

☐1 Holding the script pen at the correct 30° angle, draw the first downstroke.

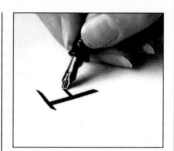

☐3 The second cross stroke is drawn in, making sure that the pen remains consistently at a 30° angle.

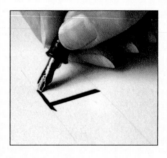

☐2 The first cross stroke is then drawn in, incorporating the correctly angled serif on the left (the correctly held 30° angle of the pen makes the cross stroke slightly thinner).

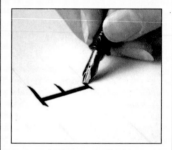

☐4 The base serif is then added. The height of the completed letter should be exactly 10 nib widths.

UNDERSTANDING THE SYMBOL

Where appropriate, a symbol indicating the suggested nib width, letter height, and pen angle accompanies each alphabet: use this as a guide only. Whatever size nib is used, the height of the letter is always determined using a 'ladder' of nib widths.

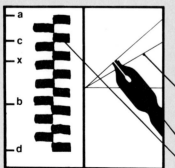

a refers to the ascender height
c refers to the height of the capital letter
x refers to the x-height, that is the height of the body of the letter
b refers to the baseline, where the body of the lower case letter sits or the base of the cap sits
d refers to where the descender finishes
pen angle hold your pen over the nib to ensure that it is at the right angle before you start; when more than one angle line is shown, this indicates there is a range of angles for that hand
nib width the correct width of the pen is shown
ladder to determine letter height

The pen angle for this vertical hand varies from 5° for the serifs to 20°–30° for most of the strokes. An angle of 45° is needed for the majority of diagonal strokes. A steeper angle is used for the slanted strokes of **M** and **N**, and a flat pen (0°) for the diagonal of **Z**. The pen moves from the top to the bottom of all vertical and diagonal strokes.

The letter height is 10 nib widths. Meticulous attention must be paid to the height and width of the letters to achieve and maintain their elegant proportions.

There are variations in the style and application of serifs and some are more difficult to execute than others. The simplest serif is added as a single separate stroke – a hairline formed by turning the pen to the flat angle (0°) for the horizontal stroke. A bolder serif can be executed as a

A Q X

A B C D E F G
H I J K L M N
O P Q R S T U
V W X Y Z

ROMAN ALPHABET

Roman letters can be written with a broad pen, held at an angle of 30° for most of the strokes. Diagonal strokes require a steeper pen angle (45°), and the middle stroke of the **Z** is made with a much flatter angle. The serifs require further manipulation of the pen, including using only the corner of the nib to complete their fine endings. The height of the letters is 10 nib widths.

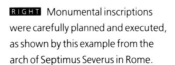

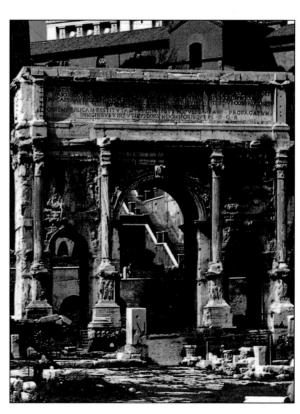

ABOVE The construction of Roman letters depends on good pen control and achieving and maintaining elegant proportions. Begin and end the vertical stroke with a small hook, which provides the foundation of the serif. To complete it, the pen is turned to 0° to the horizontal writing line.

RIGHT Monumental inscriptions were carefully planned and executed, as shown by this example from the arch of Septimus Severus in Rome.

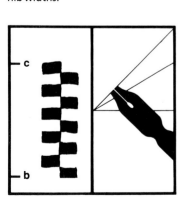

precursor to or an extension of a stroke.

The classical Roman form has a considered serif extending on both sides of the upright stroke. There is an almost imperceptible flaring of the upright before it comes to rest in the serif. These elegant endings involve much turning of the pen. Apart from in **C**, **G**, and **S**, all serifs are parallel to the writing line. A concise four-stroke pattern produces the desired effect. The first stroke is the vertical, the second the hairline – in some styles this is slightly concave toward the middle. The third and fourth strokes are identical, but reversed on either side of the vertical, joining the extremes of the hairline serif to the upright with a gentle curve. The procedure is the same for serifs at the top and bottom of the letters.

CLASSICAL ROMAN CAPITALS ALPHABET

The elegant style of classical Roman capitals survives most clearly in the stone-carved inscriptions of imperial architecture and monuments. This alphabet is a modern pen-written version based on those carved forms. The accompanying diagrams show the order and direction of the pen strokes by which the character is formed: the square-tipped pen is drawn across the paper, never pushed against the grain. The serifs, or finishing strokes, are modelled on the style originally typical of chiselled lettering; they are not natural pen forms, and they require a delicate touch and some dextrous manipulation of the pen.

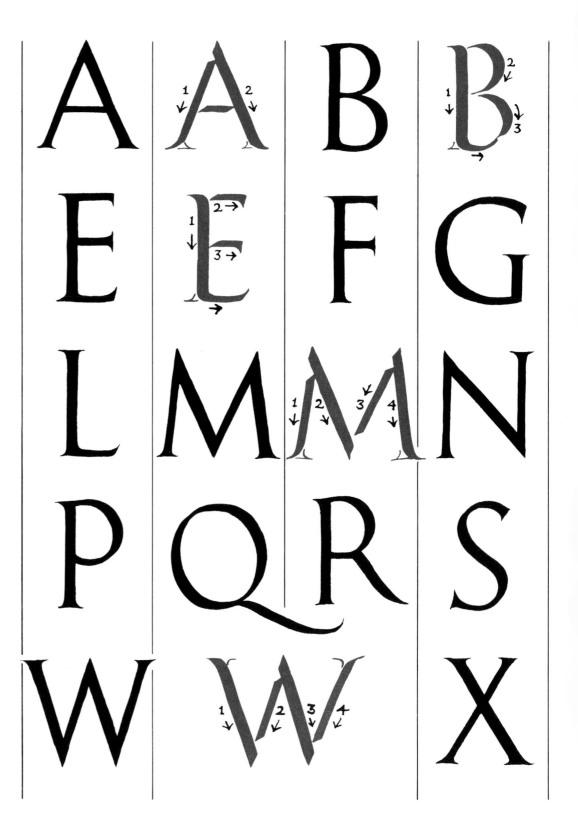

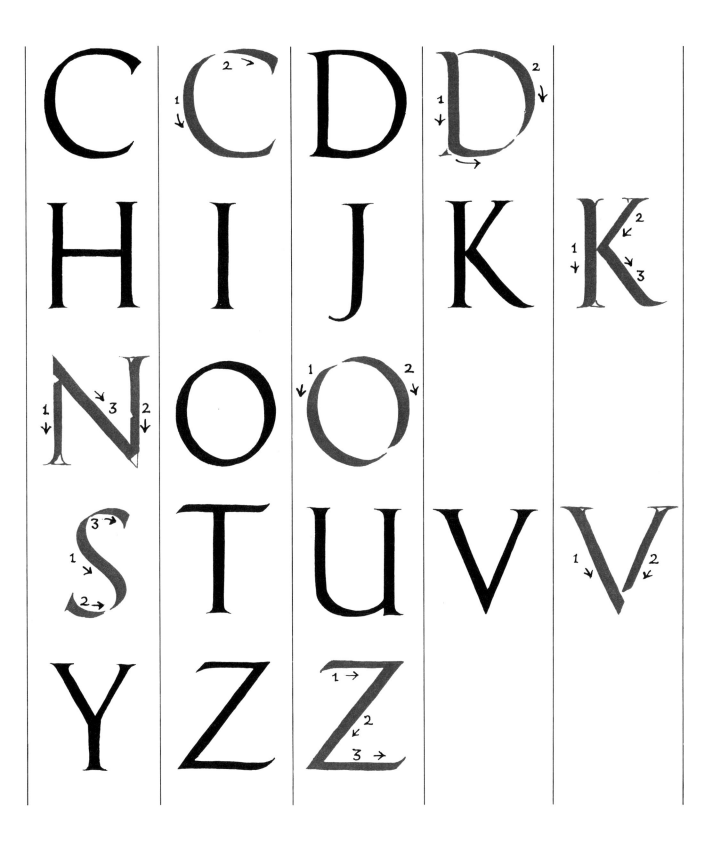

ROMAN LOWER-CASE LETTERS

This alphabet is designed as a complement to the preceeding capitals; the flat Roman serifs are seen in **k**, **v**, **w**, **x** and **y** and at the base of each letter, while the verticals have slanted serifs formed by a slight sideways and upward movement in beginning the stroke, before the pen is pulled smoothly downward. There was no directly comparable contemporary form of what are now called lower-case letters corresponding to the original Roman capitals. The shorter, more rounded forms with ascending and descending strokes were fully evolved in early minuscule scripts, which in turn were re-adapted by later writing masters and type designers to an overall style and proportion corresponding to the classical squared capitals.

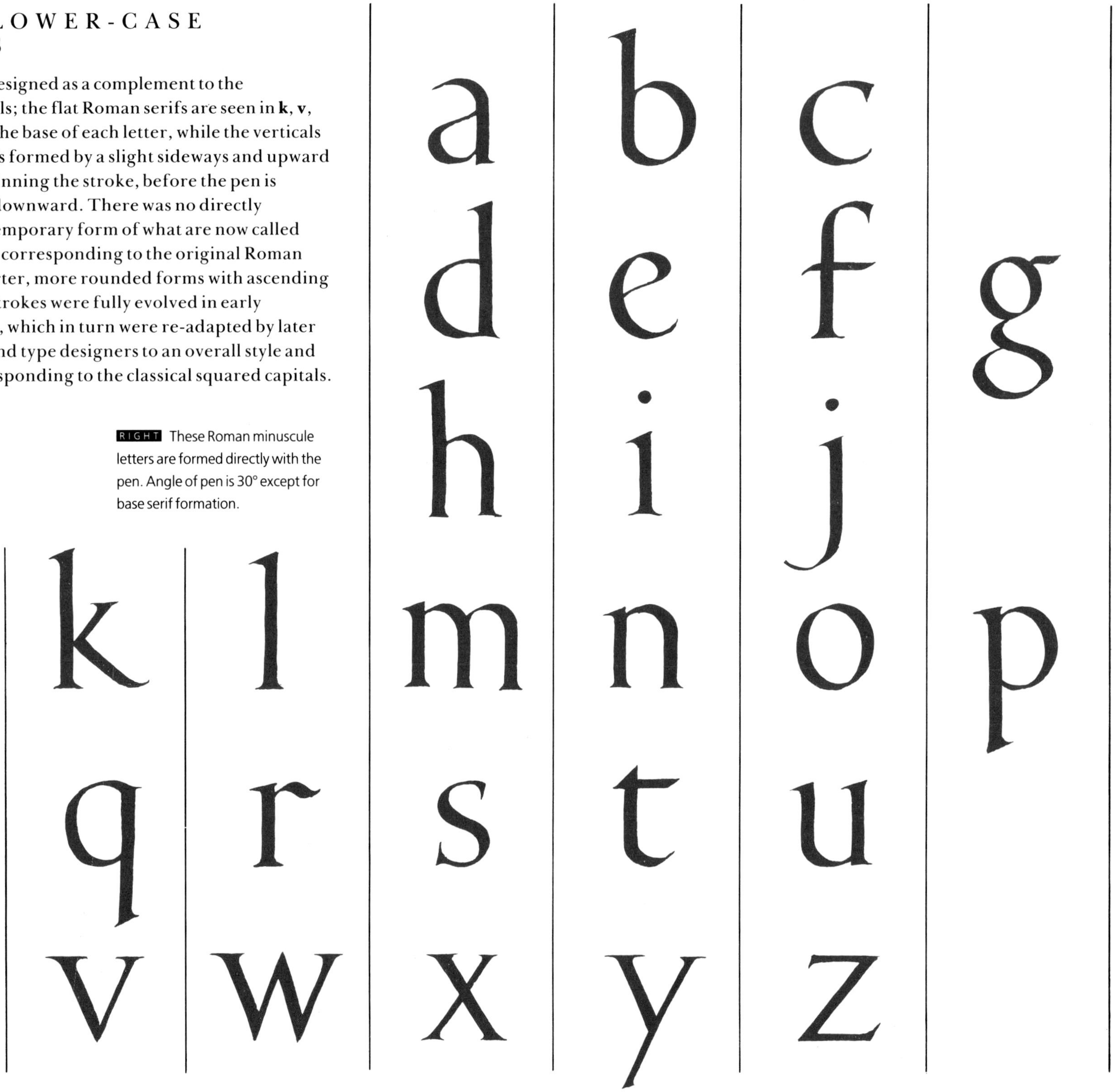

RIGHT These Roman minuscule letters are formed directly with the pen. Angle of pen is 30° except for base serif formation.

a b c

d e f

g

h i j

k l m n o p

q r s t u

v w x y z

COMPOUNDED ROMAN CAPITALS

Delicate proportions and finely varied strokes create a sophisticated modern adaptation of the Roman squared capitals. In this case, the thick and thin stroke variations do not correspond to the actual pen width: the heavier vertical stems and swelling curves are created by outlining the shape and filling in with solid colour, in a manner similar to the traditional tendering of decorative Versals. Fine hairlines are used to terminate the individual elements, cutting across the width of the vertical and diagonal strokes with a deliberate yet subtle emphasis. There is no attempt to round out the serifs as in the classical Roman capitals.

RIGHT Built up letterforms are almost always in colour. The skeleton of the letter is drawn and filled with fluid colour. The fine serif is in lieu of the Roman serif.

A B C D
E F G H
I J K L
M N O P
Q R S T U
V W X Y Z

MODERN PEN-DRAWN ROMAN LETTERING

This freely worked lower-case alphabet written by the American scribe Arthur Baker employs unusual elongation of extended strokes, although the body of the forms is rounded. Exaggerated thick/thin contrasts weight the bowls of the letters at a low angle. The slashing verticals and flourished tails cut through the solid, even texture, which is created by the use of interlocking forms and repeated letters. All these elements have been carefully thought out in the arrangement of the alphabet as a complete design form. The fluid tracks of the broad-nibbed pen show how the practised calligrapher can invest simple letterforms with a lively spontaneity while preserving an overall balance.

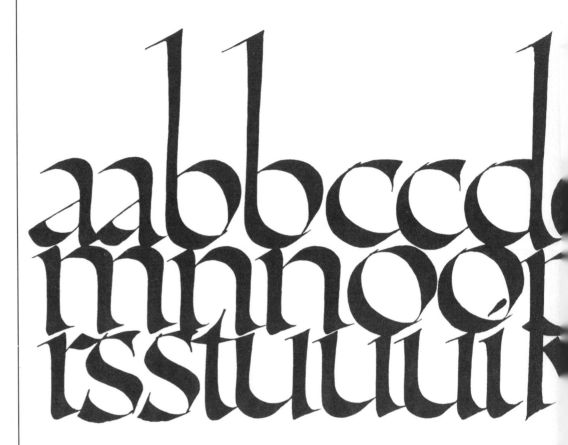

RIGHT This lively Roman lower-case letter emphasizes the pattern value of letterforms, drawn very freely, although designed *en bloc*.

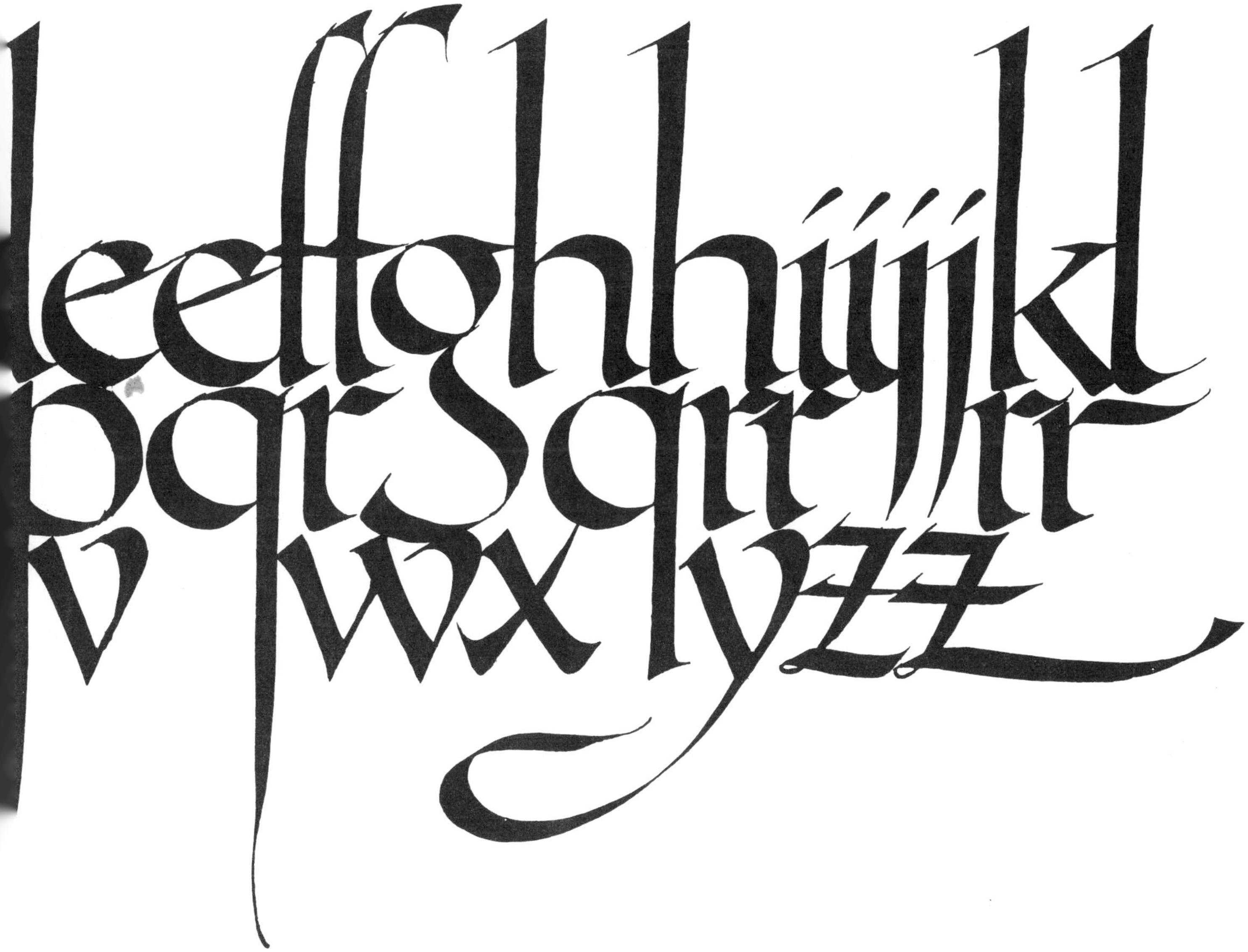

leeffghhiijjkl
pqr sqrr lrr
v vwx lyzz

Uncial and half-uncial alphabets

There are many early Greek examples of this ancient letterform and the use of Uncials spread to the Roman empire while Roman square and Rustic capitals were still in use. The 'new' hand provided some economy of strokes and more speed, but it retained formality. The Romans gave it the name Uncial from *uncia* meaning 'inch'. Study of early Christian manuscripts shows that it became the main bookhand of the period.

The Uncial hand is upright and bold, with full and rounded letters. It has an uncomplicated construction sequence with, at times, only a mere hint of the existence of ascenders and descenders. The best tools for writing Uncials are a broad nib or square-tipped brush. The nib gives a very clean, sharp outer edge to the letters.

The old style of very round Uncials was made with the pen held almost horizontally, using a letter height of three to four nib widths. The modern, more open style is executed with a pen angle of 10°–20° and a height of five nib widths. The clubbed serifs are made by forming a small angled stroke followed by the upright stroke. Some Uncials can be given a hairline serif as an extension of a non-enclosed stroke.

Spacing between the letters of this rotund hand requires some special attention. Each letter should be able to 'breathe'. Try to achieve a balance of black and white, increasing the spaces between words and lines as necessary.

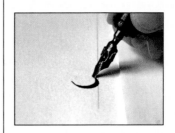

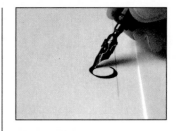

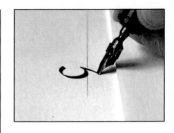

1 Uncial is a broad face, the pen being held at a very flat angle of 10°–20° to obtain the broad downstroke.

2 The pen is lifted from the paper before drawing the broad top stroke of the G.

3 The slimmer tail stroke is added. This face is characterized by full, rounded letters with very short ascenders and descenders.

When you see a page of Uncials, you get an overwhelming sense of the letters being compressed neatly between parallel lines. The need to combine Uncials with another hand frequently arises, to develop the texture of the work. Versals are the natural complement to this quite adaptable hand of thin horizontals and thick verticals.

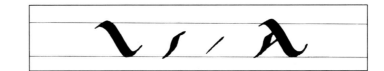

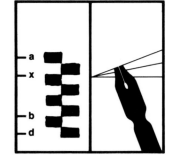

UNCIAL ALPHABET

These majuscule letters are written with the pen held at a very flat angle of 10°–20° to the horizontal, which can be difficult and uncomfortable to execute. The letters are rounded and squat, with minimal ascenders and descenders. The serif is a small wedge, formed by a slightly angled stroke, which is followed by the upright stroke. Use a broad nib or square-cut brush to form these letters, making special note of the fine thin lines that offset the thick strokes.

The stroke diagram clearly shows the quite delicate nature of the second stroke of the letter.

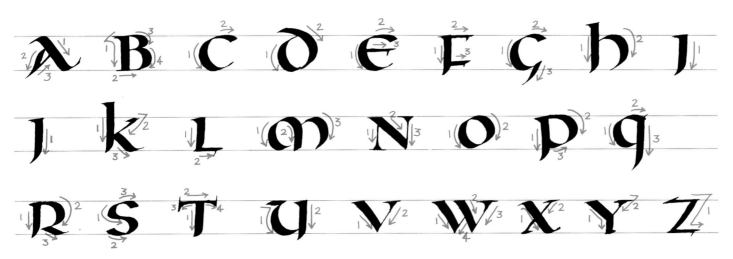

HALF-UNCIAL

The Uncial, with its minimal ascenders and descenders, is regarded as a majuscule hand. The Half-Uncial, although still seen as a majuscule, is often accredited with being the forerunner of most minuscule forms. The ascenders and descenders distinctly rise and fall from the bodies of the letters, making an immediate association with lower-case letters. The Uncial and Half-Uncial are acknowledged as the inspiration for the Celtic insular script used to produce the famous *Book of Kells*.

If you have difficulty making the first stroke, divide the task into two strokes. Make the long horizontal stroke first, and then add a small stroke on the left-hand top edge. The main stroke of the letter may need some practice to achieve the correct balance of open and closed counter strokes after the application of the final stroke.

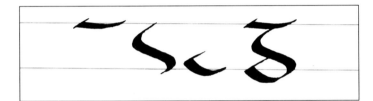

HALF-UNCIAL
ALPHABET

The Half-Uncial majuscule is closely identified with Anglo-Saxon and Celtic insular hands. The letters are four to four-and-a-half widths in height, with a flat pen angle. The letterforms are round, and have short descenders and ascenders, the latter with a distinctive wedge-shaped serif. The interlinear spacing can be kept to a minimum, although well-considered spacing between the lines creates a fine image overall. Spacing the lines by as much as four or more nib widths allows room for a single letter at the beginning of a sentence to be enlarged and decorated. These letters are excellent forms to receive decoration.

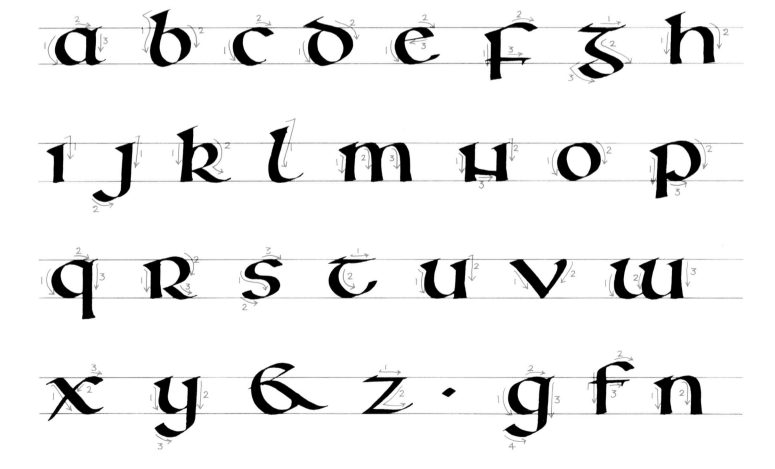

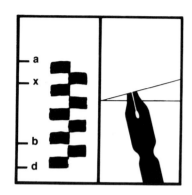

MODERN UNCIAL ALPHABET

The Modern Uncial is derived from the traditional Uncial majuscule. The letters are quite heavy, and maintain the roundness of other Uncial forms. The letters are written with a flat pen angle of 15° to the horizontal, although an angle of 30° is acceptable. The letter height is four-and-a-half to five nib widths. The short ascenders and descenders of Uncial hands are maintained. Many of the vertical strokes and descenders taper off to the left, with no serif.

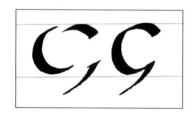

The first stroke of this letter should capture the roundness of the letter shape – based on the O. The second stroke completed this round quality. Finally, the tail of the letter is added.

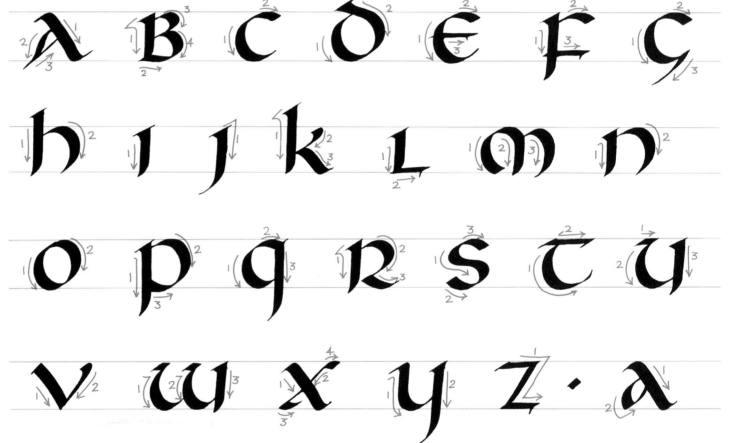

MODERN UNCIAL ALPHABET

The curving shapes of Uncial letters were more rapidly and easily written with an edged pen than were the angular capitals of Roman letters, and Uncials became the main book hand of the late Roman Empire and the primary form in Christian manuscripts up until the eighth century.

A number of variations arose in the design of individual letters: particularly in **A**, **D**, **H**, **M**, **N**, **T** and **W**, there are alternative forms which roughly correspond to the typically differentiated identities of subsequent capital and minuscule alphabets. Uncials are generally fairly heavy letters written with the flat edge of a square-tipped pen. But, as can be seen from the written sample, they form an immensely rich and descriptive texture, all the more elegant for the finely hooked terminals and hairline flourishes.

LEFT These letterforms seem to have a universal appeal perhaps because of their rich round shapes. Their weight is strong: about four nib widths to the height. The Uncial is very adaptable and although the pen is usually held horizontally, it can also produce other characteristics when drawn at an angle.

ENGLISH UNCIALS AND HALF-UNCIALS

This alphabet shows another modern transcription of the early Uncial form, followed by a Half-Uncial alphabet, the book hand which followed on from Uncials. In this case the Half-Uncials are based on early English lettering from the beautifully decorated Lindisfarne Gospels, written in the seventh century. In the Half-Uncials, the characteristics leading to minuscule, or lower-case, forms are readily apparent. This is a systematic and formal script, with deliberate ascenders and descenders breaking out of the body height of the letters. Despite the lingering reference to the capital form of **N**, this is otherwise the precursor of flower-case forms, and it is particularly noticeable that the semi-capitalized **A** still in use in the Uncial alphabet has been completely modified into the more rounded, compact character appropriate to the Half-Uncial script.

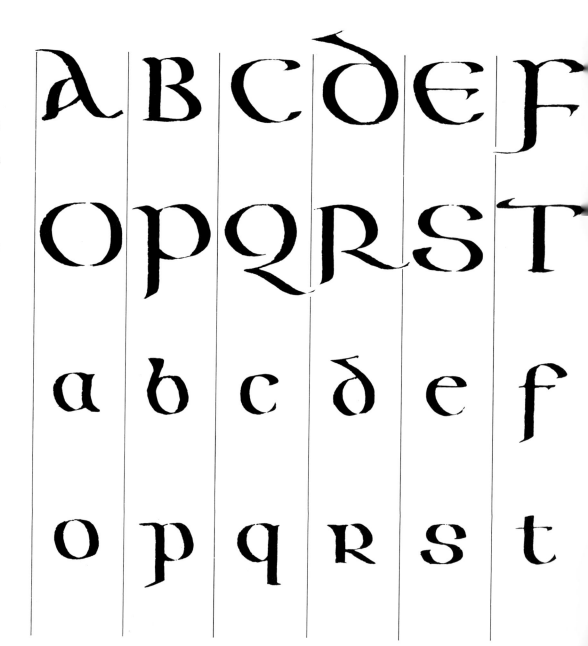

GHIKLMN

UVWXY

s h i j k l m n

u v w x y z

est in coelis: sancti

Versal alphabets

These elegant capital letters appear liberally throughout early manuscripts, but were seldom used to compose an entire block of text. Their main purpose was to serve as chapter openings, to draw the attention of the reader to an important section of the text, or to begin a paragraph or verse. Standing in any of these commanding positions on the page, these extraordinary letters were at times emblazoned almost beyond recognition. There were no minuscule forms, so the accompanying body of text would be executed in Uncial, Half-Uncial, or Carolingian letters.

In medieval times, Versal letters used as initials were simply coloured green, red, or blue. Richly burnished gold versions were limited to use in manuscripts deemed of particular importance.

The unusual feature of Versals in calligraphic terms is that they are built-up, not written, letters. The construction appears straightforward, but it is curiously difficult to master. Most of the strokes are formed in the same way, whether they are curved or straight. As a guide to height, base the letter on eight to ten times the width of the letter's stem.

It is advisable to begin by drawing a light pencil outline, so that the correct angles and counter shapes are established. Then you can work the letter stroke by stroke using a medium-fine pen, starting with the uprights. These are slightly 'pinched', tapering inward to the centre and broadening a little at the ends. The diagonal strokes are similarly constructed. Unless you are adding colour, a single stroke should fill in the letter once the outlines have been drawn. The slightly extended hairline serifs are formed with the pen held flat.

Letters with rounded counters should fall slightly above and below the actual letter height. When making these letters, complete the inner line of the counter first, so that you achieve the correct proportions. The outer curves of the letters are slightly sharper than the inner ones. In letters that have crossbars, these are placed slightly above the middle.

The spaciousness of these graceful letterforms provides much scope for decoration. You can add a contrasting colour simply by using a pen or brush to make the filling-in stroke. A heading, or the first word of a text, catches attention when it is richly embellished with colour, has hairlines added and elaborate flourishes swirled into intricate patterns. Beginning a piece of work with a single Versal also offers an excellent opportunity for gilding.

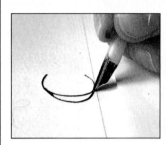

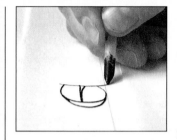

1 In this Versal capital, the inner stroke is drawn first to establish the shape of the counter, and then the outer stroke is drawn. (On straight downstrokes, the stroke is slightly pinched in the middle.)

3 The enclosing downstroke is now drawn. These hairline strokes should be lightly drawn with the pen held at 90° angle to the paper.

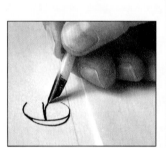

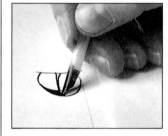

2 The two middle cross strokes start at the width of the nib and are splayed in two flaring strokes at the end to produce a wedge shape.

4 The skeleton lettering is filled in with a single stroke. Filling-in can also be done with a fine sable brush.

Contemporary design trends have provided new perceptions of works composed entirely of upper case letters. The elegant Versal works well in many contexts. A rhythmic texture can be created if careful consideration is given to the spaces the letters occupy. To achieve movement in the design, some of the letters may vary in size, but maintaining a constant letter size can result in a work of great credibility and elegance.

A B C D E F G H
I J K L M N O
P Q R S T U V
W X Y Z · O T O

VERSAL ALPHABET

These built-up capital letters are excellent forms for headings and decorating, and work well with many calligraphic hands. The inner strokes are drawn first to ensure the counter shape is the correct proportion. The pinched vertical strokes are constructed with great care; the pinching is a subtle curve and must not be exaggerated. A metal nib, fine pointed brush, or quill can be used to construct these letters. The instrument is manipulated at various angles to achieve a balance of thin and thick strokes.

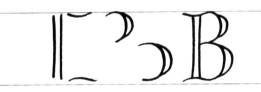

The slightly pinched vertical strokes of the letter are drawn first. Turn the pen to 0° to the horizontal writing line, and draw the serifs. The inner stroke of the counter shape is drawn first to establish the shape, then the outer strokes are added.

VERSALS – ROMAN FORM

These simple Versals are in a style based on Roman capitals, as commonly used in early manuscripts. The important characteristic of Versals, compared to other calligraphic lettering, is that the letterforms are built up gradually rather than written fluidly. The pen is narrower and more flexible than that used to write the text. In this sample, fine hairline serifs complete the forms; these are in lieu of the proper Roman serif.

RIGHT Versals are essentially pen-made with a flexible quill or metal pen. Each Versal letter is actually formed with three strokes: a vertical stem, for example, is outlined on each side, and the third stroke is quickly applied to fill the space between.

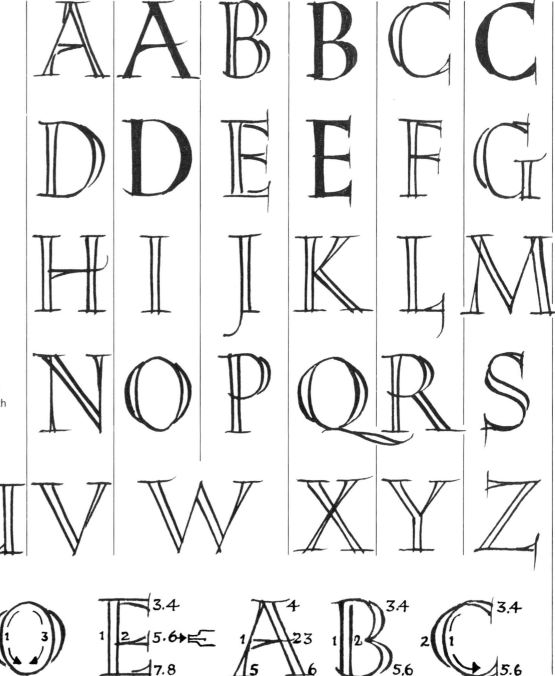

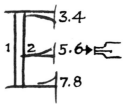

VERSALS – LOMBARDIC FORM

The curving shapes of this Versal alphabet are influenced by both Lombardic scripts and Uncial letters, as demonstrated particularly in the forms of **D**, **H** and **M**. The cross-strokes and curves are terminated with a flaring of the width cut across by a hairline, and these lines are rather more bold and flourished than in the Roman-style Versals, creating a lively textural rhythm. The fine, flexible quill or pen used to draw the Versals can be charged with ink or thinned watercolour paint. Two-colour Versals can be attractively made by drawing the outer strokes in a dark ink and flooding the inner area with colour. Red, green and blue were the traditional colours for Versals: they are strong hues which balance with black writing ink.

RIGHT These are richer forms, largely based on Uncial letters, producing free and lively expression and used continuously throughout the ages.

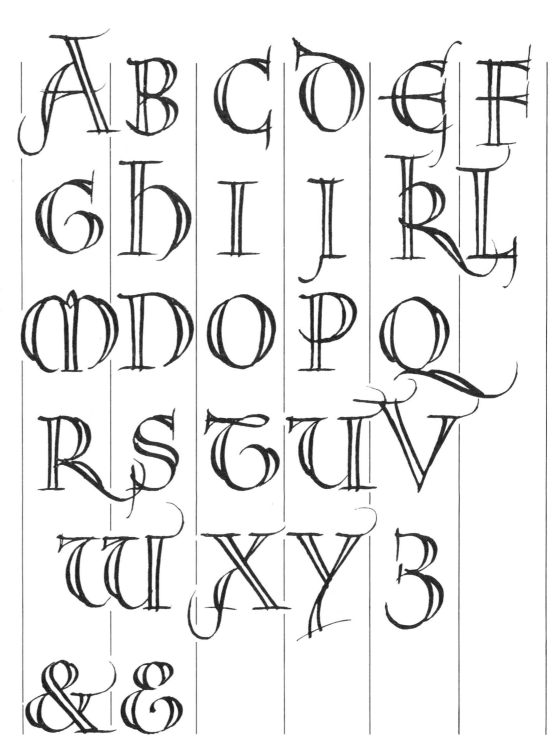

ELABORATED VERSALS

The design of this alphabet takes the rhythmic and flourished quality of the Lombardic style a little further. The construction of the letterforms is very fluid and decorative, from the exaggerated tails of **K**, **Q**, **R** and **X** to the individual details enlivening the counter spaces of **B**, **O** and **Q**. The elaboration is of a consistent style and quality, but intriguingly varied in detail to make the form of each letter not only clearly distinguishable but also individually ornamental.

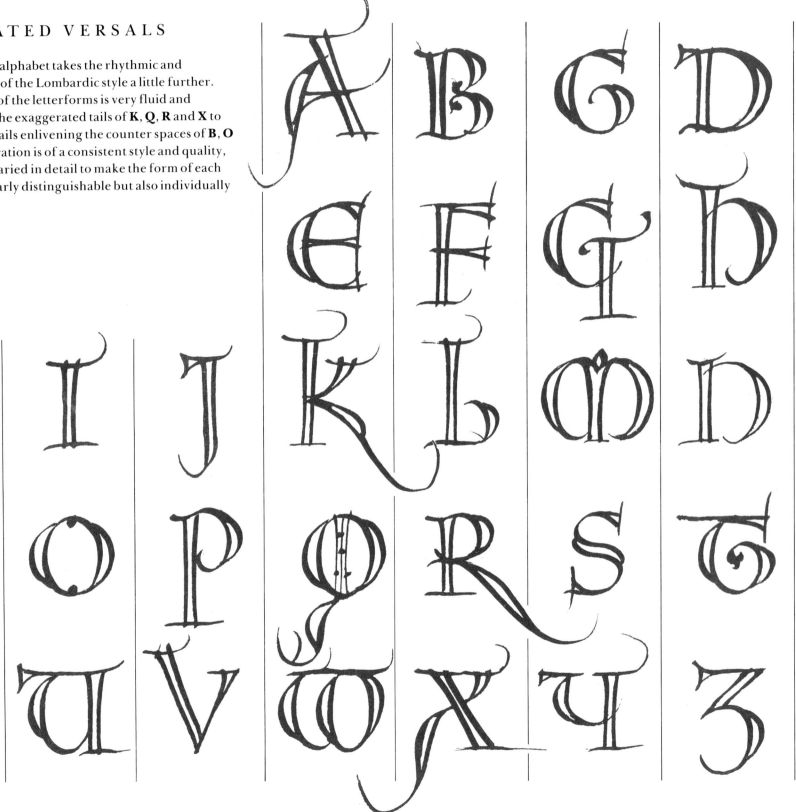

ORNAMENTED VERSALS

The weighty shapes of these Lombardic-style Versals are sufficiently broad to allow a decorative piercing of the curves and stems, in addition to flourished and ornamental detail. The drawn Versal letter can be the basis of a heavily ornamented or illuminated capital letter, decorated with abstract motifs or, as in the original miniatures of medieval manuscripts, with tiny pictures of figurative images. Colours can be introduced to add variety to the design, and Versals are also traditionally the subjects for gilding, with burnished gold leaf or painted powder gold.

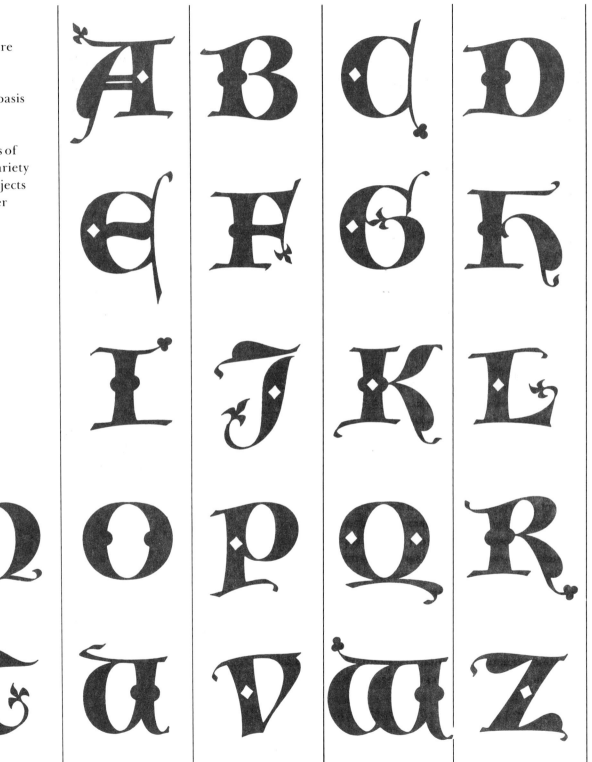

Gothic alphabets

Numerous styles of lettering evolved during the Gothic era, the period broadly straddling the twelfth to sixteenth centuries. The developments in writing reflected changes of style in architecture, where lancet arches replaced the rounded Roman arches, and ribbed vaults and thrusting flying buttresses appeared.

A variety of Gothic hands emerged sharing many common elements, including a heavy, dense black form, angular letters, rigid verticals and, often, short ascenders and descenders in relation to the height. Sometimes the emphasis on angularity renders the work almost illegible to modern readers. The many variations, both formal and informal, are attributable to the numbers of people who adapted the forms to suit their own requirements. Often small changes in structure occurred simply through the need for speed and economy in writing. Some rounded versions of Gothic lettering did persist and develop, such as Rotunda. Other Gothic forms practised today are Blackletter and Textura.

A Gothic hand can be produced using a broad pen held at an angle of 45° and a height of five nib widths. A height of six nib widths achieves a slender letter with more clarity.

A neat, tidy, and textured work results from making the white spaces within and between the letters the same thickness as the upright strokes. With due consideration, Gothic lettering can be very effective. To use it successfully, plan the piece carefully and do plenty fo rough drafts, developing your ability to space the letters consistently. When working on the final piece, execute the strokes with determination.

Originally, there were no specific capital letters in the Gothic forms. Usually, a decorated letter was dropped in, and this worked surprisingly well. The Gothic upper case now used is distinctly open, even rounded, compared with the lower case lettering. The height is seven nib widths. Gothic capitals work best on their own as individual letters. Seldom are they used successfully for an entire word.

In the lower-case letters, a square serif is used which sits atop the strokes. In the upper-case forms, the same square serif is seen, but more usually sited on the left-hand outside edge of the upright strokes.

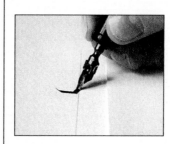

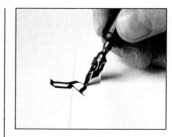

1 The first stroke of this Blackletter letter is formed by holding the pen at an angle of 35° and making a fine line diagonally to the left. Almost immediately the pen is pulled down into the strong vertical line. Before this stroke reaches the base line it is stopped, and a strong diagonal stroke is pulled down to the right, and onto the base line.

3 The final stroke begins with a hairline drawn from the end of the diagonal stroke resting on the baseline. It travels down to the left. To complete the descender, a wave stroke is made to the right, where it joins up with the middle of the descender.

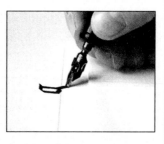

2 The pen returns to the top of the letter, and rests at the pen angle where the first stroke began. The pen is pulled to the right, beyond where the next vertical line will begin. The vertical stroke that becomes the descender curves out to the right before it reaches the baseline. At about two nib widths below the baseline, the stroke is pulled back to the left, and to the thinnest part of the stroke, where it stops.

4 The splendid Gothic S is easier to execute than it appears on first viewing. Breaking it down into its constituent parts to work out how it is made, it transpires that it is constructed of similar strokes travelling in the same direction, as the stroke diagram illustrates.

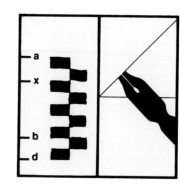

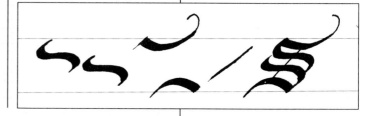

BLACKLETTER

Blackletter was born of a need for speed and economy, like so many developments in writing. The style is composed of thrusting, upright strokes that create an overall vertical effect, but the eye can find rest in the horizontals breaking the spaces at top and bottom of the letters.

To write this hand, you hold a broad pen at an angle of 30°–40° to the writing line. The weight of the letter can be varied by adjusting the height between three and five nib widths. The counter spaces, the vertical strokes, and the spaces between letters are usually of identical thickness.

Blackletter is exceedingly economical, as constant condensing means more letters per line and more words per page. The spaces between lines can be reduced, and the ascenders and descenders shortened to a minimum to create a very dense texture. This occurs in the version of Gothic lettering known as Textura (page 96), which can be seen as pure pattern.

The upper-case letters, seven nib widths in height, are not conducive to use in whole words, as legibility becomes a problem.

This Gothic hand works surprisingly well with decorative capitals, and there are many fine historical examples. Contemporary uses for Blackletter occur in various contexts, including presentation documents.

GOTHIC BLACKLETTER ALPHABET

The upper-case letters of seven nib widths in height have a roundness which contrasts well with the angularity of the lower-case letters of five nib widths height. The distinctive, angular O is a good guide for the lower-case letters. The short ascenders and descenders permit tight interlinear spacing.

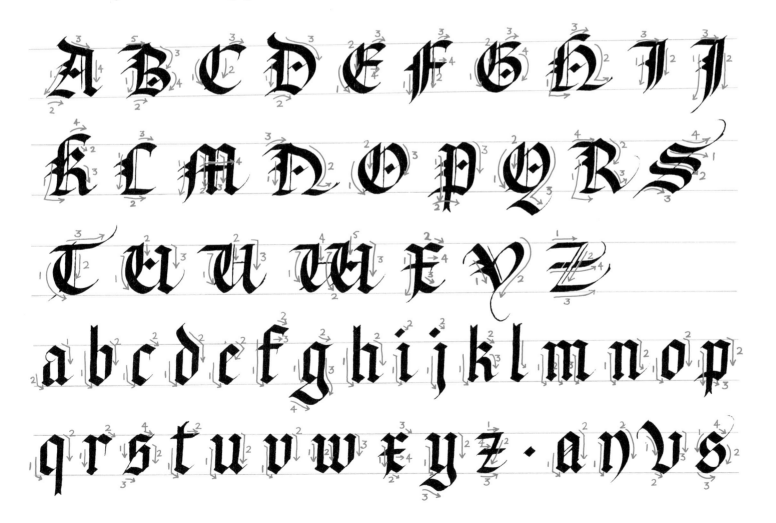

GOTHIC CURSIVE ALPHABET

This elegant hand is perhaps less well-known and therefore not widely used. A single upper-case letter used with lower-case letters can be used for a heading with eye-catching effect. The lower-case letters are written four-and-a-half to five nib widths high.

The letters have a distinctive almond (mandorla) shape, thought to have been a Middle Eastern influence. The letters are pointed where they touch the baseline, and some have fine line extensions from this point. Some of the descenders end in sharp fine line extended strokes. The upper-case letters are written six-and-a-half to seven nib

widths high. Many of these capital letters are more recognizable as lower-case forms. It is evident when looking at the lower-case letters, that this hand evolved to be written at speed.

The Gothic cursive upper-case **A** is presented in a shape more recognizable as a lower-case letter. The cross stroke, which begins the letter at the top, holds and balances the rest of the letter. The fine lines must contrast with the bold strokes to give this hand its own particular identity.

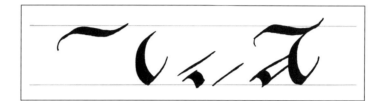

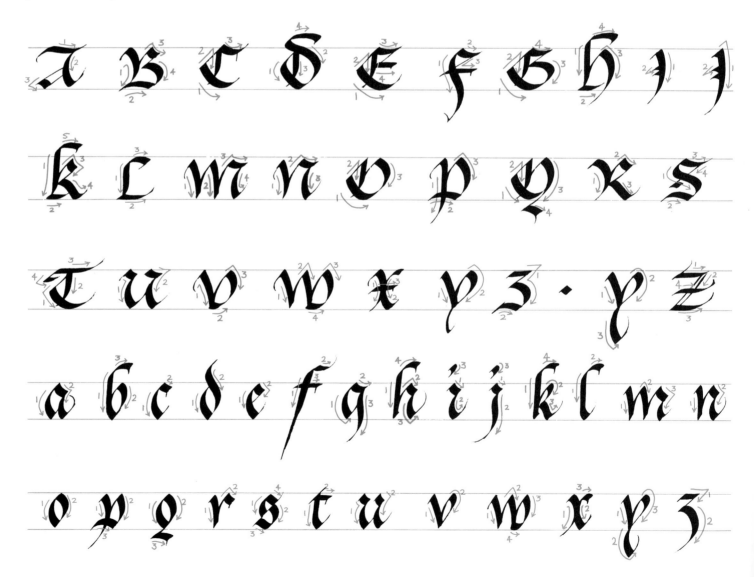

ROTUNDA (ROTONDA)

Variously referred to as Italian Gothic, Half-Gothic, or round Gothic, this crisp hand was used as a bookhand in medieval and Renaissance Italy. While in northern Europe, the hard, dense Blackletter style flourished, in the southern countries there was a distinctly softer form, especially by comparison with the compact and angular Textura, a style never seriously pursued in Italy. However, a further comparison with the Gothic hand practised in the north reveals that in the spaciousness of Rotunda there is a slight angularity, particularly pronounced on letters with enclosed counter spaces.

Medieval Italian manuscripts show the form exquisitely. The ascenders and descenders are often minimal, which creates a very even linear texture. The space between both letters and words is often pronounced, but there still exists a balanced letter structure of bold upright strokes and fine, thin strokes.

The serif style varied according to the preference of the scribe. Fine hairline extensions are often applied, and many strokes simply terminate with the pen angle. There are a few examples that show the use of the truly Gothic-style lozenge-shaped serif.

The simple, clean letters need to be carefully formed in order to display their pleasing proportions. The letters are written with a pen angle of 30°.

This rounded, open hand was skilfully combined with splendidly illuminated Versals. Some early manuscripts include pen-drawn capitals constructed in a similar manner to letters in the body of the text, but they are more rounded.

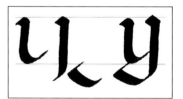

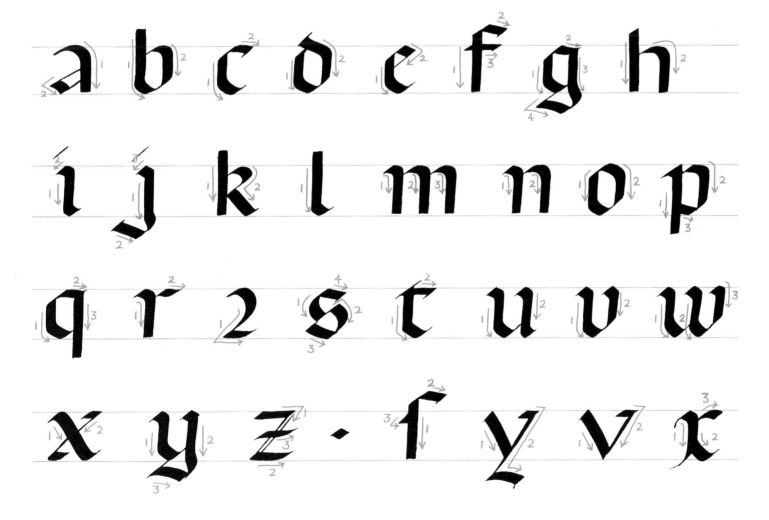

ROTUNDA MINUSCULE ALPHABET

The Rotunda minuscule is a more open and rounded Gothic hand. The letters are written four-and-a-half to five nib widths high, and with a pen angle of 30° to the horizontal. The letters maintain some of the obvious Gothic characteristics. The ascenders and descenders are short, but the distinctive lozenge-shaped serif is seldom used. Many of the letters have strokes which have square endings. There is a distinct softening of stroke compared to the more familiar angularity of some Gothic hands.

Rotunda minuscules need practice to obtain the roundness of the counter shapes, and still retain the slight angularity of the corners, so typical of gothic hands.

RIGHT RENATE FUHRMANN – A fine example of Textura – a dense Gothic hand which at its most extreme displays no difference in thickness between vertical strokes, counter strokes, and letter spaces. Delicate tonal changes occur throughout the text, which has been written using watercolour. Distemper and wood tar are the other materials used.

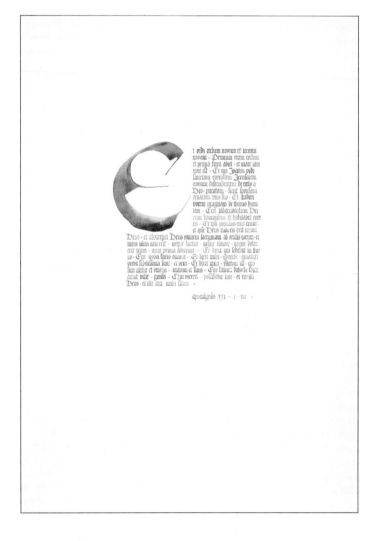

TEXTURA

This Gothic script, which was mostly practised in northern Europe, takes its name from the Latin *textum*, meaning 'woven fabric' or 'texture'. Used as a bookhand and widely found in early psalters and prayer books, this lower-case alphabet developed in many formal and informal styles. Two of the formal hands were *textus precissus* and *textus quadratus*. The former was characterized by strong upright strokes standing flat on the baseline, the latter by distinctive diamond-shaped serifs and forking at the tops of the ascenders.

The Textura hand, as its name suggests, is built of condensed, bold black verticals. These are identical in thickness to the counter spaces and the spaces between the letters. The spacing between lines is minimal, which is ideal for accommodating the typically Gothic short ascenders and descenders.

To execute this hand, you hold the broad nib at 40°. The letter height is six nib widths. Variations in height create further interest in the texture of the overall design.

The letters have a distinct angular stress. Extra hairlines can be added by lifting one corner of the pen at the end of a stroke and dragging a little wet ink outwards to become the hairline extension.

A recognizable feature of manuscripts written in Textura is the line filling. Where a line finished short of the right-hand margin, the scribe would complete the line with exquisite patterning. If the line was short by only one or two letters, a simple flourish or pen pattern would serve the purpose. This is a solution that can be utilized for many design problems. The patterning must pay respect to the lettering style: thus, for Textura, it must be quite solid.

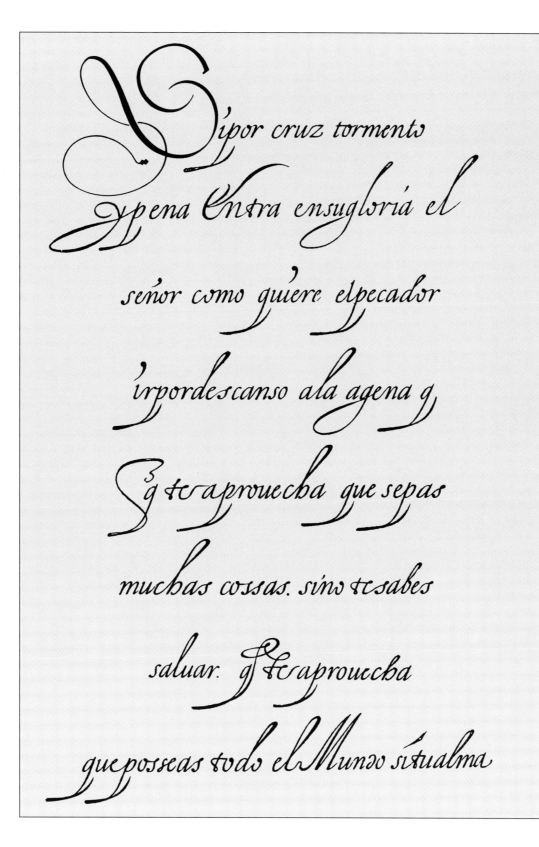

A sample combining the elaborate, Gothic-influenced Neudorffer capital with an early Copperplate script by Spanish calligrapher Morante demonstrates the influence of Copperplate technique on the forms of the letters — the tendency towards fine and fluidly swelling strokes as compared to the emphatic thick/thin contrasts of edge pen lettering. From the time when the practical constraints on calligraphy were removed by the use of mechanical printing for most types of publication, calligraphers have applied considerable invention and eclecticism to their work. Even more than those earlier writing masters, modern calligraphers and graphic artists can draw upon a vast range of styles and techniques as the basis for new designs and combinations of letters.

TEXTURA ALPHABET

The forms of Gothic script, known as Blackletter, are instantly recognizable from the compressed, angular and vertically stressed letters. The original proportions of Textura were based on three strokes of the pen, so that the counters or interior spaces were the same width as the pen strokes. This regularity can make the combined letterforms very difficult to read as a script. This version shows a slightly more open form with serifs which are naturally contrived in the pen angle at the top of the stroke. The bases of the letters are finished with the characteristic lozenge-shaped feet corresponding to the width and consistent 40° angle of the edged pen. These feet are set slightly off-centre on the vertical stems. The form is ornamental and evocative of its period. Development of Blackletter scripts continued through the introduction of printers' types in Europe, and they became the models for the first mechanical letters.

FRAKTUR ALPHABET

Less angular than the Gothic Textura, yet equally characteristic of its time, is the Blackletter script known as Fraktur, identifiable by the forked ascenders. This curious branching of the vertical stroke derived from the cutting of a quill pen with the tip slit to one side rather than centrally, so a slight flick of the pen would create an unevenly broken terminal. This alphabet has the basically vertical, compressed emphasis typical of Gothic lettering, but a more generous width and deliberate curving of certain shapes which relieves the occasional rigidity encountered in the more formally constructed styles.

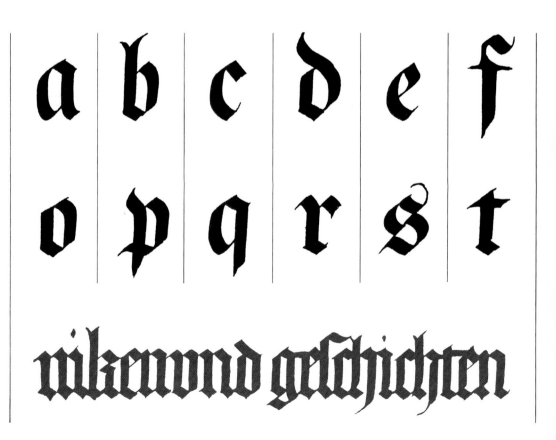

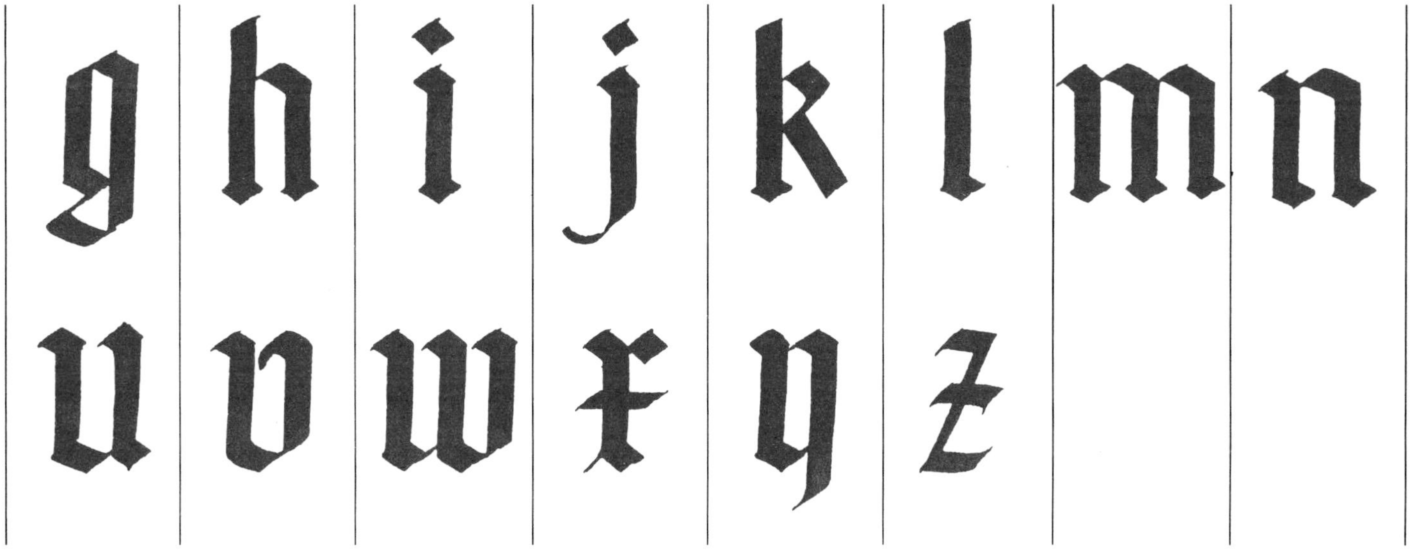

g h i j k l m n
u v w x y z

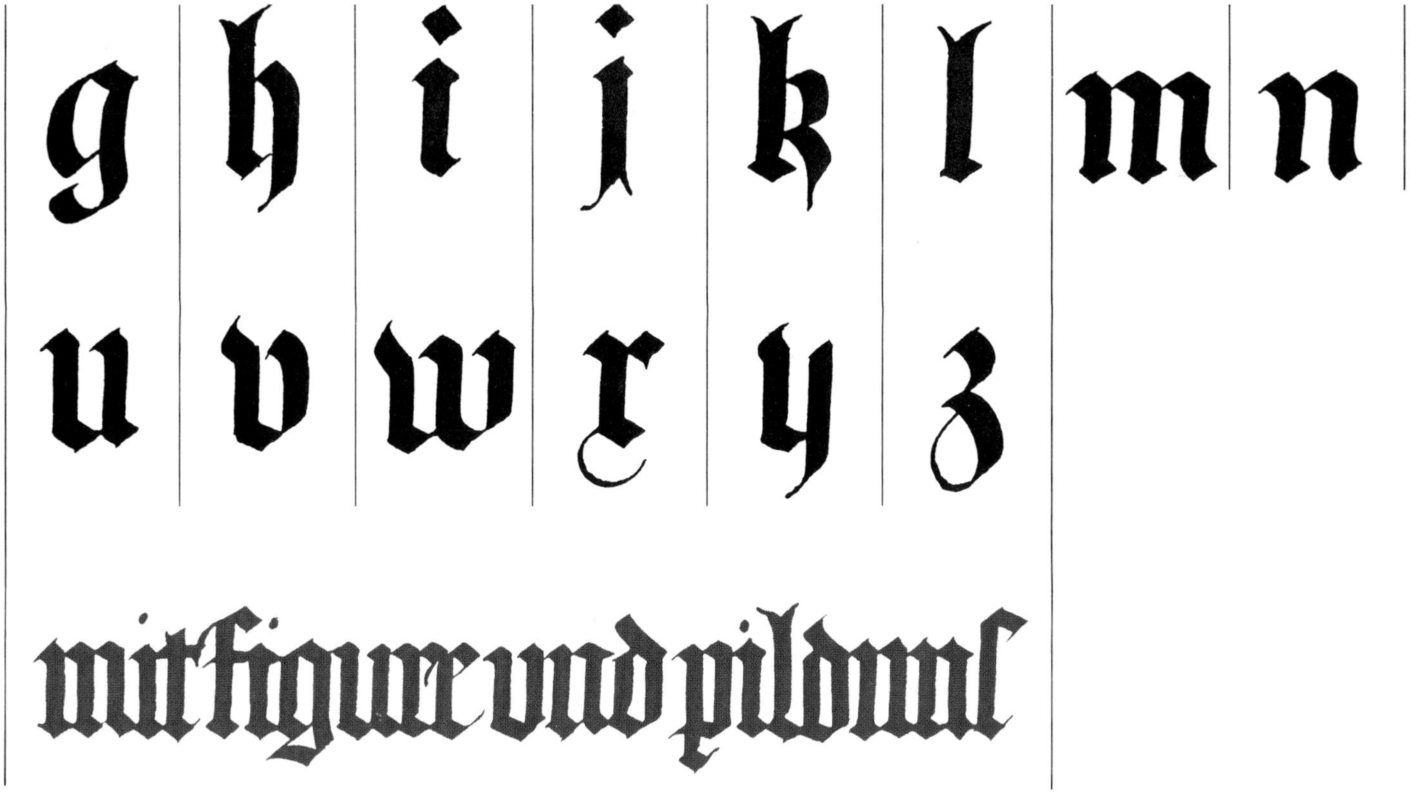

g h i j k l m n
u v w x y z

mit figure vnd pildnuf

GOTHIC MAJUSCULE

These majuscule letters are noticeably rounded and open in form, texturally far less dense and heavy than other styles corresponding to the Blackletter script. This suggests that the alphabet derives from capital letters used as decorative initials, since the strokes are of medium weight by reference to the body size of the letterforms, providing interior spaces sufficiently open to allow for ornamentation of the form. They include pen-drawn decoration in the features extending from the structural outlines – small flicked protrusions and double hairlines attached to the counters and vertical stems. The curving strokes show the influence of Lombardic and Uncial lettering.

RIGHT An unusually light alphabet, the capitals have a filigree detail. The Uncial influence is clearly seen in **U** and **M**.

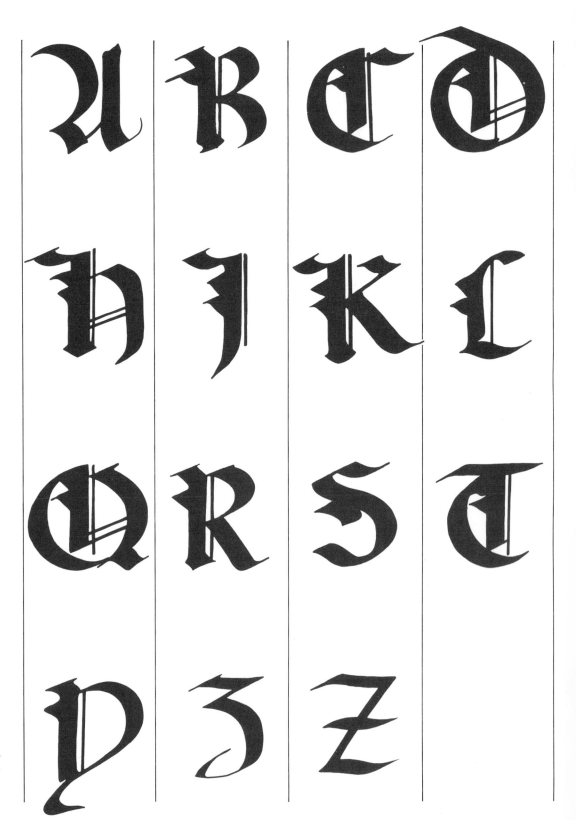

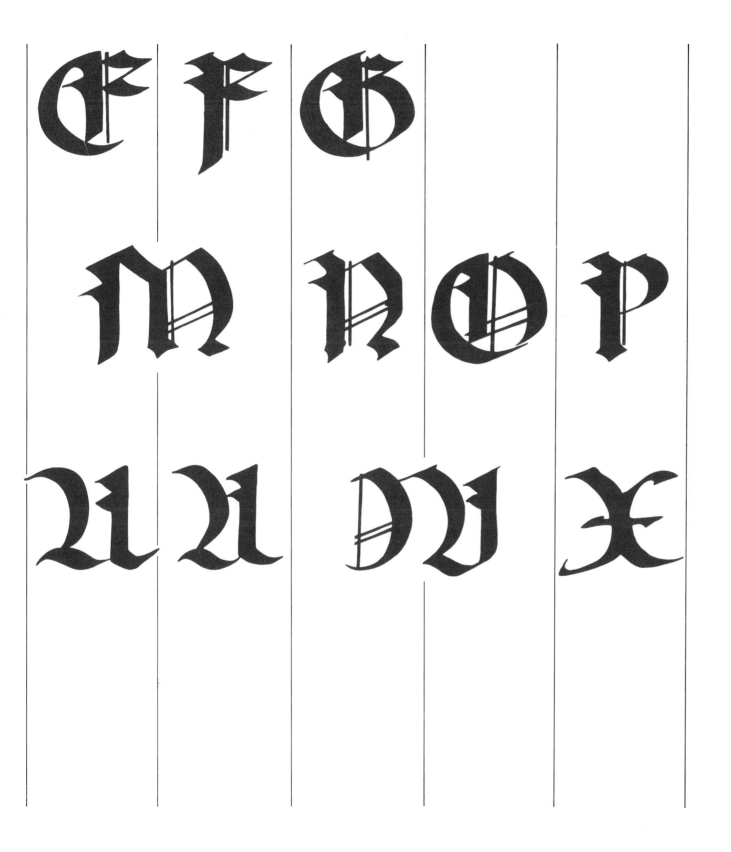

MODIFIED GOTHIC CAPITALS

A modern revision of Blackletter styling gives these capital letters a squared and open character with the rich black texture of Gothic but a more pronounced variation between thick and thin strokes. Tiny twists and flourishes of the pen give the curving stems and bowls a lively rhythm. There is some influence from the basic constructions of Uncial letters; and although these are relatively simple, broadly described shapes, they have a sophisticated style and consistency derived from the well-judged proportions and the economy of the pen movements.

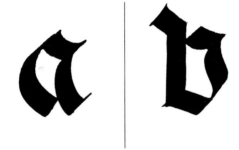

MODIFIED GOTHIC SCRIPT

A simplified version of a rounded Gothic script corresponds to the capital letters in the sample. Here again, the influence of Uncial letters is visible in the forms of **d** and **h**, for example, and the compactness of the forms is maintained by the shortened descenders in **p** and **q**. Although a formalized, heavily weighted style, having the typically dense texture of Gothic scripts, this alphabet has a variation in the letter construction that makes it a more distinct and legible script for most readers than the more stylized, angular Textura.

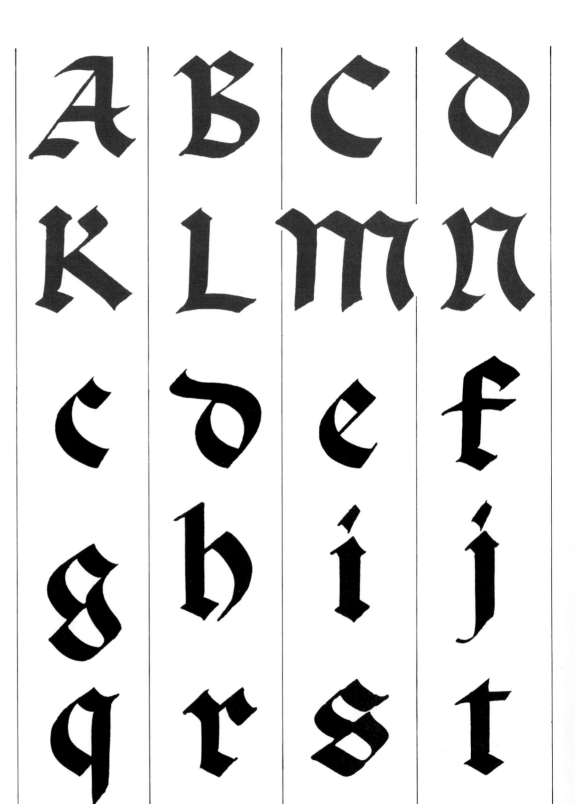

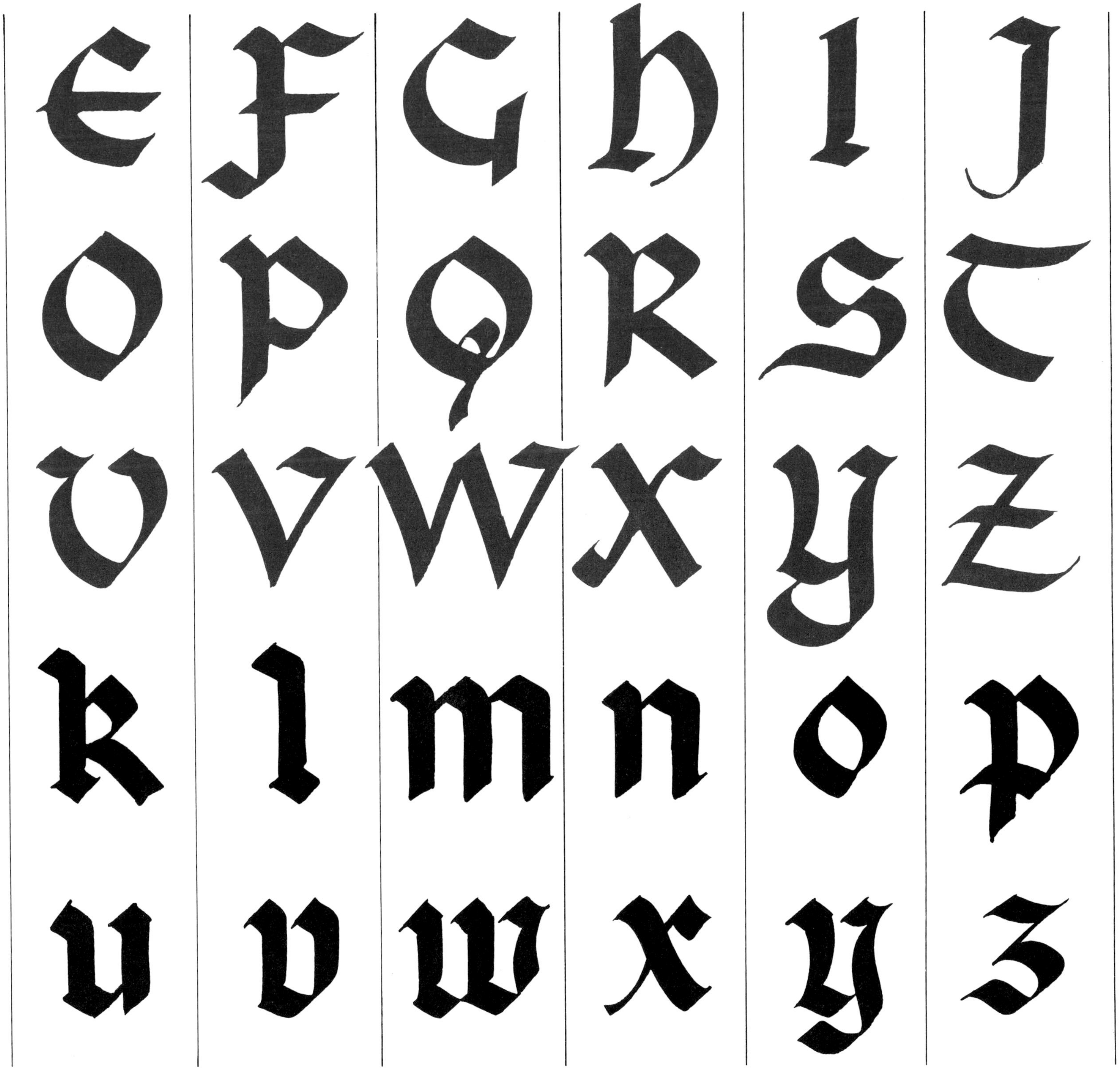

E F G H I J
O P Q R S T
V W X Y Z
k l m n o p
u v w x y z

DECORATED GOTHIC CAPITALS

This alphabet is a modern version of capital lettering based on features of Gothic style. Although not an authentic historical form, it is constructed from the elements of the original Blackletter, but with a loosely curving and flourished manner which creates a more elaborate patterning through the forms. The letters are regularly proportioned and designed in logical relation one to another, enlivened by rhythmic motion in the vigorous pen strokes and controlled flourishes. The looping of stems and tails is carried through consistently, adding to the richness of the textural quality. The broken counters of **D**, **O** and **Q** relate to an ornamental device often seen in illuminated Gothic capitals.

RIGHT A heavy, decorative Gothic letter with the unusual feature of a base loop, making a rich textural effect.

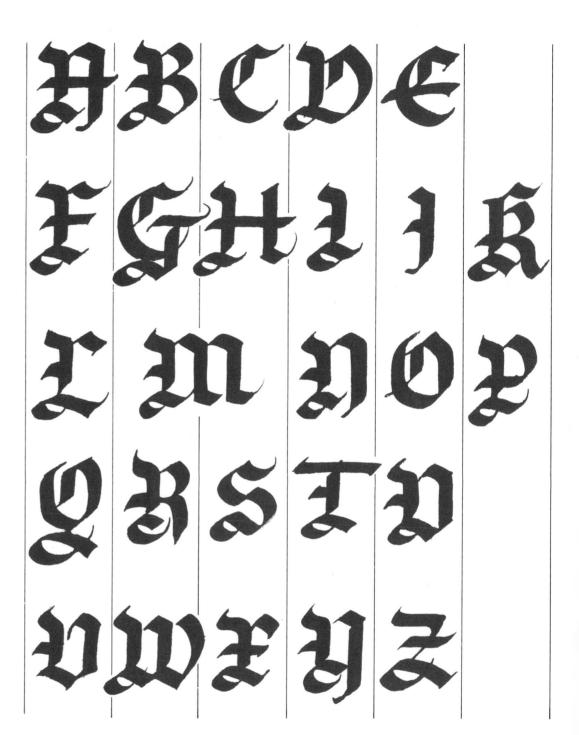

DECORATED GOTHIC MINUSCULE

Following from the decorated capital letters, the minuscule form corresponding to the previous example shows the same generously curving construction. The elaboration extends into the unusual curling tails and ascenders and the brief, finely flourished loops attached to the vertical stems of certain letters. The generally heavy, even texture of the alphabet is inspired by the authentic Blackletter forms, and the characteristics of Gothic script are clearly seen in **m** and **w**, though these are more widely proportioned than is typical in the original style on which they are based.

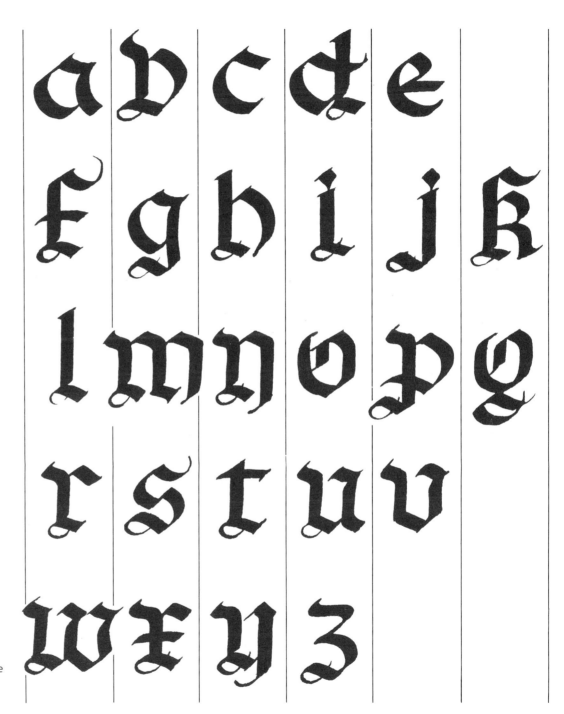

RIGHT The accompanying small letter of the alphabet shown opposite maintains the characteristic loop of the capital forms.

SKELETON GOTHIC CAPITALS

This modern revision of capital letters loosely based on the style of Fraktur is written with a double-stroke pen to form an even, open pattern. The double stroke demonstrates clearly the basic form of each letter and the variation between thick and thin occurring naturally in the pen strokes according to the direction of the pen. In this case, the thick/thin modulation appears as a transition from a double to a single line. Fraktur has a spiky, ragged quality echoed in the pointed tails and terminals of these letters. The Gothic origin of the style is particularly apparent in the heavily bowed **T** and the horizontal crossbar of **X**. The curling elaboration of the forms is appropriately applied, and despite the patterned quality of the design each letter retains its recognizable identity.

RIGHT The skeleton forms of this Fraktur-based letter, German in origin, create a light and airy effect. The large initial letters would produce a suitable foil for a simpler text.

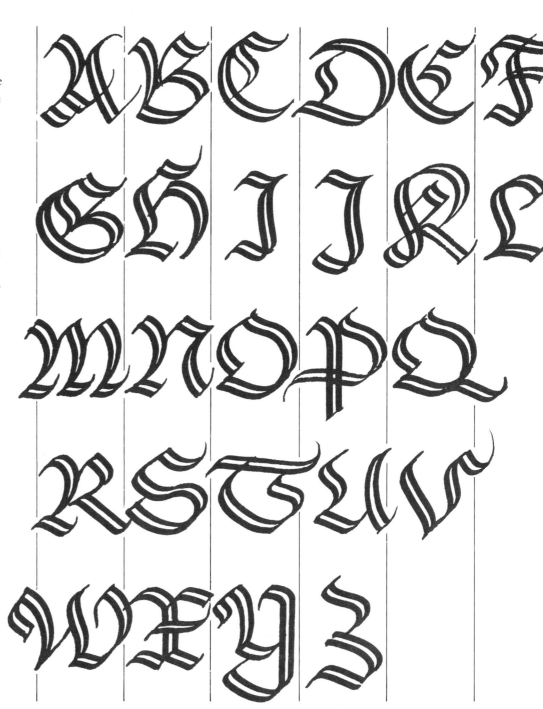

SKELETON GOTHIC MINUSCULE

Script letters form the bulk of a text and are characteristically less elaborate than their capital counterparts because of the need for legibility. In these minuscules the termination of the strokes is relatively abrupt; the tails and ascenders, as in **d** and **g**, minimally flourished. Outlining of the form relieves the heavy textural density that is typically a feature of Gothic lettering. Though the letters, composed mainly of straight strokes, still have a degree of angularity, the overall design is broad and open, the counters generously rounded. This feature is typical of later Gothic scripts, in the forms known as Bastarda and Rotunda.

RIGHT Evidence of construction is apparent in these simpler lower-case letters designed to accompany the alphabet. Closing of the open tops to the letters is optional.

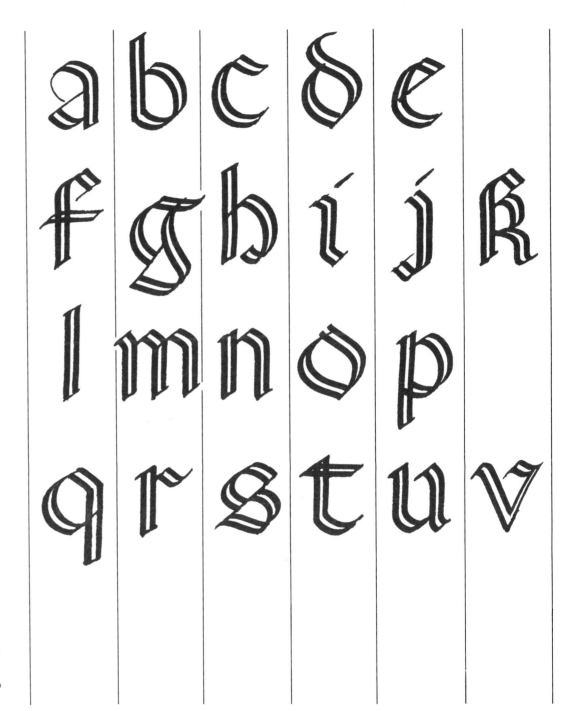

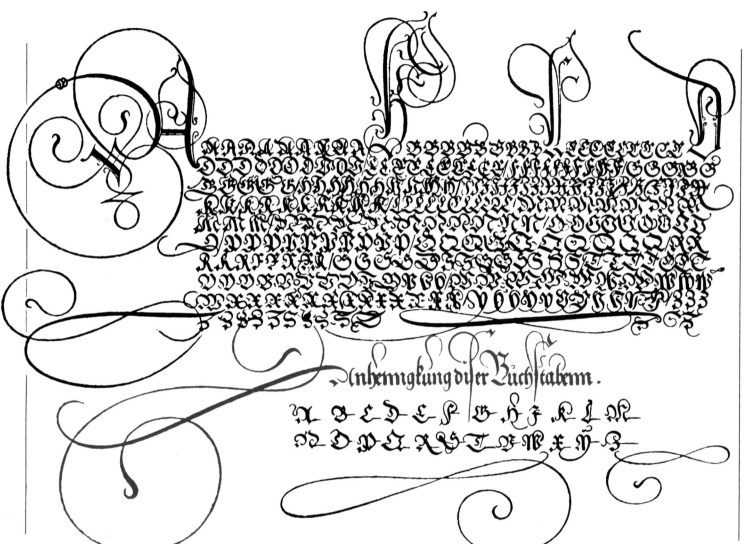

RIGHT This richly patterned alphabet is emphasized by repetition of letters and its placing on the page.

FLOURISHED GOTHIC CAPITALS

A Swiss writing master of the sixteenth century produced this finely drawn interpretation of Gothic capitals, densely packed to form a block of richly baroque texture and elaborated with loops and flourishes woven through and around the letters. Writing samples of this type have more to do with virtuoso pen work than with function and legibility, but it is interesting to trace the usually heavy Gothic forms when they are revised into a finer and more fluid pattern. The ornamentation applied to the capital letters, however, is not carried through in the script sample accompanying the alphabet block, which is restrained and readily legible by comparison.

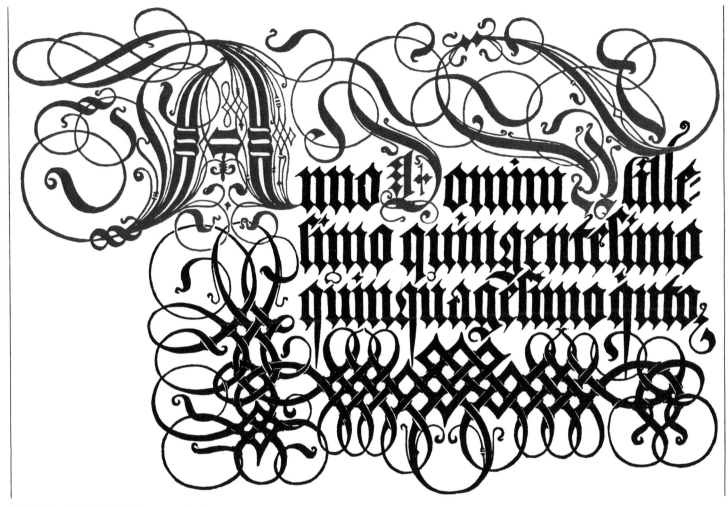

ORNAMENTED GOTHIC SCRIPT

A sixteenth-century sample of Gothic script by the Swiss writing master Urban Weyss (fl 1548) returns to the regular vertical stresses of Textura. The letterforms are of simple and regular construction, but with twisting, pointed terminals more typical of later Gothic style. These create a ragged, angled counterpoint in the rich black texture of the letters. The sample is heavily ornamented with interlocking ribbons and arabesques. These match the text for weight and density but develop freely into fine loops and curls, an unexpected but effective contrast against the angularity of the letters. The combination is contrived in terms of an overall design with balanced internal spaces. The tapering tail of **q** repeated three times in the bottom line of text is an elegant linking device.

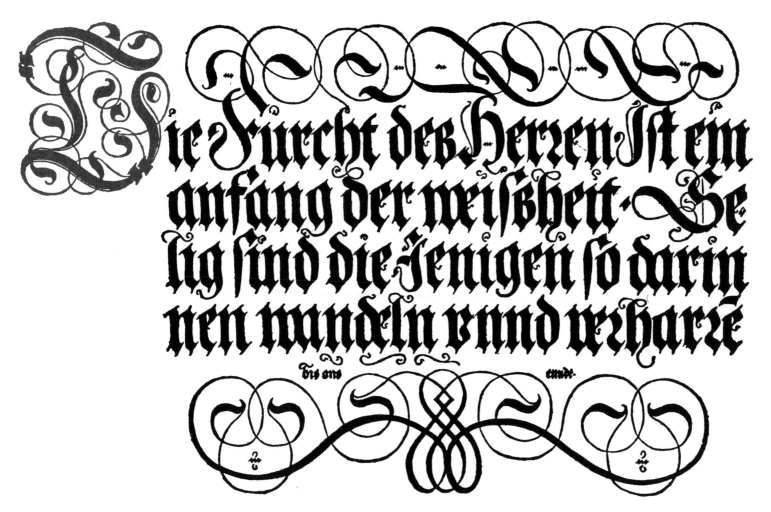

FLOURISHED GOTHIC SCRIPT

Tiny curling flourishes create an effect of fine tendrils escaping from the more solid forms of this slightly rounded Blackletter script. The repetitive vertical emphasis is controlled by the spacing of the letters, although occasional ligatures complicate the pattern of the words. The serifs are based on the lozenge-shaped form first developed in Textura script, but a deliberate twist of the pen curves the lozenge into fine hairline points at each end, instead of the simple blocked shape corresponding to pen width seen in the earlier style. The ornamental devices bordering the text are generally kept separate from the letters, which are linked only briefly by the rising strokes in the top line.

MODIFIED GOTHIC CURSIVE — CAPITALS

The cursive quality in lettering is similar to that of ordinary handwriting. Letterforms are written with a fairly rapid travelling motion rather than the precision and order needed to maintain the more formal styles. The modern alphabet based on Gothic cursive capitals is a highly designed form with a logical structure and proportional system, but the vigour and fluidity of the writing gives the letterforms a delightful spontaneity. Lightly flourished hooks and curves contribute to this quality and indicate the movement of the pen along the writing line. There are elements of italic styling in the branched arches of **M** and the lively points of **W**, but this is an upright rather than slanted form and the speed of cursive writing is more fully incorporated in the development of compressed and slanted italics.

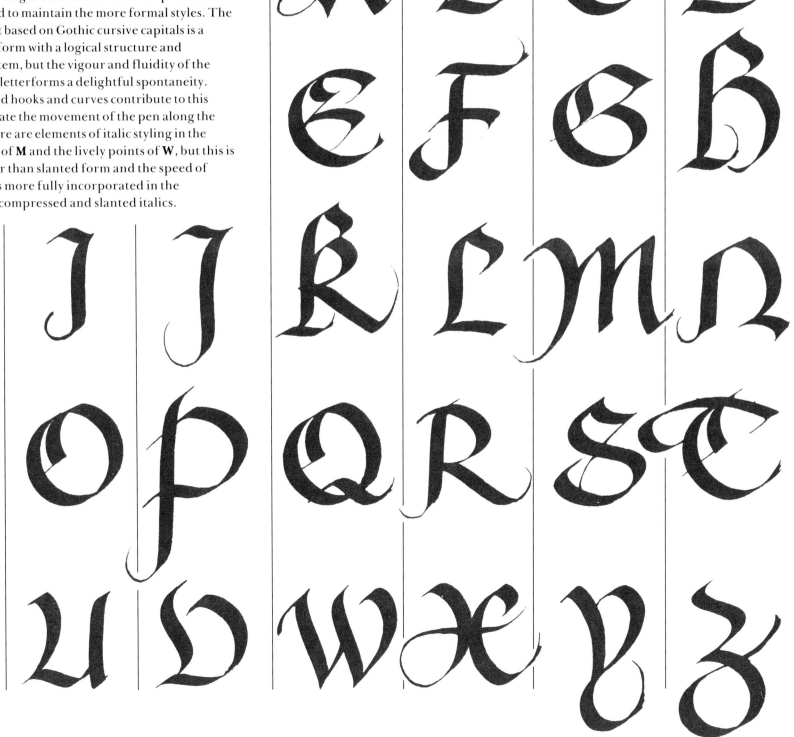

MODIFIED GOTHIC
CURSIVE SCRIPT

A widely influential running hand of the Gothic period was notable for the almond-shaped **O** borrowed from Middle Eastern sources and introduced to Europe following the Crusades. In this modified revision of Gothic cursive script the almond (mandorla) shape influences the construction of all the curved and bowed letters. As compared to the capital alphabet, the script is obliquely written so that the letters readily become linked when a text is written at speed. The numerals are simply designed with the same fluid, rhythmic qulaity as the letterforms.

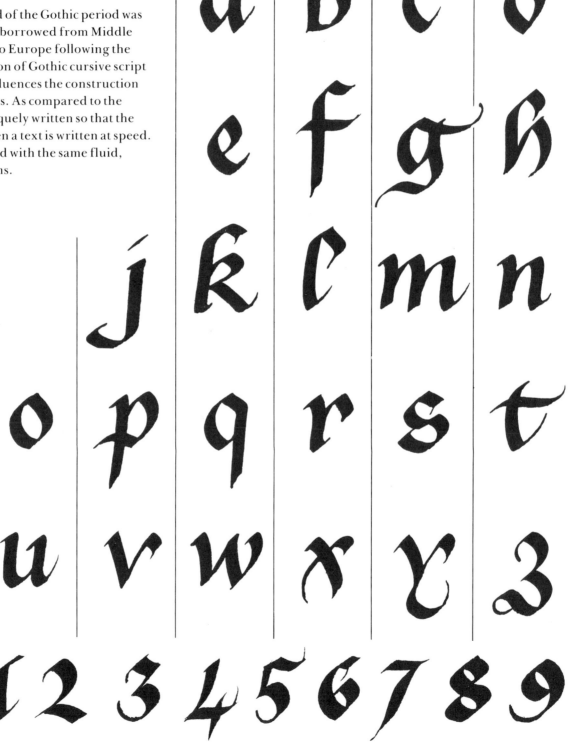

Italic alphabets

The Italic hand developed in Renaissance Italy. There was a need for greater speed in writing, particularly for copying large amounts of text. Through studies of classical manuscripts of the ninth century, Italian scholars evolved this compressed and more than usually slanting style.

The compression is based on an elliptical **o**. The slant is maintained at an angle of 5°–10° to the vertical. The broad pen is held at an angle of 45°, which achieves the characteristic contrast of thick and thin strokes. The hand has simple serifs and ascenders and descenders that can be varied in length. Simple or elaborate flourishing and swashes can be introduced as an extension to many letters.

Together, these characteristics constitute a truly elegant hand that, with practice, should retain its graceful proportions even when written at speed. These are the factors that render the formal Italic hand so suitable for use as the basis for many fine handwriting styles in common use today.

The height of the lower-case letters is five nib widths, of the upper-case letters seven nib widths. Ascenders and descenders are usually about three to four nib widths. A lighter weight can be achieved by increasing the lower-case letter height to six nib widths.

Italics work well in many situations. The style is excellent for work that needs to be easily read and comprehended. It has a curious ability to be appropriate in both formal and informal settings. Blocks of text rendered in Italic can be given textural variation by the introduction of another hand, for example, Foundational, for headings and sub-headings. With the addition of suitable flourishing, menus, name cards, invitations, and certificates can be rendered as designs of character and elegance without loss of legibility. Try not to overdo the amount of flourishing: too much makes the lettering difficult to read and less pleasing to the viewer.

There is plenty of room for inventiveness on the part of the calligrapher, such as experimenting with double letters and connecting letters. The two main connectors are horizontal and diagonal lines. The object is to achieve a join that appears to be a natural extension of the letters.

Another area for exploration, which is sure to arise when you use Italic, is where you find noticeable space between the last letter of a line and the natural end of that line. The piece may not be justified on the right-hand margin, but sometimes too much white space looks out of place in the overall design.

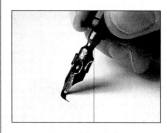

1 The elegant proportions of the Italic hand are achieved by maintaining a constant pen angle of 45°, and modelling the letters on the elliptical **O**. The letter **G**, shown here, shares the same characteristics as **A, C, D, E, O,** and **Q**. The first stroke moves from the pen angle to the right. It is almost a straight stroke and forms the top of the letter.

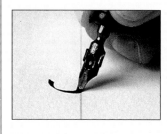

2 The second stroke begins at the same place as the first. It pulls around to form the first half of the elliptically-shaped bowl of the letter.

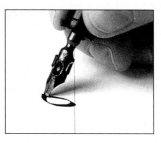

3 The stroke continues around until it reaches the thinnest part, and then climbs steeply toward the top of the letter.

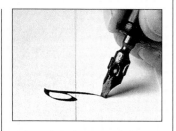

4 The backbone of the letter is the third stroke, which begins at the top, and plunges down into the descender. The stroke finishes in a slight curve to the left, which becomes the thinnest part of the stroke.

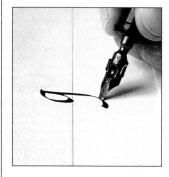

5 The last stroke of this letter starts in the white space to the left of the descender. The small finishing stroke is pulled to the right to meet the slightly curved end of the descender.

ABCDEFGHIJKLM

NOPQRSTUVWXYZ

abcdefghijklmnop

qrstuvwxyz · fgry

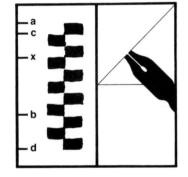

ITALIC ALPHABET

The Italic alphabet provides a good model as a first hand to learn calligraphy. The lower-case letters are five nib widths in height and executed with the pen nib at a 45° angle. The slant of the letters is maintained at an angle of 5°–10° to the vertical, depending on personal preference. Whatever angle is selected, it must be consistent throughout the work.

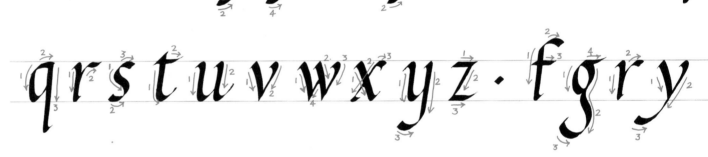

An important feature of the lower-case letters here is the way the arching stroke is made. The construction of the **K**, **B** and **P** is similar to the **H**, **M** and **N**.

This construction shows how the serif can be written as an integral part of the first stroke, or the pen can be lifted off the paper, and the serif added.

Line filling can be approached from two main directions. The first is to extend the last letter: unfortunately, this does not work with all letters. The second approach is to fill the line with a subtle arrangement of, for example, dots made with the broad nib. Consider the ideas explored in borders on pages 44–5 and you will find some satisfactory solutions.

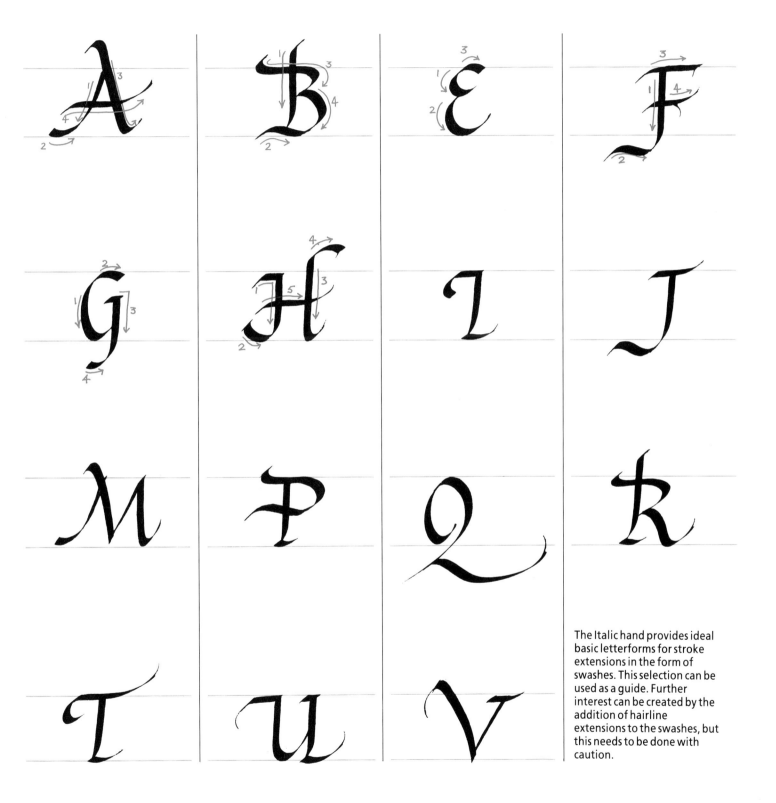

The Italic hand provides ideal basic letterforms for stroke extensions in the form of swashes. This selection can be used as a guide. Further interest can be created by the addition of hairline extensions to the swashes, but this needs to be done with caution.

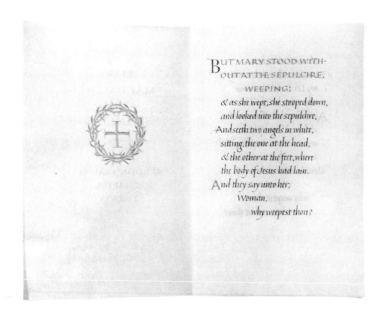

LEFT JOAN PILSBURY — These opening pages of a manuscript book display a spacious and well-considered layout, with generous margin widths and interlinear space. The story of Mary Magdalen is written in black and green on vellum. A burnished gold letter introduces the words, which are rendered in a beautiful example of formal Italics. (The informal style is recognizable by ligatures which join individual letters, creating the cursive Italic.)

BELOW DAVE WOOD — The Italic hand, with its informal and formal styles, has great flexibility. Bolder or more condensed forms can be created by decreasing or increasing the letter height (by varying the number of nib widths). This logo is a speculative design, presented as a possible solution to a particular visual problem. The Italics do not dictate a specific image; they make the design accessible (and in turn the product/client) with a timeless and ageless quality.

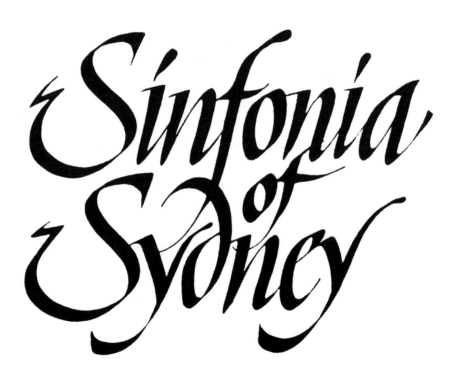

ITALIC CAPITALS

Notably narrowed and slanted, these letters are a
sophisticated modern Italic written with a consistent 45°
pen angle that creates a fluid modulation in the strokes.
Italic capitals are basically a compressed version of the
Roman form and have a similar regularity of proportion
governing the relationships between the different letters.
Flowing extensions of the stems and tails break through the
baseline to emphasize the elongated construction. As the
squared capitals were the characteristic formal lettering of
the Roman Empire, so Italic was the typical pen form of
scribes and scholars in Renaissance Italy.

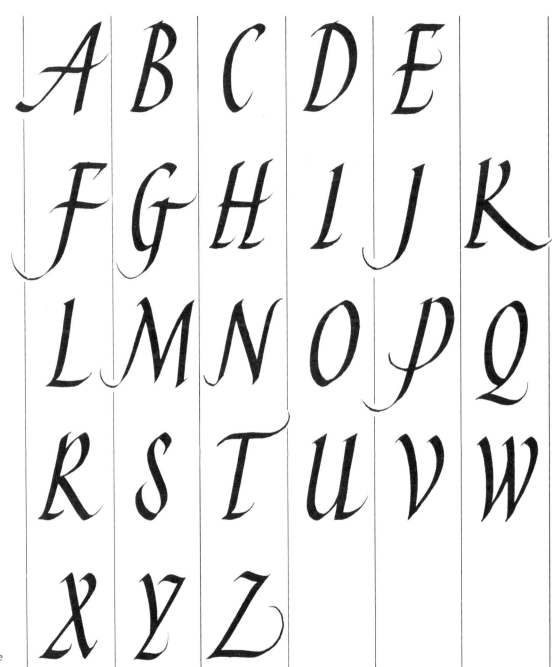

RIGHT The capitals in this modern
version of the Italic alphabet are tall,
elegant, and work well together. The
length of flourishes on tails, etc is
optional.

ITALIC LOWER CASE

Italic is a cursive hand, originally developed as a formal script that could be rapidly written without losing the fineness of its proportions and basic structure. In this version of the lower-case Italic alphabet, the curved ascenders and flourished descenders give greater emphasis to the slanting of the letters. The extension of these strokes achieves a length slightly exceeding the body height of the letters, but it is not so exaggerated as to destroy the balance in the patern of the lettering. Apart from the slanting and compression of the letterforms, the main characteristic of Italic is the branching of the arches from the main stems in the letters **h**, **m** and **n**. There is a similar construction in the bowls of **b**, **k** and **p**, and this creates the angular nature of Italic script.

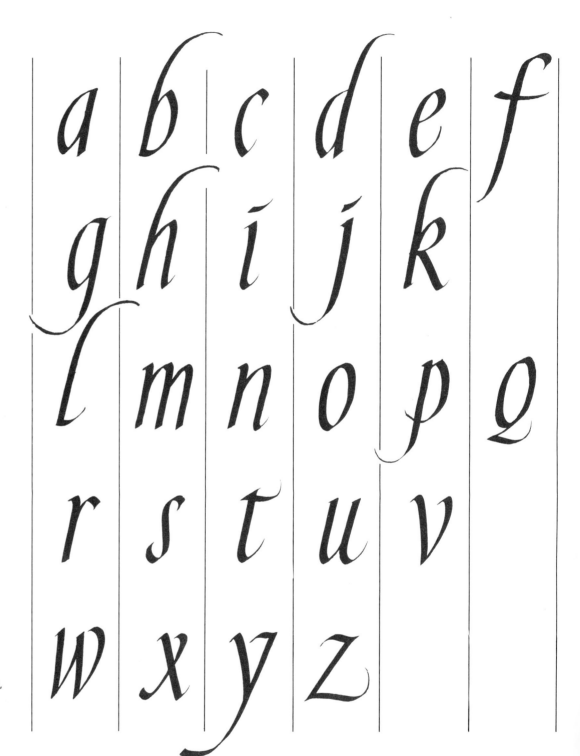

RIGHT As with most Italics, these letters branch from the main stroke, are compressed but consistent in width, with flowing ascenders and descenders.

COMPRESSED HAND – LOWER CASE

Compressed lettering is a development from modern reinterpretations of tenth-century minuscule letters. These are characteristically elegant, simple forms, which may be described as tilted but not emphatically slanted. The bowed letters are basically oval rther than rounded or angular, and this dictates the lateral compression affecting the proportions of the other letters. Ascenders are finished with a natural pen curve, as are the descenders of **g** and **y**, while in **p** and **q** the dropped stems are neatly terminated with a sideways twist of the pen.

RIGHT The Italic alphabet is so called because it originated in Italy. These simple lower-case letters are based on an oval, and the pattern of the counter and interspace should be drawn as consistently as possible. The arches are rounded, rather than branched.

COMPRESSED HAND – CAPITALS

The compressed capital letters are compact forms of medium weight. They have a clean, unelaborated style consistent with the lower-case letters, the same subtle slanting and oval counters being the characteristic qualities The thick-thin variation of the movement of the edged pen is not particularly pronounced in these letterforms. Vertical and slanted strokes are begun with a slightly angled serif. The bases of the letters are neatly finished with hooked terminals or sturdy horizontal feet.

RIGHT The capitals in this modern version of the Italic alphabet are tall and elegant and work well together. The length of flourishes on tails, etc, is optional.

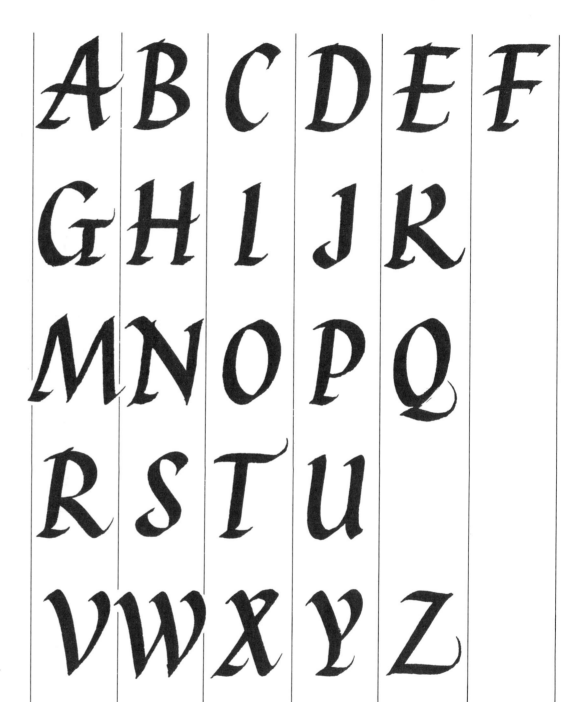

COPYBOOK ITALIC

The Italic and Humanist scripts of the Renaissance were widely disseminated through the medium of printed copybooks, the first of which was published in 1522 by Ludovico degli Arrighi (fl 1510–27). This finely textured, even Italic is an extremely practical hand, as demonstrated in the text sample, which appears to have been rapidly written without any loss to the elegance of the lettering. It is interesting to note that in the alphabet samples the lower-case letters have a deliberate slant while the capitals alternate different versions, one which is squared and upright in character while the alternative form is compressed, elongated and fluid.

RIGHT Arrighi was a sixteenth-century Italian calligrapher living in Rome. He produced writing manuals and designed type, his Italic typefaces being the finest of the period. This is a reprint of his first copybook of 1522, based on the Humanist script.

LITERA DA BREVI

A a b c d e e f g g h i k l m n o p q r s s s t u x y z

~: Marcus Antonius Casanoua :~.
Pierij vates, laudem.si opera ista merentur,
Praxiteli nostro carmina pauca date'.
Non placet hoc; nostri pietas laudanda Coryti'est;
Qui dicat hæc; nisi vos forsan uterqz mouet ;
Debetis saltem Dijs carmina, ni quoqz, et istis
Illa datis. iam nos mollia saxa sumus .

A A B B C C D D E E F F G G H H I
K L L M M N N O P P Q Q R R S
S T T U V V X X Y Z & & Bi & Bi

Ludouicus Vicentinus scribebat Roma' anno
salutis M D XXIII

FLOURISHED ITALIC

Although cursive Italic scripts were generally developed in Italy and southern Europe, this particularly exuberant alphabet is the work of the Dutch cartographer and mathematician Gerardus Mercator (1512–94), who in 1540 published a beautifully designed volume of writing samples, It offers a number of variations on the basic forms of the letters, demonstrating long ascenders and flourished tails, and also including the special features of ampersands and ligatured letters. This is a finely written Italic with little modulation in the letterstrokes. The controlled vigour of the flourishes ensures that they flow naturally from the lettering and do not interfere with the legibility of the characters.

RIGHT This Italic, produced by Gerardus Mercator, the leader of Dutch and Flemish cartographers, is restrained yet exuberant.

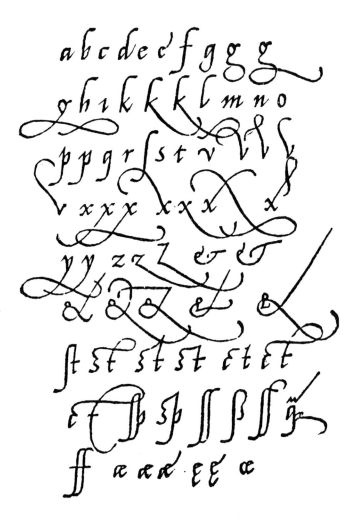

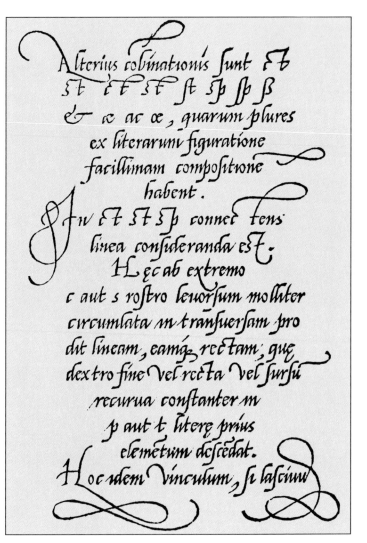

ELABORATED ITALIC

The original manuscript from which this Italic lettering sample is taken is an Italian discourse on hawking written around 1560–70. That text occupies the first part of the book and is followed by a number of writing samples. The light-textured capitals with their extended flourishes show the possible variety in the basic letterforms. The final version of **Z** is a particularly curious and decorative construction. The capitals are followed by a script sample containing further elaboration and finely drawn ornamentation. As with earlier forms of lettering, Italic became widely used throughout Europe, and during the main period of its prevalence, the style developed differently in different countries and regions.

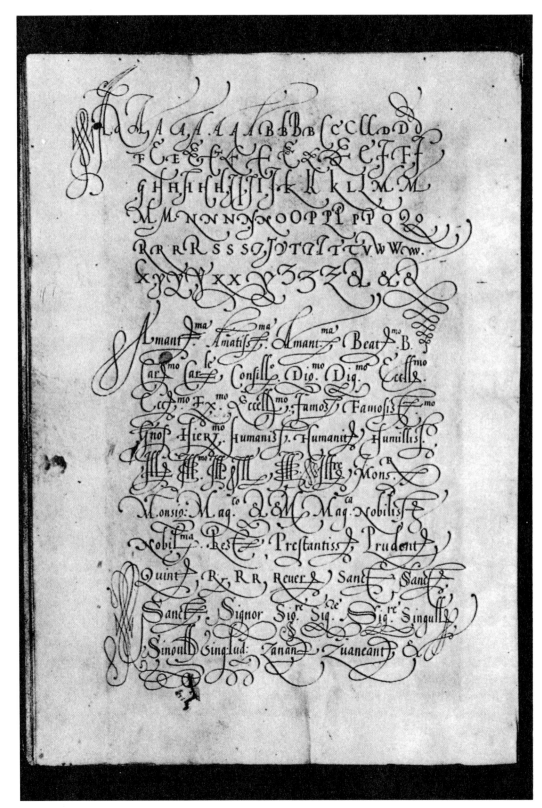

RIGHT An incredibly rich example of Italic capital and lower-case letters. Although heavily flourished, it is an interesting source of invention and inspiration.

SPANISH ITALIC CAPITALS

Francisco Lucas (*c* 1530 to after 1580) was an important influence on the development of Spanish calligraphy, perfecting his interpretations of the late Gothic cursive Bastarda, the Renaissance Humanistic scripts and the rounded minuscules of Rotunda. This sample is a delightful exposition of variations in calligraphic form in an alphabet of capital letters: compact structures contrast with looped and flourished forms. The six different versions of **M** are a particularly descriptive lessons in lettering design.

SPANISH ITALIC SCRIPT

This is a very fine and controlled Italic script, with a neat balance between the rising and descending lines and their relationships to the body height of the letters. The letterforms are well-proportioned and evenly textured, the subtle slanting carried through in the tall curved ascenders and clubbed descenders. Distinctive variations of form include the forward and backward facing bowls of the **g**, the straight and curving versions of **j**, the abbreviated **r** and the long and short forms of **s**. The alphabet is reproduced in woodcut, the letters being cut into the ground of the wood block rather than left raised upon the surface, thus printing as white on black.

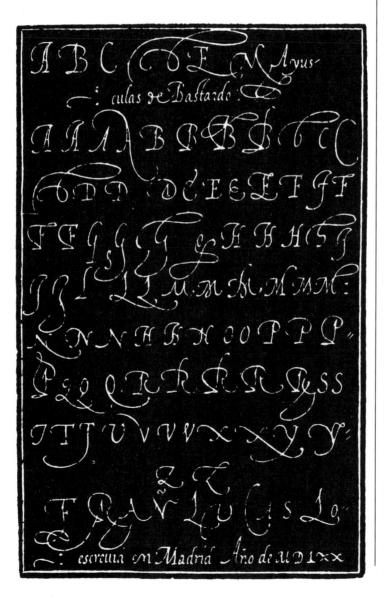

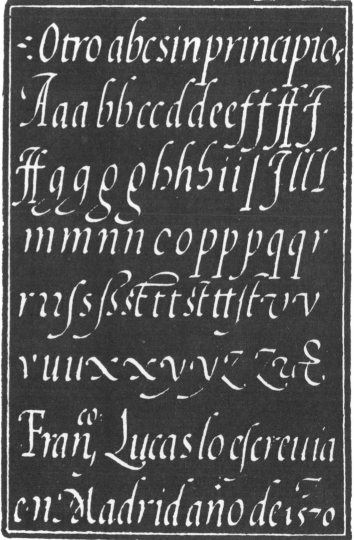

DECORATIVE ITALIC

This is a sixteenth-century copybook form, another sample in which the sharply elegant slanted Italic evolves under the influence of Copperplate engraving into a finely flourished, trailed and ornamented style of capitals. As was the usual practice in writing manuals, each letter is given in different versions. In this case these vary from the oblique to the rounded, with decorative features from hooked or curving terminals to scrolled and woven ornamentation. The thick and thin variations of the letter strokes are not pronounced and suggest the original use of a pointed pen, with pressure applied to splay the nib slightly in order to broaden out the fine lines and soften the longer flourishes. The engraved sample was published in England, but shows the influence of Italian writing styles.

HUMANISTIC CURSIVE CAPITALS

Humanistic scripts were originally a southern European development based on the rounded ninth- and tenth-century minuscules. These upright and cursive hands were a product of the Renaissance period in Italy, in their turn giving rise to the compressed and angular Italic which is categorized as a Humanistic hand. The alternative forms in these cursive capitals reflect both the earlier influence and the development of the style. The slight slant is typical of Italic, as are the sharply turned angles of **M** and **N**, in this case incorporating fine, tight loops at the joining of the strokes in the head of each letter. But the letters also include a more fluid, rounded form of construction, still with an Italic-style branching of arch from stem but with a clearly defined curve at the top of the letters and generous space between terminals at the base. The device of a leftward, looping flourish from top to bottom of a form helps to balance the spidery, tilted lettering.

RIGHT Another modern interpretaion of a humanistic majuscule alphabet. The fluid, looped forms in **E** and **W** suggest the beginning of early Copperplate characteristics.

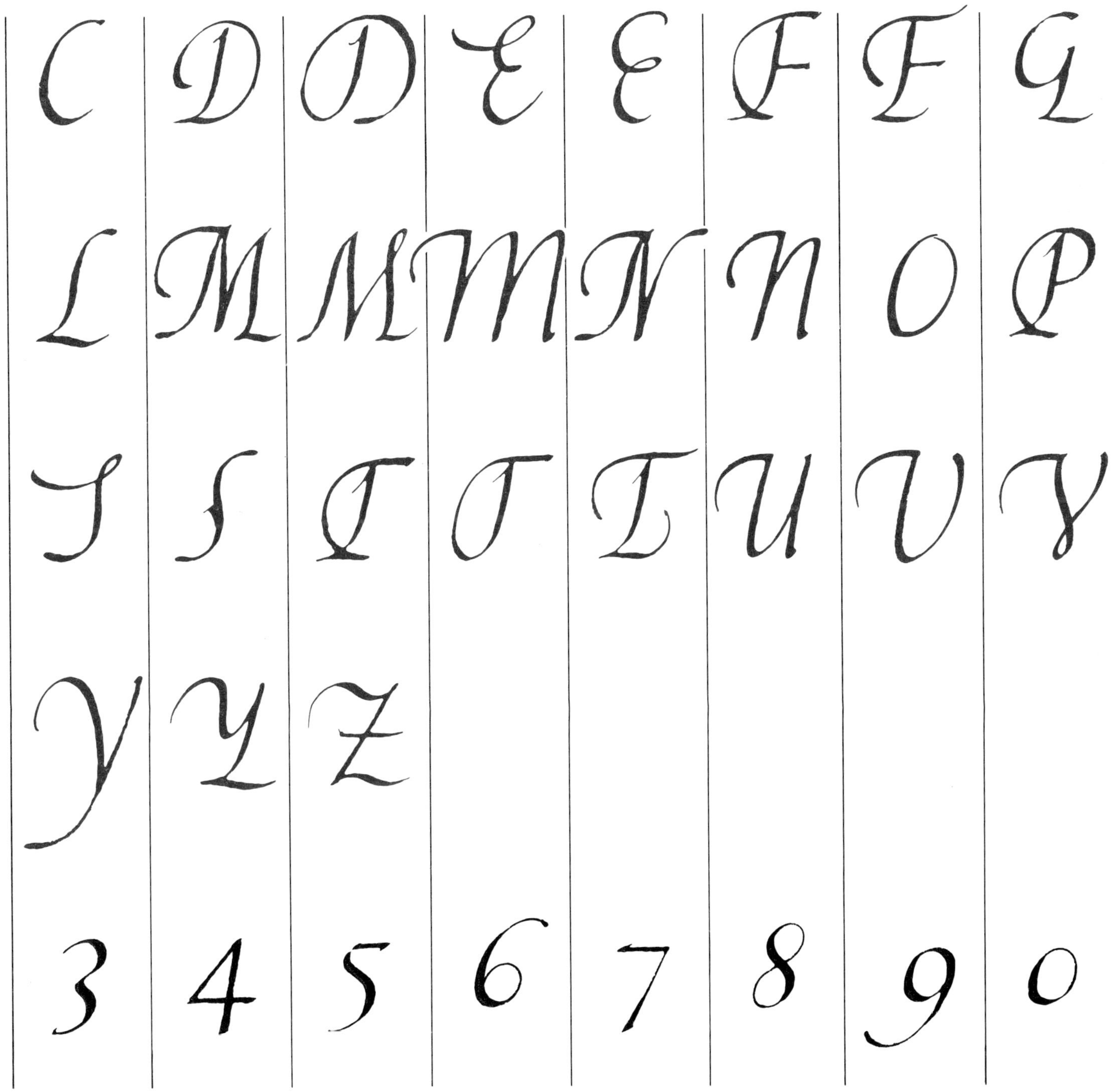

C D D E E F F G
L M M M N N O P
I J J T T T U V Y
Y Y Z
3 4 5 6 7 8 9 0

SLANTED GOTHIC

The characteristic slant of Italic is here applied to an elaborate style of lettering based on earlier Gothic forms. The sample is from a sixteenth-century Dutch copybook. The letterforms are inventively constructed, with full advantage taken of the fine pen line, which is twisted and looped into curious interpretations of each form. In the more imaginative versions, notably of **B**, **G**, **P** and **S**, the character of the letter is taken so far beyond its

recognizable shape and structure that seen out of context it would appear as a decorative abstract motif, calligraphic in influence but not necessarily identifiable as lettering. In designing an alphabet sample it is acceptable to develop these ornamental qualities because the form is identified by its place in the letter sequence, though in a general text they might be less appropriate. This design shows a keen appreciation of line, texture and spatial balance and demonstrates the graphic value and aesthetic pleasure of highly developed calligraphic skill.

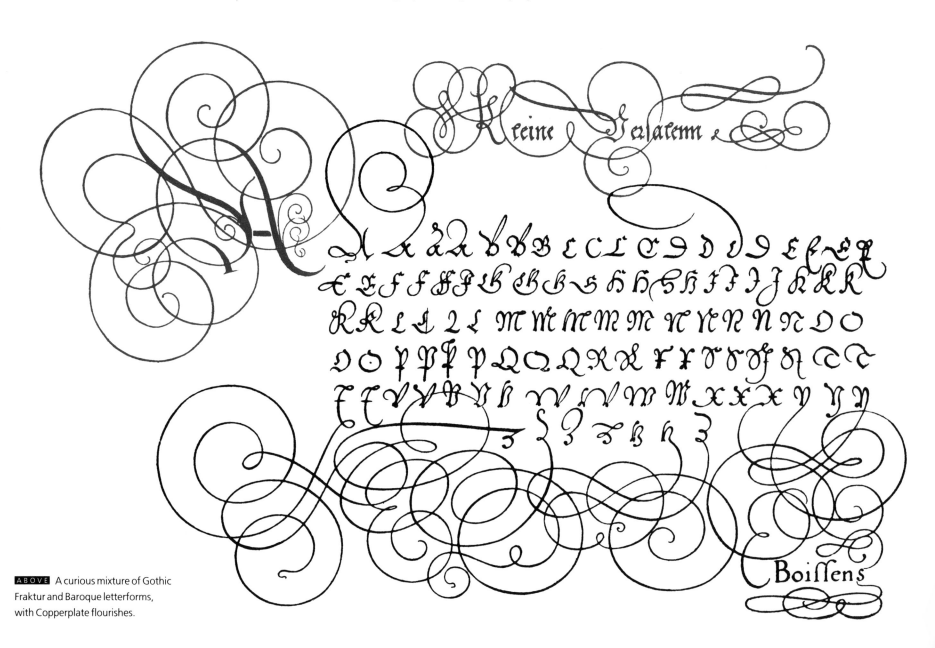

ABOVE A curious mixture of Gothic Fraktur and Baroque letterforms, with Copperplate flourishes.

Copperplate alphabets

In the sixteenth century, the quality of rolled copper sheeting supplied to engravers improved dramatically. Lettering engravers were finally able to work with their burins on a surface comparable to the paper or parchment used by scribes. Inspired by, or envious of, the newfound freedom expressed by the engravers, scribes abandoned their broad square-cut quills for flexible, pointed nibs. A fine cursive writing emerged; it could be rapidly written, dispensing with the need to lift the pen off the paper except for punctuation and word and line breaks. The result was elegant lettering that flowed across the page.

A pointed flexible nib responds to the pressure placed on it by the writer. A major feature of Copperplate is the slight swelling of the downward strokes. This is acquired by applying a modicum of pressure to the pen as the stroke is made, thus forcing a little extra ink to flow through the now slightly separated point of the nib. Similarly, by releasing almost all the pressure on the upward stroke between letters, an extraordinarily fine line is achieved.

Other easily identifiable characteristics of this hand are the occasional looped ascenders and descenders and the graceful, flowing forms written at a slant of 54°. It is extremely awkward to write beautiful Copperplate without the correct equipment – either a pen with an elbow-angled nib, or an angled nib holder. The angle of the nib or holder provides the slant.

The improvement in engraving techniques coincided with increased levels of literacy that had developed after the advent of printing from movable type. People wanted to write and in response to this interest, scribes prepared instructional copybooks. These were printed from metal plates, incised by engravers who executed exquisite, fine lines that flowed and flourished, with an unlimited measure of decorative ornamentation.

Copperplate lends itself to ornamentation, particularly energetic flourishing. If you look at old manuscripts written in any of the numerous cursive scripts, you will find grand pieces of penmanship rendered almost illegible. Here are beautifully executed letters disappearing in a subterfuge of ornament.

Copperplate became associated with more than handwritten lettering and printing. The lettering engravers exercised their art on items made of, for example, precious metal. Other craftspeople followed suit. Glass engravers, clockmakers, and metalsmiths acquired the elegant hand for their own purposes.

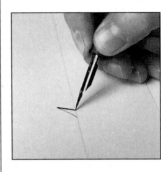

1 The letter shown here is being written with a fine straight nib. The letter begins with a hairline stroke, made with virtually no pressure on the nib so that it glides gracefully over the page. Gentle pressure is applied to the first vertical stroke, which finishes with a square end.

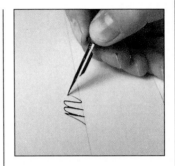

3 Unlike the first two vertical strokes, which finished with a square end, the final stroke curves around into a hairline. This hairline is usually extended and becomes the first stroke of the next letter.

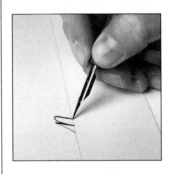

2 The second vertical stroke is preceded by another fine hairline stroke. Observe where the hairline leaves the first vertical stroke. Notice the shape of the white space formed by these two strokes.

COPPERPLATE

ALPHABET

This elegant script is composed of four basic strokes. The first is the hairline which begins most of the letter. There is a further hairline which serves as a ligature to join the letters. There are some strokes which have square ends. The final stroke to consider begins and ends with a hairline but swells in the middle as pressure is applied to force more ink through the nib.

The letters can be written with an elbow-angled holder or nib, or, with practice, a fine pointed nib. The slant of the writing is 54°, giving fine and flowing lines. The looped or flourished ascenders and descenders are generally of a greater length than those which finish straight.

COPPERPLATE SCRIPT

This rather weighty Copperplate form, although rolling and cursive in style, is derived from an attempt to subject script lettering to a geometric system of construction. The letters are remarkably even and regular in proportion. The very straight and clean-cut ascenders and descenders are offered as an appropriate contrast to the elegantly curving tails. The relatively emphatic thick/thin modulation of the strokes refers back to the characteristic texture of edged pen writing, but in this case it is artificially constructed by drawing with a pointed pen, outlining and then filling the broader width of stems and curves, as may be seen in the samples of letter construction developed in a skeleton form within a carefully constructed grid format.

abcdeffghijkllm

nopqrſsttuvwxyyz.

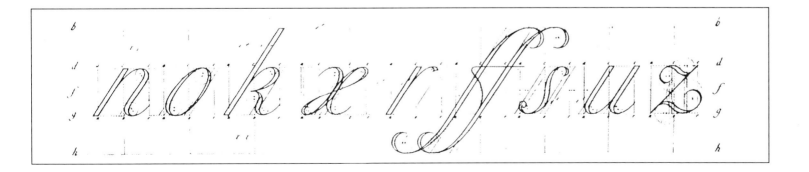

FLOURISHED CAPITALS

By the end of the sixteenth century, fine engraving on copper plates had superseded the broader printing technique of woodcut as a method of reproducing writing samples for publication. As the solid forms appropriate to woodcut had caused some modification to earlier pen lettering styles, so the fineness and fluidity of copperplate engraving itself began to influence the fashion in writing styles, giving rise to the curling linear forms that became known as Copperplate scripts. The delicate swelling and narrowing line made by a graver corresponds to the travelling mark of a pointed pen guided under varying pressure. This impressive sample of Copperplate capitals has great movement, style and energy, but it is controlled in the execution to produce harmoniously balanced relationships between the letters.

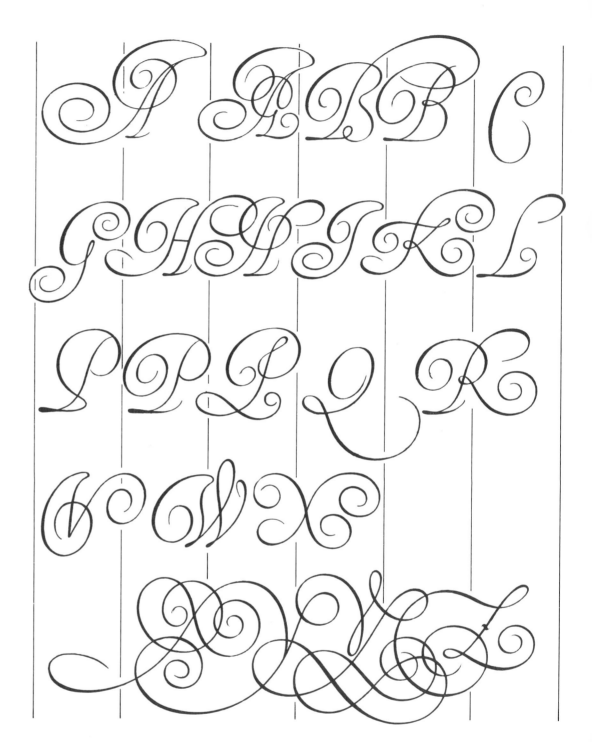

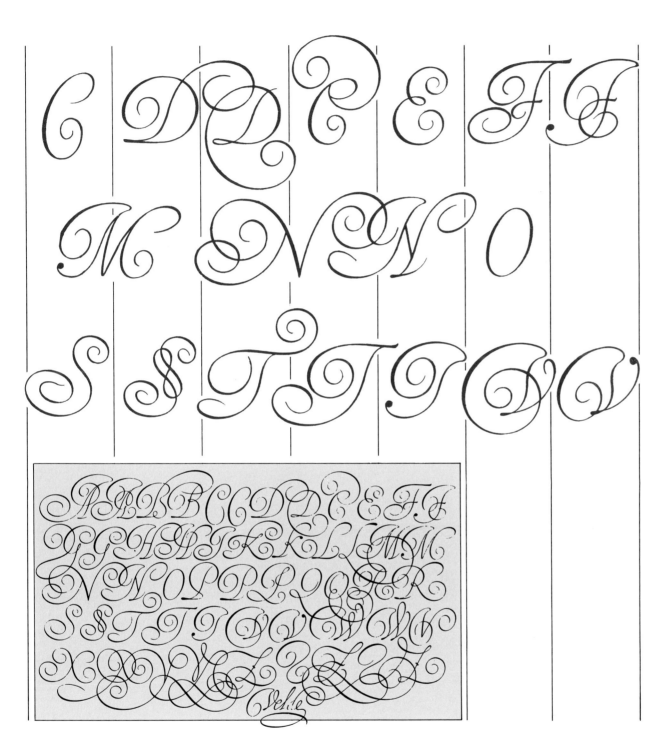

ROUNDHAND

English Copperplate script of the eighteenth century demonstrates a refined and even hand in which the smoothly curving letterforms are slanted and cursive. This is a prime example of lettering designed specifically to be reproduced by engraving. The pointed pen moves fluidly through the form of each letter, and the varying pressure used to modulate the pen line has been subtly applied and carefully controlled. This is a decorative but not elaborate script, the lower-case letters being finely balanced and embellished with loops while the capitals are evenly matched and developed with elegantly restrained flourishes. The engraving, though not the original lettering, was carried out by the English calligrapher and master engraver George Bickham (*c* 1684–1748), whose collection of writing samples published serially under the title *The Universal Penman* was highly influential on contemporary writing style.

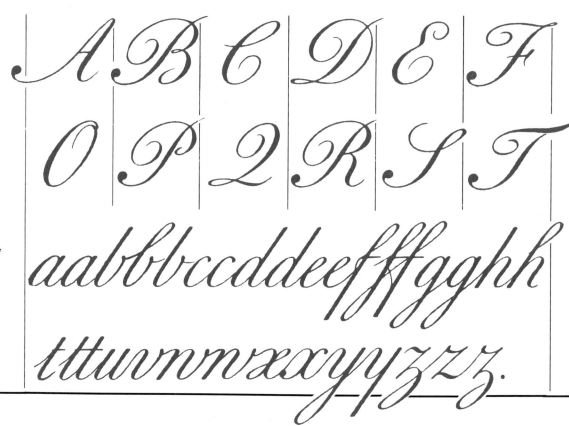

POINTED PEN LETTERS (1)

This is an extremely refined, formal cursive script typical of the development of pointed pen lettering under the influence of Copperplate engraving in the eighteenth century. Its elegance derives from the compressed and elongated style. In the lower-case form, the length of ascenders and descenders exceeds the body height of the letters, but the evenness of the proportions maintains the overall balance of the script. The rounded capitals are elaborated with flowing, looped flourishes while the subtly fluid stems of **H**, **I**, **J** and **K** are topped with an intriguing double curve. The numerals, though consistent with the overall style of the lettering, are a little more generous in width but carefully contained within a fixed body height.

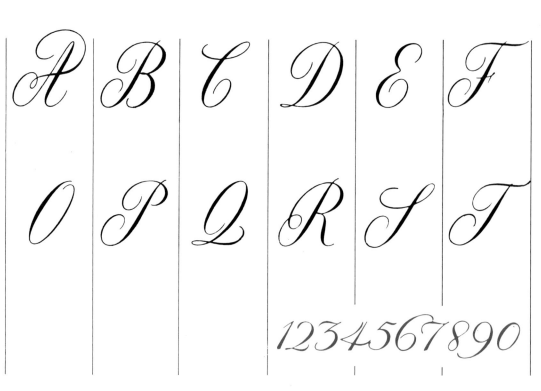

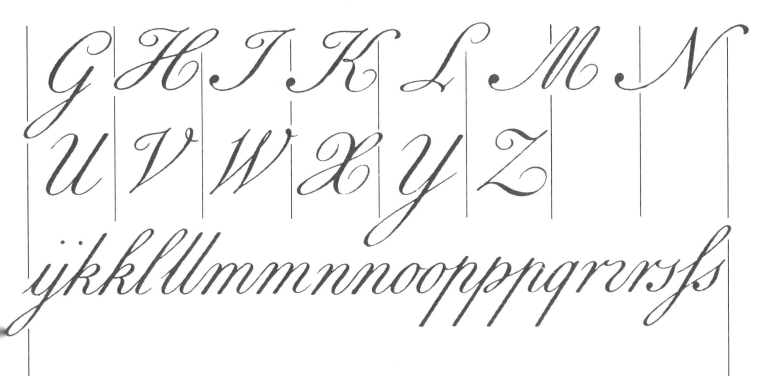

G H I J K L M N
U V W X Y Z
ijkkllllmmnnooppppqrvrsfs

G H I J K L M N
U V W X Y Z
abcdefghijklmnopqrvrstuvwxyzz

POINTED PEN LETTERS (2)

The lightweight, flowing texture of pointed pen writing has a gracefulness seen at its best when an alphabet form is designed, like this sample, as a series of well-proportioned, unelaborated shapes. The loops and curls are restrained and naturally in harmony with the basic structure of each letter. The cursive nature of the script is demonstrated in the finely slanted joining strokes forming discreet links between the letters. The relationships between the script, capitals and numerals are completely consistent and appropriate, including the alternative rounded and angular forms shown for the capital letters **M**, **N**, **V** and **W**.

RIGHT This alphabet combines round and pointed capitals with some alternative letters in both styles.

FINE GOTHIC-STYLE SCRIPT

The fashion for copybooks in the eighteenth century encouraged the most versatile displays of calligraphic skill and the technique of Copperplate engraving was not employed solely to reproduce the style of current pointed pen lettering. Whereas the Gothic-influenced script, which the original publication terms 'German text', refers to the earlier style of edged-pen letters, the tools of engraving require that a heavy black line be built up from several finely cut lines. This sample shows a modification to the letterforms with regard to the influence of that technique. The lower-case letters are made light in texture and slightly flourished. The tails and ascenders, though complementary, do not extend naturally from the angular, pointed structures but seem to be an addition based on contemporary fashion. The capitals are more heavily defined but decorated with finely looped ornamentation. This balance of texture ensures that the letters emerge as distinct and legible despite the elaboration.

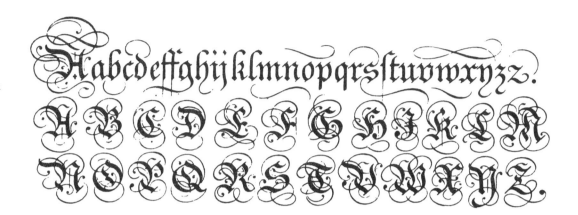

ROUND TEXT

The round hand is, like the earlier forms of Italic writing, an elegant but extremely practical hand, well adapted to the natural movement of hand and pen. This cursive sample shows the linking of letters through the flowing motion of the pen along the writing line, facilitated by the slanting of the letters. The body height of the letters is equal to the length of the ascenders, and a subtle balance is created by the extended drop of the descenders looping below the baseline. The forms are compressed but the rounded bowls and arches maintain the even texture of the script in the relationship between height and width of the letters. This evenness is also due to the consistency of the pen strokes, in which the minimal variation of pressure and density is fluidly and restrainedly applied.

SQUARE TEXT

Square text is the name given in the original copybook publication to this eighteenth-century calligraphy based on Gothic forms. It is an appropriate designation: although the letters are angularized by the pointed terminals and lozenge-shaped serifs borrowed from Blackletter styles, these are grafted onto an adaptation of rounded letters which gives the script a broad, squared quality and medium-weight texture identifiable of its own period, though influenced by the historical source. In the capital letters, the extended, looping hairlines enhance the lively character of the text. Certain authentic medieval letterforms show this type of hairline embellishment, but in this case again, the manner of execution seems to owe more to contemporary fashion than to the origin of the device. But the overall structure of the capital letters and the divided counters of **C**, **G**, **O**, **Q** and **T** have a convincing period flavour.

ROUND HAND

This round hand sample has all the marks of the standard form in its evenly spaced and weighted letters, deliberate proportions and controlled execution. The purpose of copybooks was to distribute widely both the forms of letters considered of particular excellence and functional value and styles of decorative lettering designed to demonstrate the writing master's skills and tax the discipline of the pupil. Round hand was a ubiquitous style of the eighteenth century used as a model script until the early twentieth century and taught in schools as the standard of elegant writing. It is indisputably a formal, attractive hand, though recent fashion in calligraphy has tended to reject the finer Copperplate styles in favour of edge-pen letters derived from earlier sources.

REVISED HUMANISTIC SCRIPTS

These two samples draw upon the characteristics of Renaissance hands to develop script letters of sharp angularity matched by more generous, flowing capitals. The first is an inventive, eclectic script; the pairing of capital and small letters suggests that it is developed within its own terms of reference rather than strictly based on a known traditional style. The cursive script originally designated the 'secretary' hand, which forms the second sample, is a very tightly constructed, logical and balanced form which, as the name suggests, was intended to be highly functional in day-to-day tasks requiring writing that was rapid but refined, consistent and legible.

ABOVE The alphabets on this page were engraved by George Bickham and show a variety of hands current in the eighteenth century, some still retaining Gothic influences. Sometimes the two styles were combined.

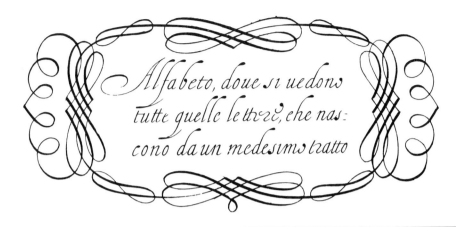

FLOURISHED SCRIPT LETTERS

Despite the rococo ornamentation typically applied to Copperplate styles, this alphabet has a curiously spare and simple character. The letters are grouped in rows according to the basic body height or presence of an ascender or descender. Within each row the stylization is systematically applied, the extended rightward-leaning ascenders finished by a rounded terminal showing heavy pen pressure, the leftward-flowing tails and descenders sharply turned on a backward angle, except in **g**, where the tail is generously looped. A peculiar inconsistency occurs in the final grouping of letters, which, compared to the rest, are more broadly formed and developed as if to pose an alternative to the original style. A written heading shows, however, that applied as a script this lettering does have an unexpectedly convincing appearance and consistency.

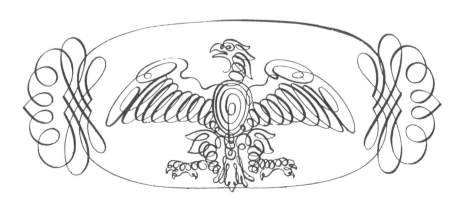

LEFT The curved tops of these simple characters are reminiscent of the looped tops used by Cresci in the sixteenth century.

FLOURISHED CAPITALS (1)

The proportions of these letters depart completely from the influence of standard traditional or classical forms. The proliferation of styles that occurred with the widespread publication of copybooks led to much inventiveness in the design of letters, with greater and lesser degrees of success. In this sample of looped capitals there is a consistency in the relationships of the rounded letters, but **A**, **H**, **M**, **N** and **R** are noticeably compressed, while **X**, **Y** and **Z** are converted to comparatively broad forms. Each letter appears to be developed in terms of its own structure, with less regard to the relationships between forms, especially in such details as the double curve of **Q** and the scrolled elaboration of **X**. However, the key to the variations may lie in the fact that the alphabet, with its surrounding ornamentation, is conceived in terms of the overall design effect and each grouping of letters has a definite internal coherence, as does the writer's signature in the central panel, which shows the functional properties of the lettering.

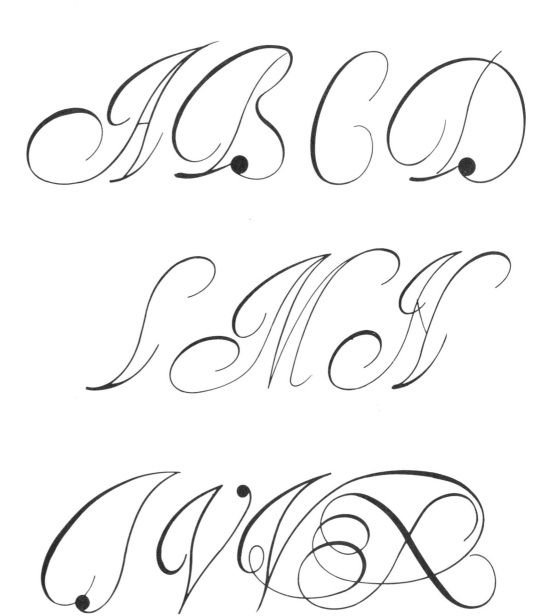

RIGHT These are extremely finely engraved letters with unusual dot endings and elegant curves.

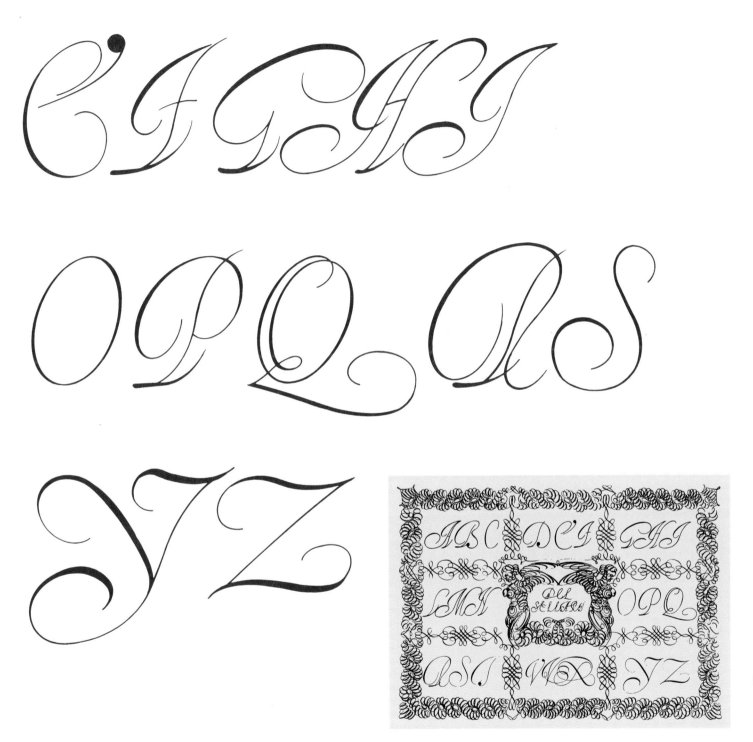

LEFT When grouped together, as in the panel, their decorative qualities can be seen to best effect.

FLOURISHED CAPITALS (2)

These finely developed scrolled capitals demonstrate the versatility of Copperplate style. The thick-thin contrast betrays their origin as edged-pen rather than pointed pen letters, though the narrow nib width creates a fluid and lightweight appearance. The construction of each letter is carefully controlled by the evenly spaced writing lines governing body height and internal features. The extended, looping flourishes at the heads and bases of the letter are systematically fitted to these guidelines. The calligrapher, French writing master Charles Paillasson (fl 1760), has allowed himself a final extravagant gesture in the billowing flourished tails wrapped under and around the letters on the bottom line of the alphabet.

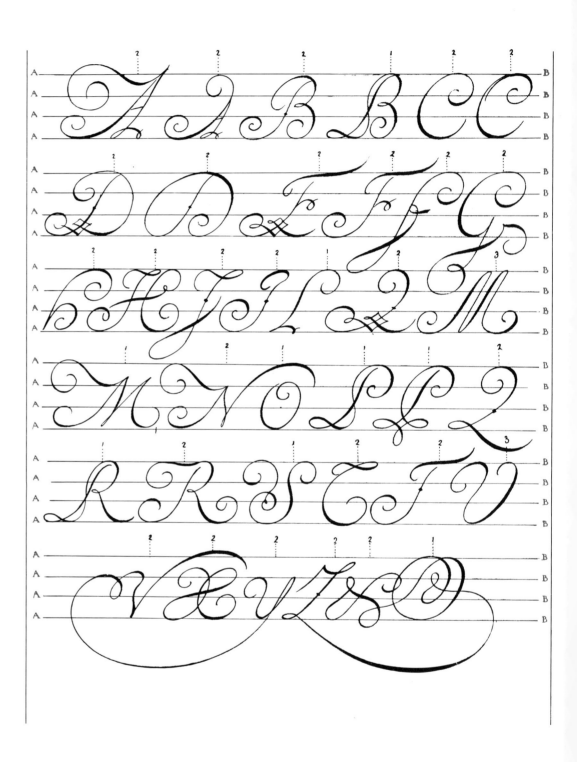

RIGHT Free-flowing majuscule letters with unusual additions of interlaced strapwork in **D**, **E** and **L**.

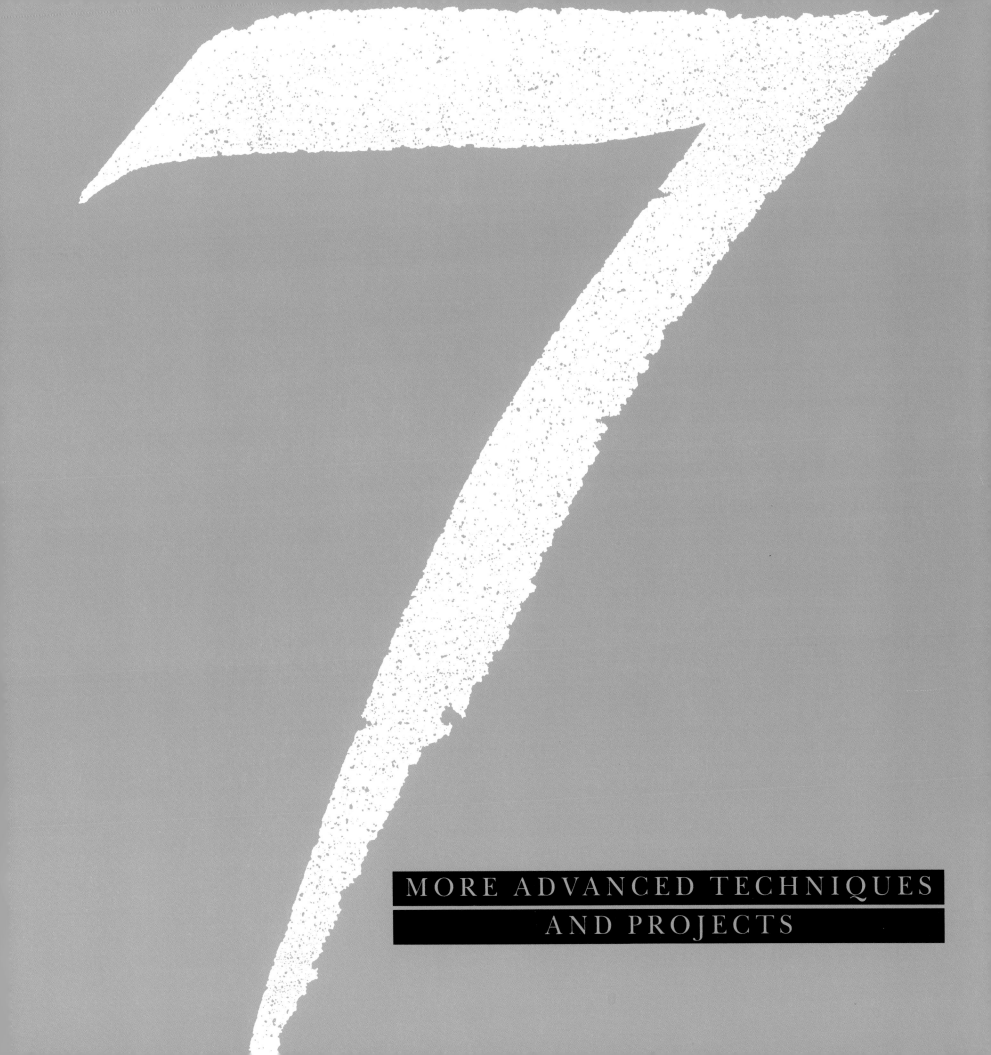

7

MORE ADVANCED TECHNIQUES
AND PROJECTS

Deciding on a text area

There are traditional margin proportions which have been used for many years in the laying out of single sheets and double-page spreads. The unit values of head, foredge, foot and inner (or spine) margins were based on proportions of the quarto and octavo folds of given sheet sizes. In the UK, a full-size sheet of any size is called a Broadside; a Broadside folded in half is called a Folio; a Folio folded in half, making four sheets, is called Quarto and a Quarto folded in half, making eight leaves, is called an Octavo. Sheets of approximately the same sizes are available internationally.

When deciding on the size of sheet to use for a specific project, and the layout and margins to be used, the amount of text and the nature of the work must be taken into account. This section is devoted to continuous text and the margin proportions and width of measure which relate to this particular aspect of layout. The proportions given here will be adequate for most works and are given as a point from which to start laying out text. They can be changed to suit a particular requirement, but remember, when changing the unit values, to allow more space at the foot so that the column of text does not look as if it is slipping off the sheet area.

Take a sheet 8¼in (210mm) by 5⅞in (149mm), known as A5, taken from the paper size A system. A5 is used for leaflets and brochures. The A system is unique, as the sheet proportion remains in the same ratio even when folded in half or doubled up in size.

To decide on a text area, the width of the A5 sheet, 5⅞in (149mm), must be divided by 10 to obtain a unit width, that is 14.9mm. Round this up to the nearest whole millimetre to 15mm. (Clearly, in this example it is easier to use the metric measure.) This will be the basic unit and it will be used to create the margins and text area of the sheet. One unit should be left at the head of the sheet, one unit for both the foredge and the spine and 1½ units at the foot. This leaves a text measure of 119mm in width and 172mm in depth.

The size of text can be dependent on the amount of copy to be contained within the format, but emphasis here will be put on continuous text, as in a manuscript or booklet of several pages. The golden rule in continuous text lettering is that the optimum in readability is a line-length of ten words. In the English language this is equivalent to 60 characters, as the average word is six characters long, including word spaces. Therefore the line length can be

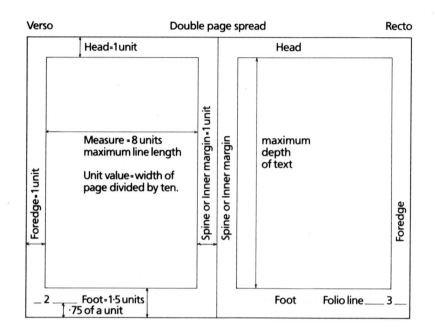

Verso — Double page spread — Recto

Head = 1 unit

Foredge = 1 unit

Measure = 8 units maximum line length

Unit value = width of page divided by ten

Spine or Inner margin = 1 unit

Spine or Inner margin

Head

maximum depth of text

Foredge

2 Foot = 1.5 units
·75 of a unit

Foot   Folio line   3

between eight and twelve words, or 48 and 72 characters. Given this information a nib size can be chosen to give approximately 60 characters to the line in the letter style decided upon. A typewritten manuscript can be easily fitted by counting the characters in one line, multiplying this by the number of lines and dividing the result by the number of characters contained within one line of the layout.

Roman Serif has been used for the example given here and various nib sizes were tested out – B2, Italic broad, Italic medium and Italic fine – before Italic fine was finally settled upon. Some interlinear space must be allowed to ensure that the ascenders and descenders do not clash. So, letter a few lines with half a nib width and a nib width space before deciding on the latter. The depth of text will be 25 lines per page. The text in this example has been ranged left. This in itself produces an inherent problem in that the right-hand margin will appear larger than the left, because of the ragged optical white space being produced. When producing the finished manuscript a minor adjustment for this will be made, by leaving more white space in the left-hand margin to compensate.

'What are moon-letters?' a
/ B2 nib

'What are moon-letters?' aske
/ italic broad nib

'What are moon-letters?' asked the Hobb
/ italic medium nib

'What are moon-letters?' asked the Hobbit full of
/ italic fine nib

'There are moon-letters here, beside the plain
runes which say "five feet high the door and
three may walk abreast".'
'What are moon-letters?' asked the Hobbit full of
/ italic fine nib - ½ nib width interlinear

'There are moon-letters here, beside the plain
runes which say "five feet high the door and
three may walk abreast".'
'What are moon-letters?' asked the Hobbit full of
/ italic fine nib - 1 nib width interlinear

LEFT Testing nib sizes for line length.

Using rough sketches and thumbnails

If the work is for an invitation card, consider its distribution. If it is to be posted, then there will be a limitation on convenient size. Unless you make the envelope yourself, you will need to know the availability of envelopes and matching paper or card. Check with a stationer which envelopes are available in small quantities to avoid having to use the same envelope and paper again and again. The card used here measures 4¼in (105mm) by 5⅞in (149m) (or A6), which fits into a C6 envelope.

Is the invitation formal or informal? This will determine the type of layout chosen. Centred layouts are generally used for formal occasions but a ranged-left layout can be equally elegant. The use of a ranged-right layout in this instance would be unsuitable, because the work entailed in producing such a layout is too great for lettering a large number of cards. A justified layout can also be disregarded as this is used only for continuous text. An asymmetrical layout could be used for an informal card, if desired. For this project, the copy has been treated in an informal manner using a ranged-left layout.

Before a rough layout can be made, decide which elements should be prominent. The words underlined here are those which will have the most impact for this design, with remaining copy being coded 1, 2 and 3 in order of importance.

Large-sized lettering, which makes up display headings, attracts the attention of the reader. Secondary information should be smaller than the display but in a size that can be read easily. Subsidiary details can be lettered smaller. The aim of the calligrapher is not only to produce a tasteful letterform but also to lead the reader through the information in a sequence that relates to the order of importance of the text.

In the same copy, the words 'Birthday Party' have been underlined, as they are the key words. The person's name has been given code 1, the invitation text, time and place have code 2 and finally 'RSVP' receives code 3, as it is the least important.

ROUGHING OUT

The next step is to rough out some basic ideas in pencil before using pen and ink. This initial work is done on layout paper at a size scaled down from the finished invitation. In this instance half the size is adequate to become familiar with the words and to create an interesting layout by committing any initial thoughts to paper. Rough layouts should be both landscape and portrait formats to discover which shape accepts the text more readily and uses the area to its best advantage.

Begin by drawing some vertical and horizontal boxes in pencil, scaled down to represent the card. To achieve this, draw the card on a piece of layout paper and divide the rectangular box diagonally from the top left-hand corner to the bottom right-hand corner. Then divide the top line of the box into two; on my card this measures 2⅛in (52.5mm) to the centre line. Draw a vertical line down from this centre point to where the vertical line meets the diagonal. This is the depth of the card at half-scale. Then draw a horizontal line from the diagonal to the left-hand vertical. The area just defined is a half-size of the original card area. Naturally at a half-size, the measurements could just be divided in half and a rectangle drawn, but on a larger format, where it may be necessary to work on roughs a sixth or an eighth of the original size, this method saves time and calculations. It is also useful when scaling illustrations or drawings up or down. This is discussed in more detail in the illustrations.

BELOW RIGHT Preparing scaled-down boxes.

BELOW Deciding on the priorities to be given to lines of text.

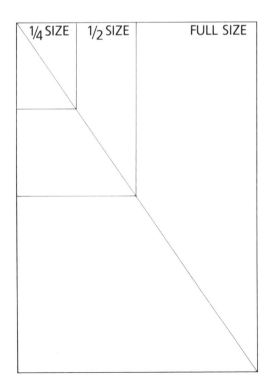

1 Jane Silvester

2 would like you to

2 come to her

birthday party

2 on 24th September

2 at 8pm Flat 3,

2 Long Lane

2 Hampstead,

2 London NW3 (RSVP)
3

| ¼ SIZE | ½ SIZE | FULL SIZE |

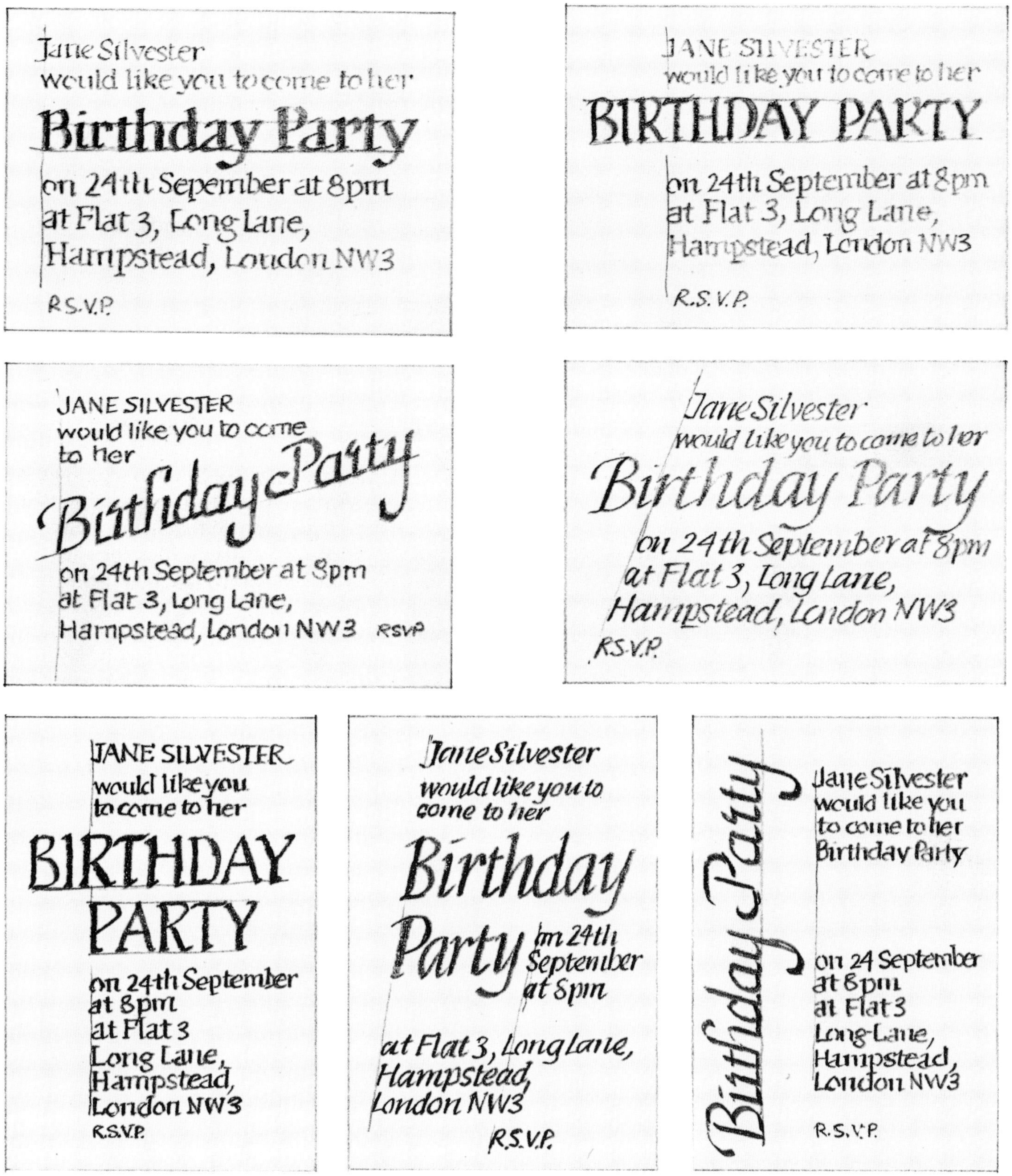

Jane Silvester
would like you to come to her
Birthday Party
on 24th Sepember at 8pm
at Flat 3, Long Lane,
Hampstead, Loudon NW3

R.S.V.P.

JANE SILVESTER
would like you to come to her
BIRTHDAY PARTY
on 24th September at 8pm
at Flat 3, Long Lane,
Hampstead, London NW3

R.S.V.P.

JANE SILVESTER
would like you to come
to her
Birthday Party
on 24th September at 8pm
at Flat 3, Long Lane,
Hampstead, London NW3   RSVP

Jane Silvester
would like you to come to her
Birthday Party
on 24th September at 8pm
at Flat 3, Long Lane,
Hampstead, London NW3
R.S.V.P.

JANE SILVESTER
would like you
to come to her
**BIRTHDAY
PARTY**
on 24th September
at 8pm
at Flat 3
Long Lane,
Hampstead,
London NW3
R.S.V.P.

Jane Silvester
would like you to
come to her
*Birthday
Party* on 24th
September
at 8pm
at Flat 3, Long Lane,
Hampstead,
London NW3
R.S.V.P.

Birthday Party

Jane Silvester
would like you
to come to her
Birthday Party
on 24 September
at 8pm
at Flat 3
Long Lane,
Hampstead,
London NW3

R.S.V.P.

LEFT Some initial small roughs to decide on layout.

Begin by using the margins discussed in 'Deciding on a text area' (pages 144–5), that is, one unit at the head and side margins and 1½ units at the foot. However, it is important to remember that for the roughs these margins must be half-size to keep the same proportion. It may be advisable to reduce the foot margin as the format is quite small and, provided there is more space at the foot than the head, this is quite in order. The text should be placed optically in the depth of the card. Then, using an HB pencil sharpened to a chisel edge, begin to describe the text on the rough layouts (also known as thumbnails owing to their small size).

From the rough layouts the landscape format works best with 'Birthday Party' lettered diagonally across the card. The angle has been fixed at the point at which the italicized letters coincide with the vertical edges of the text area. This gives stability to the layout and a reference point for the eye.

WORKING UP THE DESIGN

The rough now requires 'working up'. This is a term which refers to lettering out sample lines which one hopes will fit the working layout. The rough needs to work at actual size before the finished card can be lettered. From the small rough, an intelligent guess can be made as to the nib sizes to use by multiplying the stroke width by two, remembering the roughs were half size. Here a B4 nib has been used for the display lettering and an Italic medium for the main text.

The layout is divided into three main parts, starting with the person's name and the words of the invitation itself, then the event, and finally the venue. The main display line holds the text together and determines how large the main copy can be.

It is first necessary to draw up the card area and borders on a sheet of layout paper, but full-size this time. Start by lettering the display heading in an informal script with the B4 on a separate piece of layout paper, having first marked out the guidelines by stepping off nib widths, then drawing in the lines with a sharp 2H pencil. Once this has been lettered it should be measured against the layout, to check that the line length is correct. If it is overrunning the measure, an adjustment to letter and word spacing may avoid changing to a smaller nib.

Once the heading fits satisfactorily, the main text is then tackled. Step off the nib widths and draw in the guidelines.

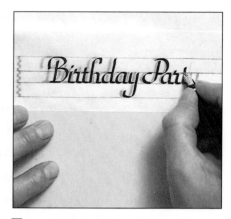

1 Drawing up the card area.

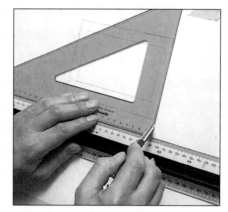

4 Closing up the letter spacing.

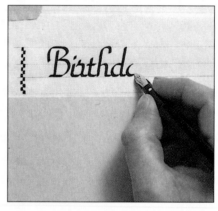

2 Lettering 'Birthday Party' using guidelines.

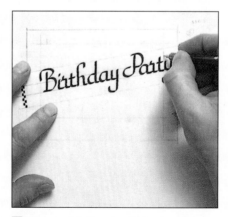

5 Checking that the words fit the text area.

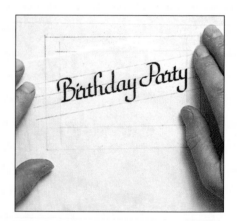

3 The words being checked against the text area for line length.

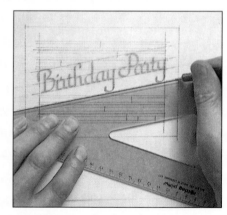

6 Positioning 'Birthday Party' and marking out guidelines.

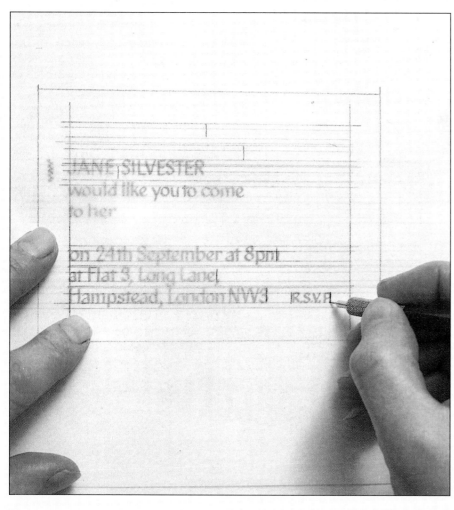

Allow a half nib-width interlinear space in the event of descenders and ascenders clashing and also leave space between the first three lines and the second three lines. After lettering the text, compare it to the layout and mark off the guidelines from the top margin for the first batch of text and from the foot margin for the second. A vertical pencil mark at the end of each line will help to gauge if lines and letters clash when the Italic line is checked against the layout.

Position the heading between the two sections of text. If it is found that there is insufficient room, use some of the extra space from the foot margin by lowering the second batch of copy. Once the position of the Italic has been established, the guidelines should be transferred to the layout sheet.

A working layout now exists, although admittedly it consists of guidelines only. It is prudent to letter in the text by tracing over the existing lines of copy before turning to the production of the finished card. There may still be some modifications to make; after all the preliminary work it is satisfying to see the completed working layout.

On viewing the finished layout, you may decide to range the 'RSVP' to the right so that it aligns with the 'y' in 'party'. This could be visually more pleasing.

7 Using a second sheet of tracing paper over the lettered text to mark off line lengths.

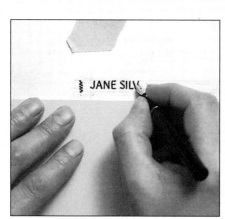

8 Beginning to letter the text.

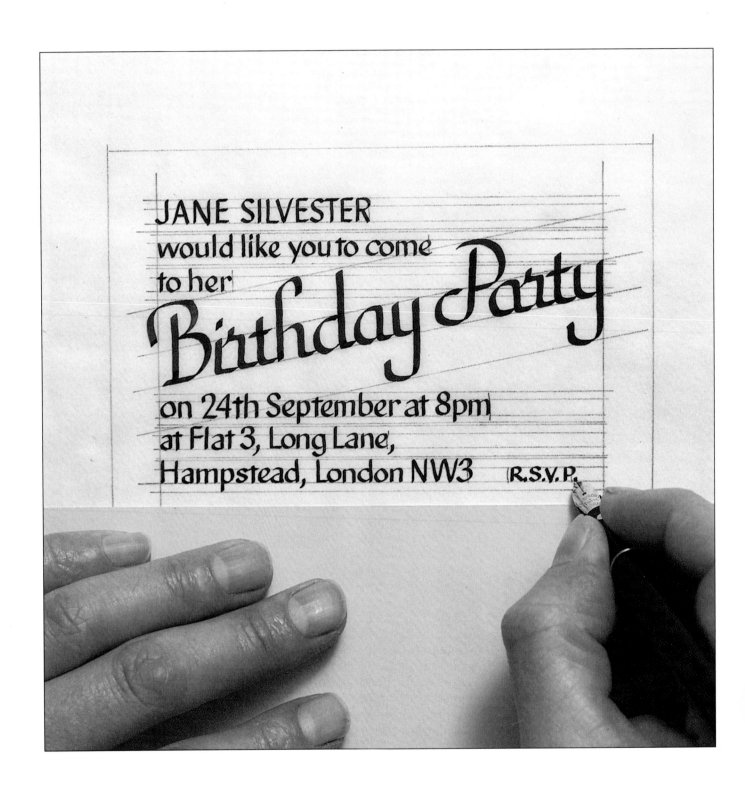

JANE SILVESTER
would like you to come
to her
Birthday Party

on 24th September at 8pm
at Flat 3, Long Lane,
Hampstead, London NW3   R.S.V.P.

RIGHT The finished working layout.

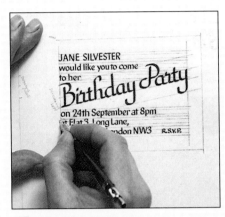

☐1 Taking measurements from the working layout.

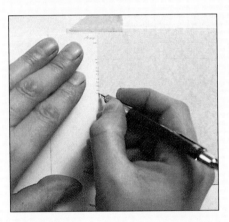

☐2 Transferring guidelines to the workpiece using a marker gauge.

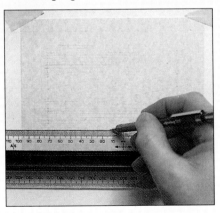

☐3 Drawing guidelines on to the workpiece.

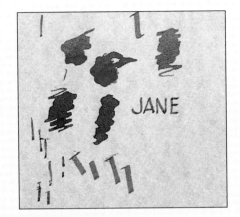

☐4 Testing various inks for colour compatability.

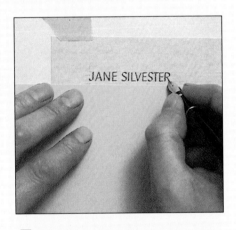

☐5 Lettering out the text using a guard sheet to keep the work surface clean.

TRANSFERRING THE DESIGN

The designed layout is then ready to be transferred to the chosen card, which must be slightly larger than the finished size, with a minimum of ½in (12mm) selvedge all round, to allow for taping the card to the drawing board. It will be trimmed off when the work is completed. The card size, margin lines and guidelines should be drawn using an HB or H pencil, being careful not to gouge tramlines into the surface – a light line is all that is required. First draw the format area, then, after stepping off the margins and guidelines on a strip of cartridge paper, transfer them to the card. The diagonal lines will have to be marked from both left- and right-hand margins.

Before beginning to letter, it is necessary to consider the colour in which the text will be written – black is hardly party-like. Here, a peach-coloured card has been chosen, with red ink for the words 'Birthday Party' and blue ink for the remaining text. A small piece of card was put to one side for trial lettering and colour checking. It is always useful to have an extra piece of the chosen material, because the action of the pen and ink may differ from surface to surface.

Position the card on the writing line, that is, the lettering position at which you feel comfortable on the board. Tape it into position and cover with a guard sheet, leaving only the first line visible. Taking the working layout, make a fold just above the x line and position it so that the first line is just below the descender line of the first guidelines on the card. Letter the line and repeat the procedure until all the lines have been worked.

It may help to reposition the piece of work after lettering the first three lines. For a small piece of work, where only a small deviation from the writing line is required, you may find it easier to move the guard downwards. However, when lettering a deep column of text it is better to leave the guard in the writing position and move the workpiece, which need not be taped to the drawing-board surface.

To letter the Italic line, the card should be turned until the text is horizontal to the writing line. The finished card should be put to one side to give the ink time to dry before removing the guidelines. This is done with a plastic eraser rather than a normal rubber eraser because it is kinder to both ink and lettering surface.

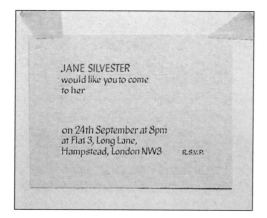

ABOVE The main text completed.

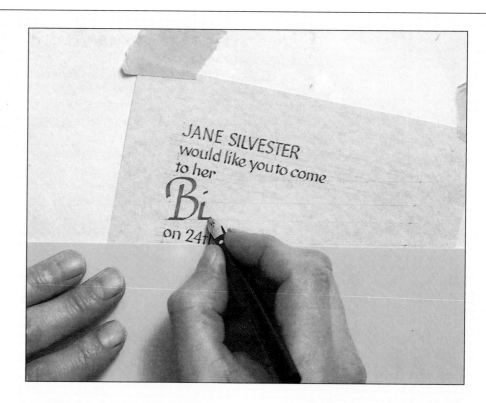

1 Lettering in 'Birthday Party'.

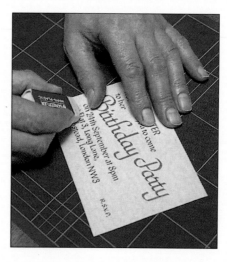

2 Erasing the guidelines once the ink has thoroughly dried.

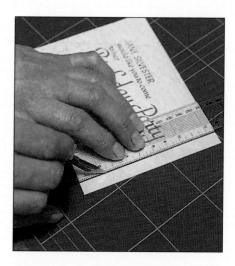

3 Trimming the card to size, with a blade, on the waste side of the ruler.

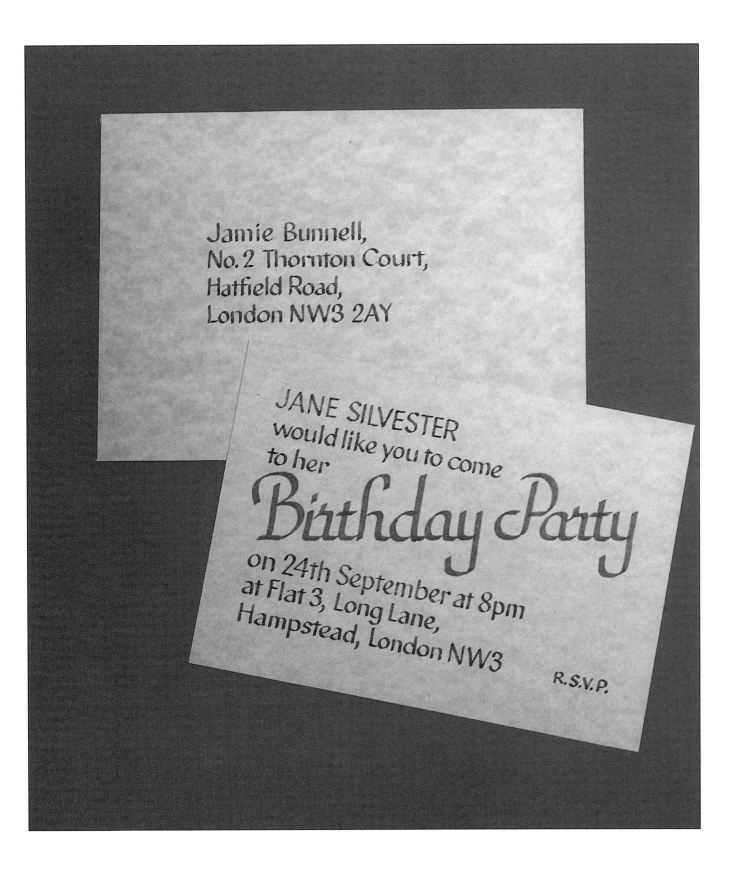

Jamie Bunnell,
No. 2 Thornton Court,
Hatfield Road,
London NW3 2AY

JANE SILVESTER
would like you to come
to her

Birthday Party

on 24th September at 8pm
at Flat 3, Long Lane,
Hampstead, London NW3

R.S.V.P.

LEFT The finished invitation and envelope.

Using a centred layout

The centred layout has an air of authority; it makes the work look official and precise. In order to illustrate the processes involved in producing such a layout, the subject chosen here is invariably displayed in a symmetrical format – the certificate.

Calligraphers are often asked to produce certificates for various organizations. Such requests can be of a one-off nature – a long-service certificate for example – or more commonly a series, when the awards for one major event are divided into sections and then sub-divided into first, second and third placings, etc. This type of certificate can be extremely complicated to lay out: because of the many copy changes, it can be difficult to obtain an overall style which is echoed in each certificate. The copy is made up from both static and variable information.

Again, ask that all important question: what is the function of the piece of work? It is, in this example, as an accolade for achievement, for winning first place in a wine-tasting competition, and the certificate will probably be framed and displayed on a living room wall.

The size of the certificate is $9\frac{1}{2}$in (240mm) by $7\frac{1}{8}$in (183m) and the text area should allow generous margins all round it. For this example, allow $1\frac{1}{2}$ units for the head and sides with 2 units at the foot. This gives $1\frac{1}{16}$in (27mm) and $1\frac{7}{16}$in (36mm) respectively (one unit being based on one tenth of the width), with a text area of $6\frac{7}{8}$in (176mm) deep and a measure width of $5\frac{1}{8}$in (129mm).

PLANNING THE LAYOUT

The copy must then be analyzed, coded 1, 2, 3 and so on in order of importance (see page 146), with any line breaks marked. The various code numbers will relate to different-sized nibs. Some pencil roughs based on the line breaks and order of importance are then sketched out. As with the invitation card, the roughs will be at either half- or third-size, just to get the feel of the words and line lengths. They need to be fairly accurate as the lettering will be used to help decide on the nib sizes required.

In a series of certificates such as these, it is necessary to use the largest amount of copy for each of the changeable areas to ensure that they will all fit into the same format. For instance, one of the other sections is just 'Aperitif Section'. It would be pointless producing a layout which allows for this one-line heading; 'The Medium Red Table Wine Section' could not fit within the same area. Likewise,

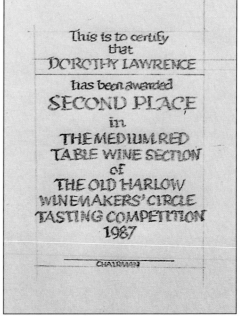

An initial thumbnail rough is produced to get a feel of the line length and copy.

Deciding on the priorities to be given to lines of text.

the longest name, Dorothy Lawrence, must be selected and the longest placing, which is 'second'.

Although the original copy supplied may have been typed out in a mixture of capitalized words and words in upper and lower case, as it was in this example, it is the function of the calligrapher to decide upon the visual balance. Those words that should be in capitals have been underlined and superfluous words have been dropped.

From roughs it is necessary to decide which one will form the basis of the working layout. The lettered stroke widths for each size need scaling up to full size and allocating accordingly. You could, for example, choose to use the following nib sizes which relate to the codes on the copy: code 1 means a B2 nib; code 2 Italic broad; code 3 Italic medium; and code 4 Italic fine. When using a fountain-type pen, it helps to have enough barrels to eliminate the changing of the nib.

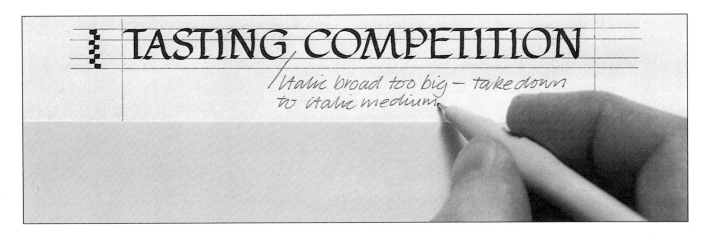

LEFT A decision must be made as to which nib size to use.

THE WORKING LAYOUT

The working layout should initially be ranged left so that you can see if the nib sizes chosen will fit the measure. Draw up the text area, 6⅞in (176mm) by 5⅛in (129mm), on a layout sheet. Take the tightest line of the chosen rough as a starting point. Some lines will fall short of the measure and are of little concern from a fitting point. Here, the longest line is 'Tasting Competition' and, as the test line, it must be lettered first.

On the same layout sheet as the text area, but above it, the measure requires marking, together with the guidelines for the Italic broad nib. The test line must be lettered to check on the width it will make. It appears just to fit, but it will be safer to drop a nib size for the whole of the section from 'The Old Harlow' to '1987'. The layout could be overpowered by this medium if it is left in its present size, but it would be best to leave 'THE MEDIUM RED TABLE WINE SECTION' in the Italic broad.

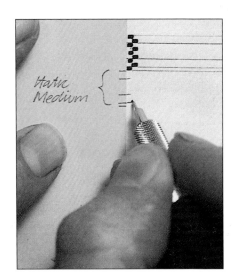

LEFT Marking out the first two lines of lettering.

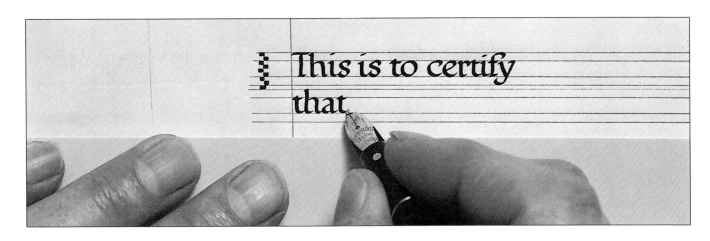

LEFT Lettering.

It is then possible to commence with the working layout. At this point, the depth that the text will have is unknown; so, by returning to the rough, it can be seen that it is unlikely to overrun, provided the space allocated is adhered to. Start by lettering the first two lines, allowing a nib-width of interlinear space. As the layout progresses, you will be shown how to arrive at line spaces between sections of text. Note down the size of nib for each line of text as a reminder when lettering the finished certificate.

On completing the first two lines, a decision has to be made as to how much space to leave between the base line of 'that' and the cap line of the name. All three lines are related phrases and, as such, should be treated similarly with interlinear space, but, as 'Dorothy Lawrence' is in a larger letterform and in capitals, the space must be optically changed to compensate for the extra area that capital letters occupy. It should be at least equivalent to the space between the base line of 'This is to certify' and the x line of 'that'.

Once lettered, the name requires underscoring with a line. It may be that the name will be filled in after the certificates are lettered, in which case don't limit the length of line to the extent of name and settle for the line being contained by the measure. As to the position of the line, there is nothing worse than underscored words which have a line so far beneath them as not to belong to the word. Here, the rule (line) is positioned two nib widths below the base line. What if the name were in upper and lower case? No problem – split the rule either side of the descender and place it closer to the base line.

Between the rule and 'has been awarded', repeat the unit of space used before, although this may need changing slightly because there are four ascending letters in the line. The spacing of the lines throughout the remaining copy will be based on this unit of space. Where there is more than one line of capitals, insert one nib width of interlinear space, using the nib being employed to letter those particular lines. Once the whole copy has been lettered and a depth arrived at, further alterations can be made if necessary.

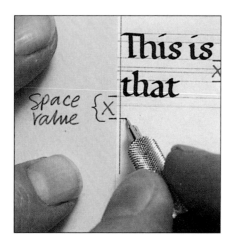
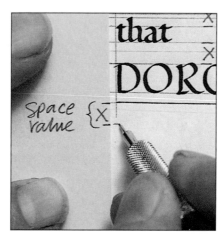

ABOVE Deciding on a space value.

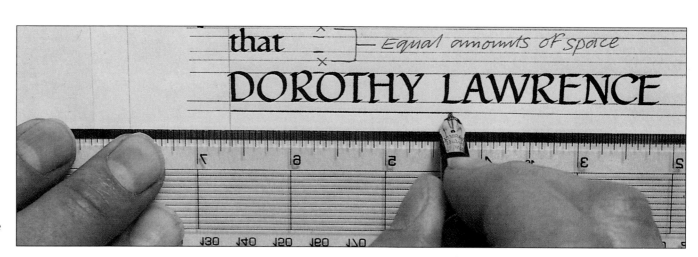

RIGHT Underscoring using the edge of the nib against an inverted rule.

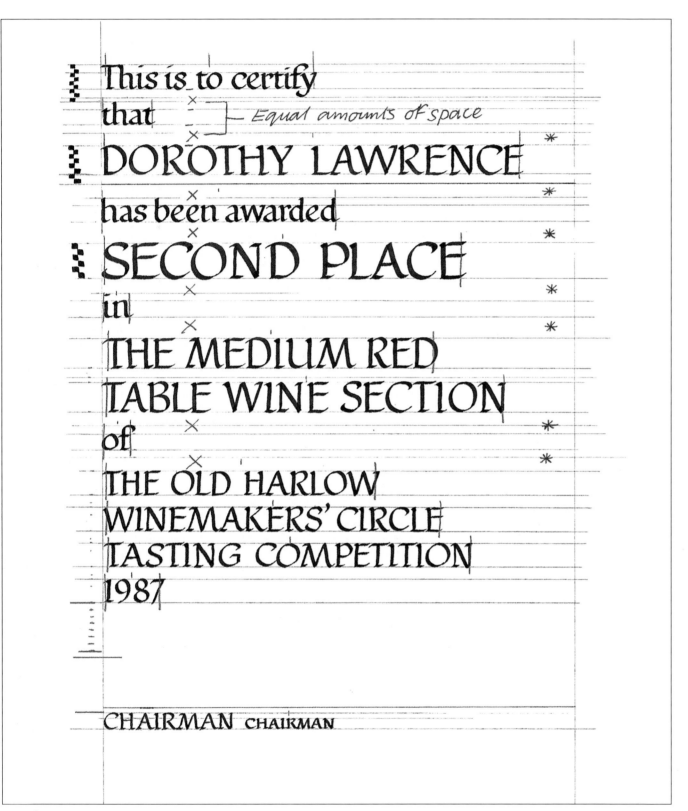

This is to certify
that   — Equal amounts of space
DOROTHY LAWRENCE   *
has been awarded   *
SECOND PLACE   *
in   *
THE MEDIUM RED   *
TABLE WINE SECTION   *
of   *
THE OLD HARLOW
WINEMAKERS' CIRCLE
TASTING COMPETITION
1987

CHAIRMAN CHAIRMAN

LEFT The finished working layout shows that extra space will be added where marked with an asterisk. The pencil lines at both ends of each line of text indicate the optical length necessary when centring the text.

Having reached the signature line, you may prefer to write the word in small capitals as opposed to the Italic fine capitals. They are drawn with the same nib but the height is limited to the x line. Small capitals can often be seen following a person's name when Honours or Degree letters are present.

The space that is left between '1987' and the rule for the signature can be halved and ample space will still be left for the signature. Take half of the present space and divide it by eight with one-eighth of the space being inserted as extra interlinear space in the seven asterisk positions marked.

CENTRING

The working layout is almost complete. In order to centre the lines on the finished certificate, it is necessary to ascertain the centre of each line of lettering or, to be more precise, the optical centre. The end of each line should be marked as if the work were to be ranged left and right, that is, the part of the first and last letter of each line which would rest on the margin line to give vertical alignment. Show these lines in pencil on the working layout.

Once the lines are marked, the length can either be measured and then halved and marked in pencil or the lines of the layout can be cut up and each line held up to the light, loosely folded until both ends of the line meet, then pinched in the centre to give a firm crease. This method is better employed where one-off pieces of work are concerned. For repeated lettering, such as certificates, it is best to keep the original layout intact as pieces of paper have an odd way of disappearing just when they are needed most. If you do decide to use the cutting method, make sure that you have made a depth gauge for the work before slicing your finished working layout into strips.

From the working layout, two gauges must be prepared: a depth gauge showing the full depth of the work, head and foot margins and each line of lettering in its correct position, together with the nib sizes and any additional

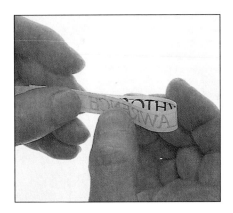

ABOVE Centring by the folding and creasing method.

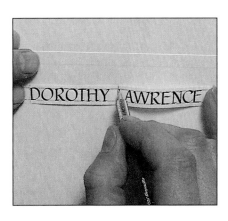

ABOVE Marking the centre crease.

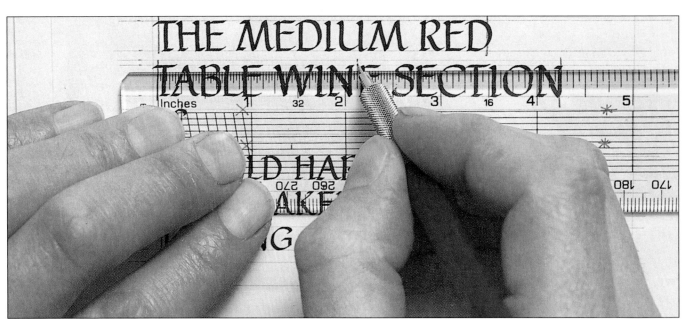

RIGHT Finding the centre by measuring with a ruler.

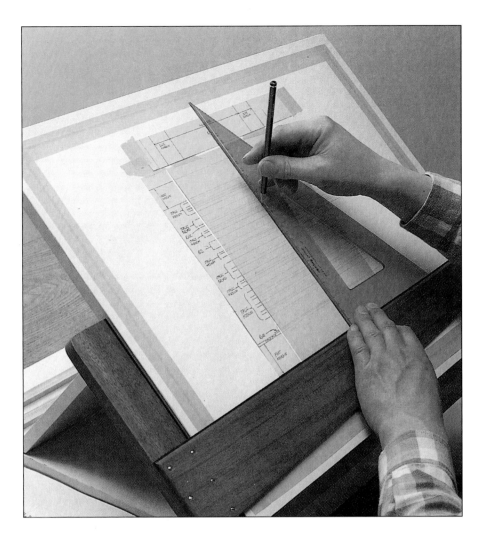

Transferring the guidelines to the finished surface.

A portion of the depth gauge used.

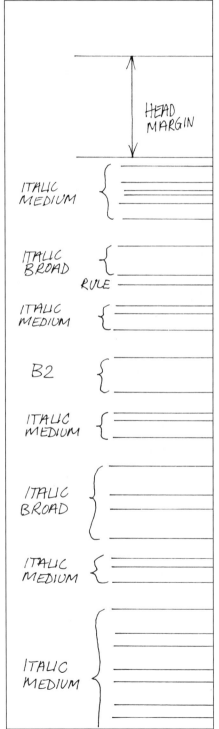

information that may be required; and a width gauge showing the side margins, measure and centre line (C/L) and any other items that are felt necessary. Each time a certificate requires marking out, the process is simplified considerably by using gauges. Naturally, the system can be used for any type of work which needs the same information to be transferred repeatedly to a finished workpiece. The gauges are taped on to the drawing board in a position above and to the left of the workpiece. All the lines are transferred to the finished working surface in H or HB pencil. The sheet to be lettered must have a paper guard to prevent it from getting dirty.

THE FINAL STAGE

Before commencing final lettering, consider the question of colour. Here a sandy-coloured paper with black and red lettering has been chosen after producing a small rough just to confirm which lines will appear in red. This rough has been produced with fine-tipped, water-soluble fibre pens which do not bleed (spread) on the paper. Only the name and placing is in red, because to include the section as well makes the layout bottom-heavy.

To use the working layout as a guide, fold it over so that the ascenders of the first line of text are on the creased edge. Then slip it behind the guard sheet with the centre line of the first line of text registered (positioned) with the centre line of the sheet to be lettered so that the guidelines are visible. Begin lettering with the appropriate pen at the start of the line shown on the working layout.

This process is repeated until the finished certificate is lettered; the layout sheet is folded each time and the finished work surface raised for each line to be lettered.

Once the certificate is completed, allow a little time to elapse before attempting to erase the guidelines. Many a fine piece of lettering has been ruined by students who are too anxious to see the finished product.

ABOVE A small rough to show colour.

RIGHT Lettering the finished certificate.

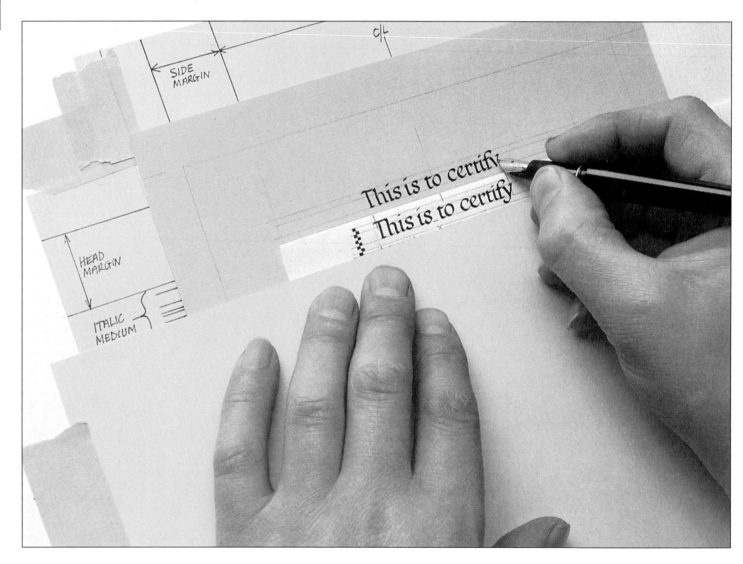

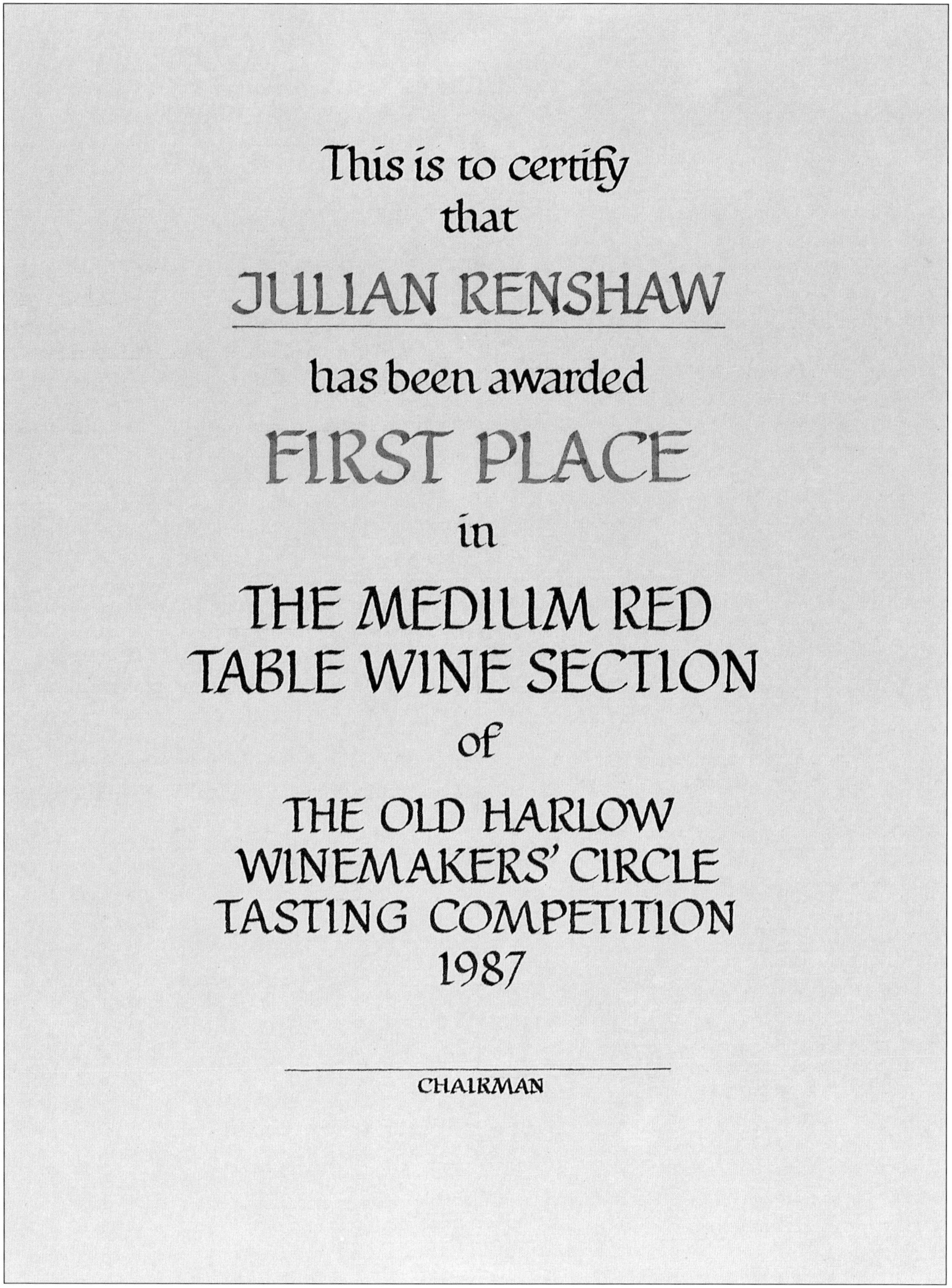

This is to certify
that

JULIAN RENSHAW

has been awarded

FIRST PLACE

in

THE MEDIUM RED
TABLE WINE SECTION

of

THE OLD HARLOW
WINEMAKERS' CIRCLE
TASTING COMPETITION
1987

_____
CHAIRMAN

LEFT The finished certificate.

Using words as images

Words not only convey information but suggest images. Language itself is born of the double need to communicate ideas in both a direct and vivid way, colouring meaning with imagery. Calligraphy, the art of writing, can add an important visual dimension.

English is a particularly rich and potent language, drawing its inheritance from a variety of sources. Through the centuries, many linguistic streams have intermingled, giving us a wonderfully precise, varied and expressive vocabulary. Poetry and prose use all these dimensions of language, capturing the sound, meaning and association of words so they resonate in the mind.

Calligraphy, with its ability to enhance words by using different styles, forms and colours, is a perfect vehicle for exploring this vocabulary further in a visual way. For instance, 'water' written in a flowing Italic hand is perhaps more evocative than water written in stiff, upright capitals.

Each style of writing has its historical connotations and its personal, interpretive qualities. For instance, Gothic is traditionally a medieval book hand, but it could be used now in a personal, idiosyncratic way to suggest other possibilities, such as fantasy or drama. Similarly with colour: certain colours have traditional and cultural associations – yellow with warmth, red with fire, green with growth, and so on. But painters can also use colour in different contexts and juxtapositions to further their vision. Painters are aware of their historical sources, but each will have a palette that is personally significant. The same is true of the calligrapher, who in some respects is a painter with words.

The traditional way to become a calligrapher is first to study historical manuscript hands. In understanding the shapes of letterforms and the influences that tools and materials have had on determining those shapes, and by the actual process of writing, calligraphers gradually evolve their own interpretations of those letters and invent new ones. By acquiring a repertoire of different styles of writing and by understanding the structure of the forms in each style, their significant aspects and inherent potential for development, so the ability to communicate ideas effectively is expanded.

Through a process of exploration, assessing the seemingly accidental shapes of letters (remembering that the shapes also indicate sound), choose only those elements that are helpful to you in that instance. Each context is unique, and what is significant in one situation is not necessarily so in another.

LEFT Calligraphy can enhance words. These three versions of water each evoke a different response. To write it in blue, traditionally the symbolic colour of water, goes even further towards capturing the essence of the word – or rather, the perceived essence, as no two people see things in the same way.

LEFT Development of letterforms in an attempt to capture the essence of the words.

RIGHT Exploring the letters and assessing their shapes and sounds enables the calligrapher to choose the elements that are relevant.

RIGHT Shine can be developed so that the active flavour of the word is visually enhanced by exaggerating the vertical stress of the I (upright lines symbolize the active principle — humans stand vertically on a horizontal plain); the added rays burst forth from a central point, suggesting a shining star of light.

RIGHT The embellishment of shone reflects the past nature of the event where the emphasis has flowed to the outside circle. If the rays are removed the resonance of the symbolism may still be absorbed subconsciously.

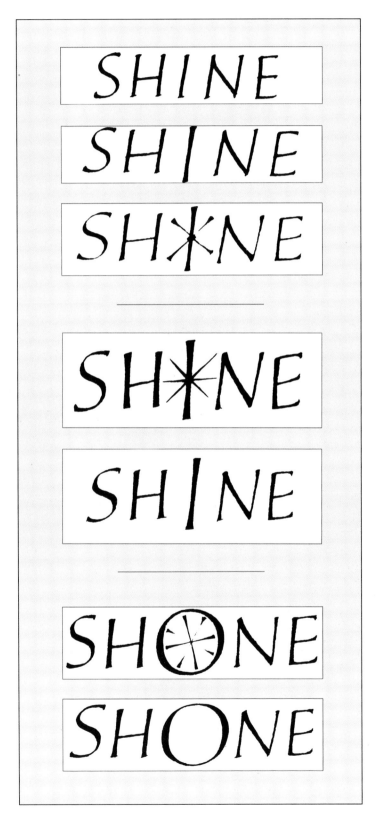

But are the shapes of letters accidental? The English language evolved mainly from Latinate and Germanic roots. From the Latin, our intellectual words are derived: for example, consider, circumstance, recognition. Many of these are compound words changing and expanding their meaning with different components. From the Germanic languages come the emotive, monosyllabic sounds: for example, grind, grieve, groan; slip, slide, sling and slink. Some of these words have obvious onomatopoeic origins.

However, there are also many etymological theories. One of these concerns vowel sound groupings. The more active and present the verb, the sharper and thinner the vowel sound: for example, sink, sank, sunk; drink, drank, drunk. Thus, shine and shone could be developed as illustrated.

Obviously, careful thought and discrimination are needed in developing letters and words in this way, as interpretation can obscure the text as well as reveal it. However, as with playing a musical instrument or reading a play, any rendering necessitates personal intervention, and in the end perhaps all we can do is believe in what we do and be as truthful as we can to our own vision of the words, though this may change as we explore.

More important, in the actual process of exploration and experimenting with the letters and words in order to portray them on the page, we discover more about the words themselves. We bring our own insights, experiences and discoveries to the making of them, and in this way find out more about how and what we think. So, exploring words can also be a way of exploring ourselves.

Illustrations

When combining illustration with calligraphy, it is important to create harmony between both elements. The illustration should reflect the square-edged pen, as do many early manuscripts, with line drawings making full use of the implement and the varied stroke widths it will produce. Textures can be built up by cross hatching (strokes in opposing directions) or by moving the pen angle from a thin stroke gradually through to a thick stroke position and vice-versa, giving a vignetted (gentle graduation of) line weight.

There is no easy way to learn how to draw with a square nib, and if you do not regard yourself as an illustrator the only way to succeed is by involvement and practice. One of the best things to do is to look at photographic and printed references.

Once you have an idea of what image you want to use to accompany a piece of calligraphy, search through your own books, photographs and pamphlets, or through those in your local library for suitable images. Searching for material will heighten your awareness of the images you see every day. A scrapbook of likely subject matter is a wonderful idea and takes very little time to add to each week. References should be as detailed as possible so that new images can readily and accurately be created from them at any opportunity.

Once the necessary references have been found, you will need to transfer them to tracing paper. If the size of the illustration required is the same as that of the reference material, it can be traced directly on to the tracing paper, using a 2H or H pencil (or lead in a technical pencil). Take care to interpret the image exactly, because what is produced on the tracing sheet will be the image traced down on to the finished piece of work. Once the tracing is completed, the sheet must be turned over and the underside of the drawing area shaded over with an HB pencil. Turn the tracing paper over again so that the image side faces upwards and position it on the finished surface of the work using masking tape at the head (top) to hold it gently in place. Then trace the drawing down by going over the lines of the image using a hard, sharp pencil, 2H or 4H. When completed, lift the tracing sheet, without unfastening, to make sure that the drawing has been successfully transferred to the finished surface. The faint image must now be inked in with a fine, square-ended nib. Build up the image slowly, referring to the original reference for the finer points.

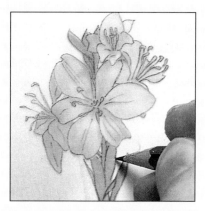
1 Tracing the image to be used from illustrative reference.

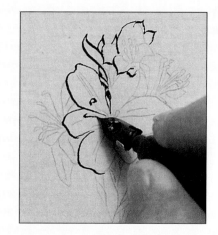
4 Inking in the initial outline.

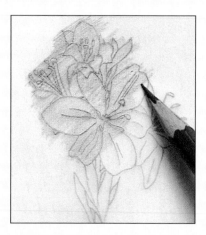
2 Shading over the underside of the tracing.

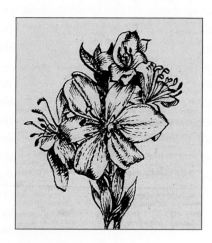
5 The finished illustration.

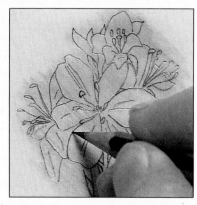
3 Tracing the image on to the finished surface.

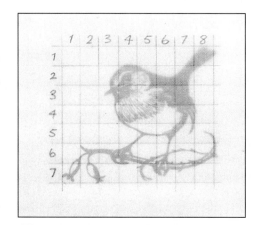

1 Confining the illustration to a gridded square on tracing paper.

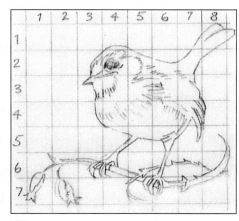

4 Building up the illustration.

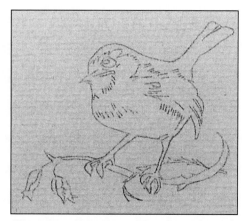

7 Traced image on finished surface.

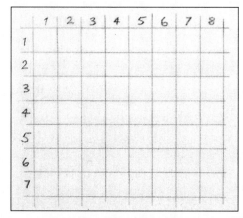

2 Drawing a gridded square to the required enlargement.

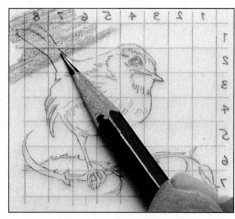

5 Shading over the underside of the tracing.

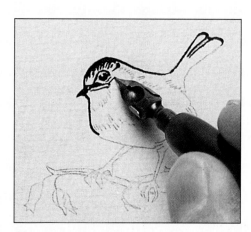

8 Inking in the initial outline.

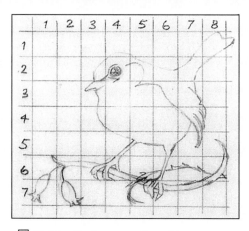

3 Plotting the image on the grid.

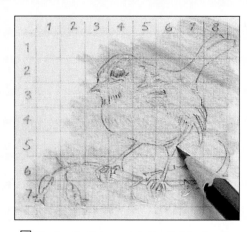

6 Tracing the image on to the finished surface.

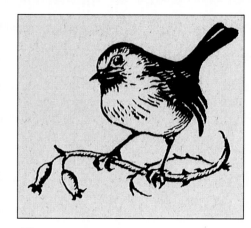

9 The finished illustration.

RIGHT AND LEFT GEORGE EVANS
— Some designs which have been
used for bookmarks and Christmas
cards.

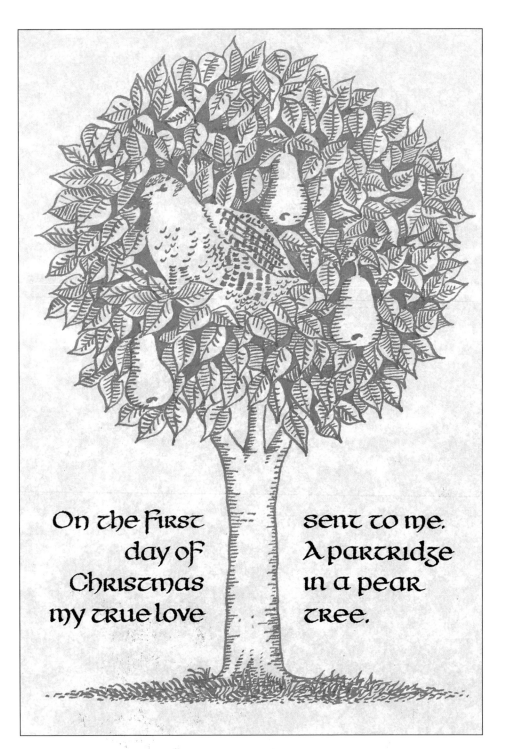

On the First
day of
Christmas
my true love

sent to me.
A partridge
in a pear
tree.

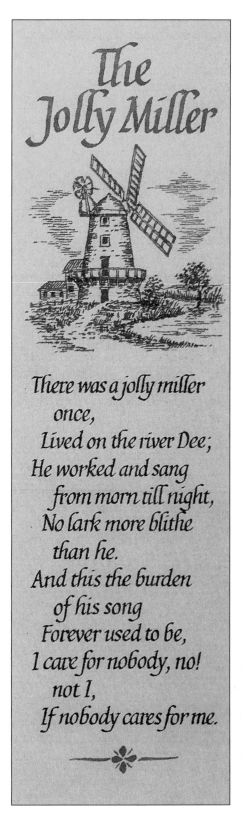

The
Jolly Miller

There was a jolly miller
once,
Lived on the river Dee;
He worked and sang
from morn till night,
No lark more blithe
than he.
And this the burden
of his song
Forever used to be,
I care for nobody, no!
not I,
If nobody cares for me.

Should the reference material found not be the correct size for the design, then it will be necessary either to enlarge or reduce the image. First contain the illustration within a square or rectangle on a sheet of tracing paper, subdividing this by small grid squares. The size required should then be drawn as a square or rectangle on another sheet and subdivided as before. Number the squares horizontally and vertically on both sheets of paper and plot your image from the reference material to the correctly-sized grid.

BELOW GEORGE EVANS — Signs of the zodiac. Some have been taken from English and German woodcuts and adapted for the pen. The Crab, Scorpion and Scales are the calligrapher's additions, as the originals were not suitable to be contained within a circle. The shading in the lower portion was necessary to give a uniformity to the twelve symbols.

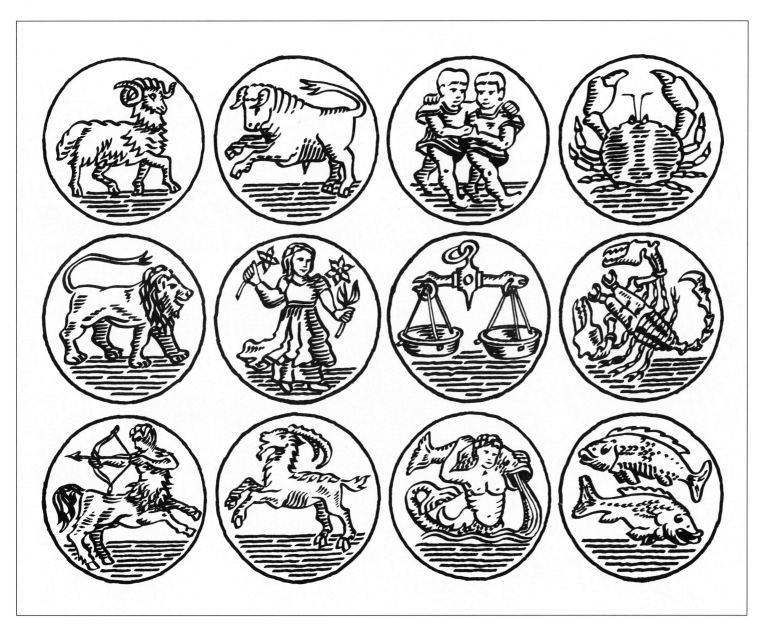

Bookbinding

The binding of a book protects the pages and enables them to open. A delicate book, made from Japanese tissue can be protected by a delicate cover. This is because the tissue and the materials are compatible in strength. As a result the reader respects the book's fragility.

JAPANESE TISSUE BINDING

This book is adapted from the *Fukuro-toji* style. The book is made square to accommodate a letter of the alphabet on each page. The letters are painted in watercolour on the Japanese tissue.

One sheet of *koju-shi* tissue will make 12 leaves. Each leaf is double thickness with the fold at the foredge. This makes only 24 pages, so that four of the letters, such as **I** and **J** or **T** and **U** need to be paired up to save using another sheet of tissue.

Japanese tissue is made on a mould constructed from slates of bamboo tied together, which makes laid lines and chain lines similar to those in Western paper. This tissue is assumed to have a short grain direction, running parallel with the chain lines. As with all books the paper is cut so that the grain direction is parallel with the spine.

When the pages are cut and folded, fit the book neatly inside the cover by knocking up the edges on the work bench. Mark a line ¼–⅜in (6–10mm) in from the spine and mark four holes along this line: one at the head and one at the tail (these should be the same distance from the edge as from the spine; the other two holes spaced evenly between them).

Use a pair of dividers to set the distance. Pierce the holes with a thin awl. Thread a needle with the mercerized cotton and knot the thread on to the needle.

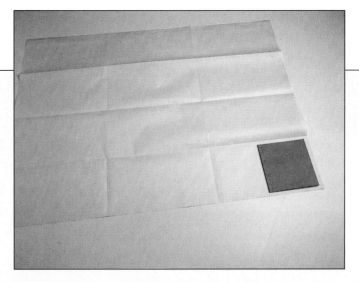

1 Fold a sheet of tissue 35 × 25½in (89 × 65cm) into 12.

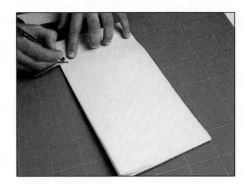

2 Trim it to 11 × 5½in (28 × 14cm). Cut one long edge, mark a line 5½in (14cm) from it and cut.

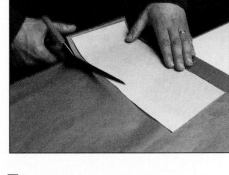

4 Use a page as a template, take some scissors and roughly cut out coloured tissue for the cover. It should be double the size of the template.

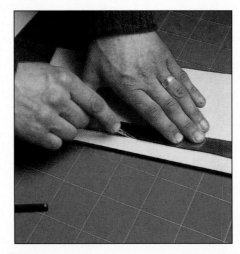

3 The short edges can be cut square using the lines on a cutting mat or with a set square.

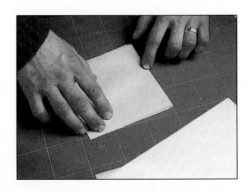

5 Fold all the pages and the cover in half.

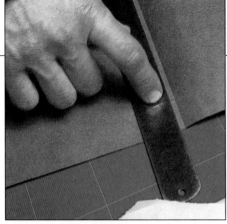

6 Make a second fold in the cover to allow for the thickness of the pages.

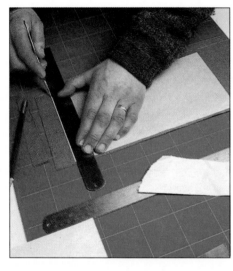

7 Use an open page to cut the cover on long edges and at 11in (28cm) from centre folds.

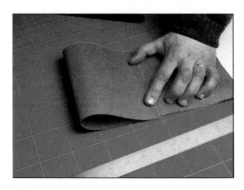

8 Fold the cover in to the central folds.

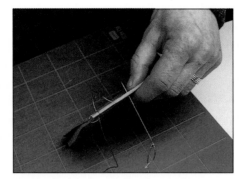

9 Work the sewing in a figure of eight, tensioning the thread as you go. Finish by tying a reef knot.

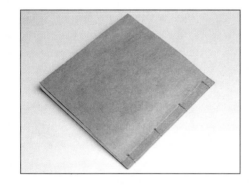

10 The finished book.

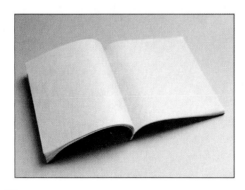

11 The stab-stitching restricts the book's opening. Take this into account when spacing letters.

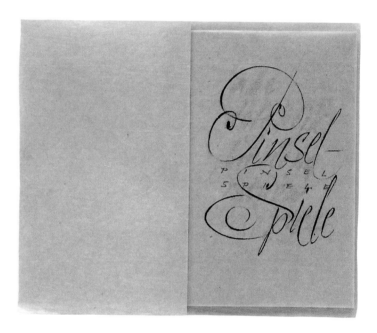

ABOVE KARL GEORG HOEFER — The title page of this small manuscript book reflects its delicate and tactile nature. A fine lightweight paper has been chosen to make the text book. Through these pages preceding and succeeding alphabets can be glimpsed. The book contains a visual feast of personal calligraphic alphabets. An alphabet book such as this should grace every calligrapher's bookshelf – a personal exploration and rendering of elegant calligraphy displayed on well laid out pages, all in a beautifully handmade book.

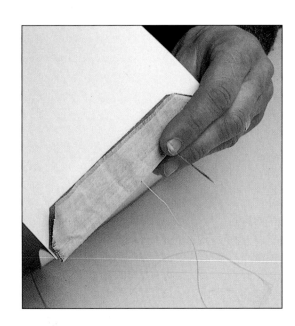

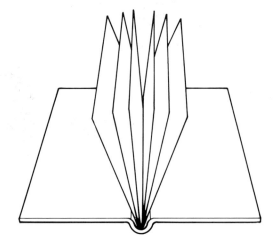

1 A strip of thin leather, reinforced by a strip of aerolinen is sewn on to the pages using a figure of eight stitch.

2 The cover opens out separately from the pages, which are held only by the thread.

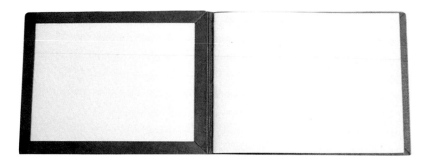

3 With the cover open flat the leather strip is pasted out with starch paste. It forms a 45° mitred joint with the leather turn-ins of the cover.

4 The structure of the book.

SINGLE-SECTION BINDING

Combining the weak pages of a single-section binding with a tough cover made from millboard and leather can be a problem. One possible solution is to use thread to act as the only hinge between the two. In this way one can avoid creating a tension between the pages and the cover when the book opens.

MULTI-SECTION BINDING

The purpose of a design binding is to attract the reader. The cover is a vehicle for the binder's self-expression. The binding itself needs to be protected in a box.

The problem of making the soft watercolour paper compatible with heavy boards and leather is solved by sewing each fold of paper on to strong, flexible supports, linen tapes, which are in turn attached to the boards. The linen tapes act as the hinges for the boards, rather than the leather. The leather has no part in the structure of the binding. The linen tapes also act as a flexible backbone for the pages so that they can open out flat.

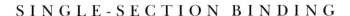

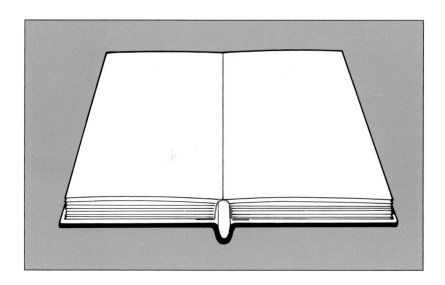

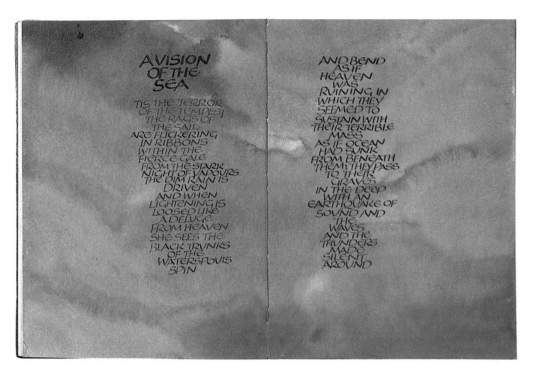

A VISION
OF THE
SEA

TIS THE TERROR
OF THE TEMPEST
THE RAGS OF
THE SAIL
ARE FLICKERING
IN RIBBONS
WITHIN THE
FIERCE GALE
FROM THE STARK
NIGHT OF VAPOURS
THE DIM RAIN IS
DRIVEN
AND WHEN
LIGHTENING IS
LOOSED LIKE
A DELUGE
FROM HEAVEN
SHE SEES THE
BLACK TRUNKS
OF THE
WATERSPOUTS
SPIN

AND BEND
AS IF
HEAVEN
WAS
RUINING IN
WHICH THEY
SEEMED TO
SUSTAIN WITH
THEIR TERRIBLE
MASS
AS IF OCEAN
HAD SUNK
FROM BENEATH
THEM THEY PASS
TO THEIR
GRAVES
IN THE DEEP
WITH AN
EARTHQUAKE OF
SOUND AND
THE
WAVES
AND THE
THUNDERS
MADE
SILENT
AROUND

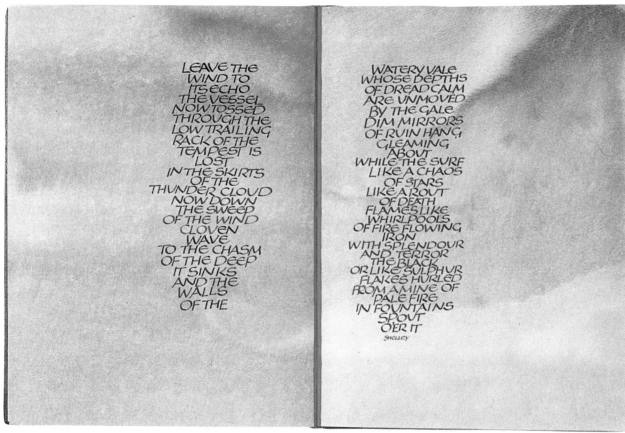

LEAVE THE
WIND TO
ITS ECHO
THE VESSEL
NOW TOSSED
THROUGH THE
LOW TRAILING
RACK OF THE
TEMPEST IS
LOST
IN THE SKIRTS
OF THE
THUNDER CLOUD
NOW DOWN
THE SWEEP
OF THE WIND
CLOVEN
WAVE
TO THE CHASM
OF THE DEEP
IT SINKS
AND THE
WALLS
OF THE

WATERY VALE
WHOSE DEPTHS
OF DREAD CALM
ARE UNMOVED
BY THE GALE
DIM MIRRORS
OF RUIN HANG
GLEAMING
ABOUT
WHILE THE SURF
LIKE A CHAOS
OF STARS
LIKE A ROUT
OF DEATH
FLAMES LIKE
WHIRLPOOLS
OF FIRE FLOWING
IRON
WITH SPLENDOUR
AND TERROR
THE BLACK
OR LIKE SULPHUR
FLAKES HURLED
FROM A MINE OF
PALE FIRE
IN FOUNTAINS
SPOUT
O'ER IT
SHELLEY

ABOVE AND LEFT WILLIAM TAUNTON — The calligraphy is written in dark blue watercolour on 300gsm (140lb) watercolour paper over multi-coloured watercolour washes.

Glossary

ARCH The part of a LOWER-CASE letter formed by a curve springing from the STEM of the letter, as in **h, m, n.**

ASCENDER The rising stroke of a LOWER-CASE letter.

BASE LINE Also called the writing line, this is the level on which a line of writing rests, giving a fixed reference for the relative heights of letter and the drop of DESCENDERS.

BLACKLETTER The term for the dense, angular writing of the GOTHIC period.

BODY HEIGHT The height of the basic form of a LOWER-CASE letter, not including the extra length of ASCENDERS or DESCENDERS.

BOOK HAND Any style of alphabet commonly used in book production before the age of printing.

BOUSTROPHEDON An arrangement of lines of writing, used by the Greeks, in which alternate lines run in opposite directions.

BOWL The part of a letter formed by curved strokes attaching to the main STEM and enclosing a COUNTER, as in **R, P, a, b.**

BROADSHEET A design in calligraphy contained on a single sheet of paper, vellum or parchment.

BUILT-UP LETTERS Letters formed by drawing rather than writing, or having modifications to the basic form of the structural pen strokes.

CALLIGRAM Words or lines of writing arranged to construct a picture or design.

CAROLINGIAN SCRIPT The first standard MINUSCULE script, devised by Alcuin of York under the direction of the Emperor Charlemagne at the end of the eighth century.

CHANCERY CURSIVE A form of ITALIC script used by the scribes of the papal Chancery in Renaissance Italy, also known as *cancellaresca.*

CHARACTER A typographic term to describe any letter, punctuation mark or symbol commonly used in typesetting.

CODEX A book made up of folded and/or bound leaves forming successive pages.

COLOPHON An inscription at the end of a hand-written book giving details of the date, place, scribe's name or other such relevant information.

COUNTER The space within a letter wholly or partially enclosed by the lines of the letterform, within the BOWL of **P**, for example.

CROSS-STROKE A horizontal stroke essential to the SKELETON form of a letter, as in **E, F, T.**

CUNEIFORM The earliest systematic form of writing, taking its name from the wedge-shaped strokes made when inscribing on soft clay.

CURSIVE A handwriting form where letters are fluidly formed and joined, without pen lifts.

DEMOTIC SCRIPT The informal SCRIPT of the Egyptians, following on from HIEROGLYPHS and HIERATIC SCRIPT.

DESCENDER The tail of a LOWER-CASE letter that drops below the BASELINE.

DIACRITICAL SIGN An accent or mark that indicates particular pronunciation.

DUCTUS The order of strokes followed in constructing a pen letter.

FACE (abb. **TYPEFACE**) The general term for an alphabet designed for typographic use.

FLOURISH An extended pen stroke or linear decoration used to embellish a basic letterform.

GESSO A smooth mixture of plaster and white lead bound in gum, which can be reduced to a liquid medium for writing or painting.

GILDING Applying gold leaf to an adhesive base to decorate a letter or ORNAMENT.

GOTHIC SCRIPT A broad term embracing a number of different styles of writing, characteristically angular and heavy, of the late medieval period.

HAND An alternative term for handwriting or SCRIPT, meaning lettering written by hand.

HAIRLINE The finest stroke of a pen, often used to create SERIFS and other finishing strokes, or decoration of a basic letterform.

HIERATIC SCRIPT The formal SCRIPT of the Ancient Egyptians.

HIEROGLYPHS The earliest form of writing used by the Ancient Egyptians, in which words were represented by pictorial symbols.

IDEOGRAM A written symbol representing a concept or abstract idea rather than an actual object.

ILLUMINATION The decoration of a MANUSCRIPT with gold leaf burnished to a high shine; the term is also used more broadly to describe decoration in gold and colours.

INDENT To leave space additional to the usual margin when beginning a line of writing, as in the opening of a paragraph.

IONIC SCRIPT The standard form of writing developed by the Greeks.

ITALIC Slanted forms of writing with curving letters based on an elliptical rather than circular model.

LAYOUT The basic plan of a two-dimensional design, showing spacing, organization of text, illustration and so on.

LOGO A word or combination of letters designed as a single unit, sometimes combined with a decorative or illustrative element; it may be used as a trademark, emblem or symbol.

LOWER-CASE Typographic term for 'small' letters as distinct from capitals, which are known in typography as upper case.

MAJUSCULE A capital letter.

MANUSCRIPT A term used specifically for a book or document written by hand rather than printed.

MASSED TEXT Text written in a heavy or compressed SCRIPT and with narrow spacing between words and lines.

MINUSCULE A 'small' or LOWER-CASE letter.

ORNAMENT A device or pattern used to decorate handwritten or printed text.

PALEOGRAPHY The study of written forms, including the general development of alphabets and particulars of handwritten manuscripts, such as date, provenance and so on.

PALIMPSEST A MANUSCRIPT from which a text has been erased and the writing surface used again.

PAPYRUS The earliest form of paper, a coarse material made by hammering together strips of fibre from the stem of the papyrus plant.

PARCHMENT Writing material prepared from the inner layer of a split sheepskin.

PHONOGRAM A written symbol representing a sound in speech.

PICTOGRAM A pictorial symbol representing a particular object or image.

RAGGED TEXT A page or column of writing with lines of different lengths, which are aligned at neither side.

RIVER The appearance of a vertical rift in a page of text, caused by an accidental, but consistent, alignment of word spaces on following lines.

ROMAN CAPITALS The formal alphabet of capital letters, devised by the Romans, which was the basis of most modern, western alphabet systems.

RUBRICATE To contrast or emphasize part or parts of a text by writing in red; for example headings, a prologue, a quotation.

RUSTIC CAPITALS An informal alphabet of capital letters used by the Romans, with letters elongated and rounded compared to the standard square ROMAN CAPITALS.

SANS SERIF A term denoting letters without SERIFS or finishing strokes.

SCRIPT Another term for writing by hand, often used to imply a CURSIVE style of writing.

SCRIPTORIUM A writing room, particularly that of a medieval monastery in which formal manuscripts were produced.

SERIF An abbreviated pen stroke or device used to finish the main stroke of a letterform; a HAIRLINE or hook, for example.

SKELETON LETTER The most basic form of a letter demonstrating its essential distinguishing characteristics.

STEM The main vertical stroke in a letterform.

TEXTURA A term for particular forms of GOTHIC SCRIPT that were so dense and regular as to appear to have a woven texture. *Textura* is a Latin word, meaning 'weave'.

TRANSITIONAL SCRIPT A letterform marking a change in style between one standard SCRIPT and the development of a new form.

UNCIAL A BOOK HAND used by the Romans and early Christians, typified by the heavy, squat form of the rounded **O.**

VELLUM Writing material prepared from the skin of a calf, having a particularly smooth, velvety texture.

VERSAL A large, decorative letter used to mark the opening of a line, paragraph or verse in a MANUSCRIPT.

WEIGHT A measurement of the relative size and thickness of a pen letter, expressed by the relationship of nib width to height.

WORD BREAK The device of hyphenating a word between syllables so it can be split into two sections to regulate line length in a text. Both parts, ideally, should be pronounceable.

X-HEIGHT Typographic term for BODY HEIGHT.

Index

Page numbers in *italics* represent illustrations

A

alignment 52
  exploring different 51, *51*
alphabets 71–142
  Bastarda 107, 124
  Blackletter 92–3, *92–3*, 95, 98, 100, 104
  Carolingian letters 86
  Copperplate alphabets 129–42, *129–42*
  Copperplate 125, 129–130, *129–130*
    flourishes *128*
    script 131, *131*
  flourished capitals 132–3, *132–3*, 140–1, *140–1*, 142, *142*
  flourished script letters 139, *139*
  Fraktur 98–9, *98–9*, 106, *128*
  Gothic alphabets 92–112, *92–112*
    cursive 94, *94*
    decorated capitals 104, *104*
    decorated minuscule 105, *105*
    fine, Gothic-style script 137, *137*
    flourished, capitals 108, *108*
    flourished, script 110, *110*
    Italian, *see* Rotunda
    majuscule 100–01, *100–01*
    modified 112, *112*
    modified, capitals 102–3, *102–3*
    modified, cursive – capitals 111, *111*
    modified, script 102–3, *102–3*
    ornamented, script 109, *109*
    round, *see* Rotunda
    skeleton, capitals 106, *106*
    skeleton, minuscule 107, *107*
    slanted 128, *128*
  Half-Gothic, *see* Rotunda
  Half-Uncial 81, *81*, 86
    English 84–5, *84–5*
  Humanistic scripts 121, 124
    cursive capitals 126–7, *126–7*
    revised, script 138, *138*

Italic alphabets 113–15, *113–15*, 113–128, *113–128*
  capitals 117, *117*
  compressed hand – capitals 120, *120*
  compressed hand – lower-case 119, *119*
  copybook 121, *121*
  decorative 125, *125*
  elaborated 123, *123*
  flourished 122, *122*
  lower-case 118, *118*
  Spanish, script 124, *124*
  Spanish, capitals 124, *124*
Lombardic lettering 100
  Versal letters *39*
pointed pen letters 134–5, *134–5*, 136, *136*
Roman alphabets 72–9, *72–9*
  capitals 24
  classical, capitals 74–5, *74–5*
  compounded, capitals 77, *77*
  letter shapes 39
  lower-case letters 76, *76*
  modern pen-drawn, lettering 78, *78*
  square capitals 80
  Quadrata 72
Rotunda (Rotonda), 92, 95, *95*, 107, 124
  minuscule 96, *96*
Roundhand 134–5, *134–5*, 138, *138*
round text 137, *137*
Rustica alphabets 24
  capitals 80
  letter shapes 39
square text 138, *138*
Textura alphabet 92, 93, 96–7, 98–9, *98–9*
Uncial alphabets 80–5, *80–5*
  English 84–5, *84–5*
  lettering 86, 100, 102
  letter shapes 39
Versal alphabets 86–91, *86–91*
  elaborated 90, *90*
  letter shapes 29, 39

Lombardic form 39, 89, *89*
  ornamented 91, *91*
  Roman form 88
ammoniac 37
anglepoise lamp 18
angles of nib 20, *20*
Arrighi *121*

B

Baker, Arthur 78–9, *78–9*
Bastarda 107, 124
Bible Historiale 43
Bickham, George 134, 138
binding 170
Blackletter alphabet 92–3, *92–3*, 95, 98, 104
Blackletter script alphabet 100
Book of Hours 38
Book of Kells 81
bookbinding 168–71, *168–71*
borders 44–6, *44–6*
  basic strokes 45, *45*
  black and white 46, *46*
  broad brush 46, *46*
  joins for 44, *44*
  letters 46, *46*
  pointed-brush 44
  with felt-tip 45, *45*
  with pointed brush 44, *44*
brush, using 26–7, *27*
  broad, borders 46, *46*
  Chinese 27, *27*
  ruling 56, *56*
  using, with colour 29, *29*
  using a pointed 32, *32*
  using a square-cut 27, *27*, 33, *33*

C

card support *16*
Carolingian letters 86
cartouche 45
centred layout, using 154–61, *154–61*
centred vs. ranged-left layouts 146
centring 50, *50*, 158–9, *158–9*
classical Roman capitals alphabet 74–5, *74–5*

cleaners 18
cleaning fluid 11
cloth, absorbent 14
Codex Aureus *37*
colour:
  applying 30–1
  density 11
  using 29–31, *29–31*
coloured ground, preparing 31, *31*
compass, using a 56, *56*
composition 53–4
compounded Roman capitals alphabet 77, *77*
Copperplate 125
Copperplate alphabets 129–42, *129–42*
  flourishes *128*
  script alphabet 131, *131*
copybook Italic alphabet 121, *121*
corners 44
Cresci 139

D

decorated Gothic alphabets:
  capitals 104, *104*
  minuscule 105, *105*
decorative devices 28–46
decorative Italic alphabet 125, *125*
depth:
  assessing 52, *52*
  planning 52
design:
  transferring 151–2, *151–2*
  working up 148–50, *148–50*
double points, using 33, *33*
drawing board 12–13, *12–13*
  making 12–13, *12–13*
  position 12
  setting up for tracing 16
  setting up generally 17, *17*
dye, retouching 11

E

Egerton manuscript *39*
elaborated Italic alphabet 123, *123*
  Versals 90, *90*

embellishment 53
English Half-Uncial alphabet 84–5, *84–5*
   Uncial alphabet 84–5, *84–5*
eraser 13
Evans, George *166, 167*

F

feathering 11
felt-tip border 45, *45*
fine Gothic-style script alphabet 137, *137*
flourished alphabets:
   capitals 132–3, *132–3*, 140–1, *140–1*, 142, *142*
   Gothic capitals alphabet 108, *108*
   Gothic script alphabet 110, *110*
   Italic alphabet 122, *122*
   script letters alphabet 139, *139*
flourishes 32–3, *32–3*
format 48–9
fountain-type pen *10*, 10
Fraktur alphabet 98–9, *98–9*, 106, *128*
Fuhrmann, Renate *96*

G

geometric design 43, *43*
gesso 34, *34*
gilding 36–7, *36–7*
   preparation for 37
gold, powdered 36–7
gold leaf 34, *34–5*, 36
Gothic alphabets 92–112, *92–112*
   cursive alphabet 94, *94*
   majuscule alphabet 100–01, *100–01*
   see also alphabets
gouache 30, 37
grease, preventing transferring 17
grinding nibs 16
gum arabic 31, 36

H

Half-Gothic alphabet *see* Rotunda
Half-Uncial alphabets 80–85, *80–85*
   letters 86

see also alphabets
headings 54, *55*
   positioning *54*
Hoefer, Karl Georg *169*
Humanistic scripts 121, 124
   cursive capitals alphabet 126–7, *126–7*

I

illumination 38–9, *38–9*
Illustrations, combining with calligraphy 164–7, *164–7*
images, using words as 162–3, *162–3*
inks 11
   coloured 29–30
   waterproof, cleaning 18
interlinear spacing 50
Italian Gothic alphabet, *see* Rotunda
Italic alphabets 113–128, *113–128*
   capitals alphabet 117, *117*
   compressed hand – capitals 120, *120*
   compressed hand – lower-case 119, *119*
   lower-case alphabet 118, *118*
   see also alphabets

J

Japanese tissue binding 168–71, *168–71*
justification 52

L

Larcher, Jean *33*
layout 50
layout:
   centring 154–61, *154–61*
   guidelines 47–56
   planning 51, *51*, 154, *154*
   working 149, *150*, 155–6, *155–6*
left-handed calligrapher 10, *10*
   position 16
   lighting 17
letter borders 46, *46*
letter construction 57–70
   terminology 58
understanding lower-case 65–68

understanding numerals 69–70
   understanding upper-case 59–64
letterforms 20
letter shapes, exploring 27, *27*
letter spacing 49, *49*, 50
letter style 50, 52, 53
letters, arranging 26, *26*
letters, combining with ornament 42, *42*
lighting 17–18
line length 52
Lombardic lettering 100
Lombardic Versal letters *39*
Lucas, Francisco 124

M

majuscule letters 58
margins 48–9
   creating 48, *48*
   proportions 144
marking up 52
materials 7–14
Mercator, Gerardus 122
minuscule letters 58
modern pen-drawn Roman lettering 78, *78*
modern Uncial alphabet 82–3, *82–3*
modified Gothic alphabets:
   capitals 102–3, *102–3*
   cursive – capitals 111, *111*
   cursive script 112, *112*
   script alphabet 102–3, *102–3*
multi-section binding 170

N

Neudorffer capital *97*
nibs *11*
   angles 20, *20*
   grinding 16
   using with coloured paint 30, *30*
nib sizes, testing out 144, *145*
numerals 69–70

O

ornament 40–3, *40–3*
   arranging 40, *40*

combining with letters 42, *42*
designing 40–2
developing methods of arranging 41, *41*
laying out 42, *42*
ornamented Gothic script 109, *109*
   Versals 91, *91*
oxgall 31

P

Paillasson, Charles 142, *142*
paints 30
palladium 34
paper 12, *12*
   sizes 144
   squared 45
papyrus 24
pens, *see also* fountain-type pen, quill, reed pen, ruling pen, steel-nibbed pen:
   control 22
   holders 11
   maintenance 18, *19*
   practice 20–22, *20–22*
pencils 13
Pilsbury, Joan *116*
pipe cleaners 18
planning layout 51, *51*, 154, *154*
pointed pen letters 134–5, *134–5*, 136, *136*
pointed-brush border 44, *44*
polyvinyl acetate (PVA) 37
positioning 18
projects 143–171
proportions 144

Q

Quadrata alphabet 72
   capitals 58
quill pen:
   cutting 23, *23*
   using 23, *23*

R

raised gold 34–5, *34–5*
reed pen:

making 24, *24*
   pen, using 24–5, *24–5*
Rees, Ieuan *33*
reservoirs 10
reversing out 51, *51*
revised Humanistic script alphabets
   138, *138*
right-handed calligrapher 10, *10*
   lighting 17
   position 16
Roman lower-case letters 76, *76*
Roman alphabet 23, *73*
Roman alphabets 72–9, *72–9*
   capitals 24
   letter shapes 39
   square capitals 80
   see also alphabets
Rotunda (Rotonda) 92, 95, *95*, 107,
   124
   minuscule, alphabet 96, *96*
rough sketches, using 146–53,
   146–53
roughing out 146–8, 147
round Gothic alphabet *see* Rotunda
round text alphabet 137, *137*
Roundhand alphabet 134–5, *134–5*,
   138, *138*
ruler 13
   cleaning 18
rules 56, *56*
ruling pen, using a 56, *56*
Rustica alphabets 24
   capitals 80
   letter shapes 39

S

scaling 146
scalpel 14, *14*
set square 13
   cleaning 18
shapes, substrate 53, *53*
Shaw, Paul *55*
single-section binding 170
skeleton Gothic alphabets:
   capitals 106, *106*
   minuscule 107, *107*

slanted Gothic alphabet 128, *128*
Smith, John *31*
space, filling 48–52, *49–52*
spacing 50
Spanish Italic alphabets
   capitals 124, *124*
   script 124, *124*
square text alphabet 138, *138*
steel-nibbed pens 10
strokes:
   basic 22, *22*
   basic for borders 45, *45*
   forming 20–22
   weights 20
   widths 20, *21*
sub-headings 54
substrate shapes 53, *53*

T

tape:
   double-sided 14
   masking 14
Taunton, William *171*
techniques 15–27
   advanced 143–171
text area, deciding on 144–5
Textura alphabet 92, 93, 96–7, 98–9,
   98–9
thumbnails, using 146–53, *146–53*
tools 7–14

U

Uncial alphabets 80–85, *80–85*
   lettering 100
   letter shapes 39
   letters 86, 102
   see also alphabets
using words as images 162–3, *162–3*

V

Van den Velde, Jan *133*
vellum 36, 38
Versal alphabets 86–91, *86–91*
   letter shapes 39
   letters 29
   Lombardic form 89, *89*

Roman form 88
   see also alphabets
watercolour paint 11, 30
Weyss, Urban 109
Wood, Dave *49, 116*
word spacing 49, *49*, 50
words, using as images 162–3, *162–3*
writing surface preparation 17